UNCIVIL WAR

UNCIVIL WAR

*Five New Orleans Street Battles and
the Rise and Fall of Radical Reconstruction*

JAMES K. HOGUE

Louisiana State University Press
Baton Rouge

Published by Louisiana State University Press

Manufactured in the United States of America
Louisiana Paperback Edition, 2011

Designer: Michelle A. Garrod
Typeface: Whitman
Typesetter: The Composing Room

Library of Congress Cataloging-in-Publication Data
Hogue, James Keith, 1954–
    Uncivil war : five New Orleans street battles and the rise and fall of radical Reconstruction /
James K. Hogue.
        p. cm.
    Includes bibliographical references and index.
    1. Reconstruction (U.S. history, 1865–1877)—Louisiana—New Orleans.   2. Violence—
Louisiana—New Orleans—History—19th century.   3. New Orleans (La.)—History—19th century.
4. New Orleans (La.)—Social conditions—19th century.   I. Title.
F379.N557H64 2006
976.3'061—dc22

                                                                          2005030434

ISBN 978-0-8071-4361-2 (pbk: alk. paper)—ISBN 978-0-8071-4391-9 (pdf)—ISBN 978-0-8071-4392-6
(epub)—ISBN 978-0-8071-4393-3 (mobi)

To the members of the West Point Class of 1980

Contents

Maps

Acknowledgments

The idea for this book originated in James McPherson's graduate seminar, "Emancipation and the Transition to Freedom," at Princeton University. This seminar attracted as intellectually stimulating a group of graduate students as I suppose I shall ever likely see in academic life, and the cross-fertilization of ideas that emerged from it was correspondingly rich. Members of the seminar were Tom Carhart, Paul Cohen, Cliff Doerksen, John Giggie, Judith Jackson, Felicia Kornbluh, Paul Kramer, Jessica Meyerson, and Nat Sheidley. Under Professor McPherson's sage guidance, we covered the range of historical questions that have absorbed a generation of historians determined to see beyond the myths that continue to obscure the era of the Civil War and Reconstruction and shed new light on the motive forces behind what remains the most dynamic and pivotal period in American history.

Out of those exchanges came the germ of the idea to explore the problem of war and politics in the period after the Civil War. Professor McPherson immediately proved receptive to the idea of a study of the history of political violence in Reconstruction Louisiana and served as advisor to the dissertation, as well as to other matters academic ever since. He remains the master that every apprentice in the historical craft ought to have.

Additional reflection on some of the themes in this work was provided by a number of professors and colleagues. Professor McPherson and Prof. John Murrin, in their "War and Society" course, gave me the first opportunity to uncover the roots of Reconstruction violence in Civil War armies through a seminar paper. Prof. Arno Mayer's seminar on modern European history provided pause to consider my topic in a comparative historical context. Professor Mayer's iconoclasm knows no bounds, and his probing of the underlying assumptions of my work has been a source of constant stimulation. Prof. Peter Paret of the Institute for Advanced Study, the world's foremost expert on Carl von Clausewitz and the theory of war, generously agreed to supervise an individualized reading course and serve as the outside reader for the dissertation. Paul Miles Jr. occupies a unique position as both a friend and a colleague.

At West Point and Princeton, he has been an expert guide to every aspect of the history of modern war.

Financial support came from several sources. The Harry Frank Guggenheim Foundation made the completion of the dissertation possible. The Princeton Center of International Studies and the Mellon Foundation provided a postdoctoral fellowship and grant, which allowed me to think about the special problems of post–Civil War America in the wider context of contemporary civil wars and reconstructions under the direction of Prof. Michael Doyle, whose knowledge of contemporary United Nations peacekeeping operations is unrivalled. The University of North Carolina at Charlotte provided a series of faculty research grants that made it possible to turn the dissertation into a book.

Last in order but first in my heart, I thank my family. My wife, Patricia, has borne my scholarly pursuits with more grace and forbearance than duty alone required. Our daughter, Michelle, has waited patiently for the arrival of "Daddy's book" for almost as long as she can remember.

I dedicate this book, with lasting affection, to all my comrades in the West Point class of 1980. It is those of them who remain on active duty, at a time when the U.S. Army is embarked on another vast project of reconstruction, who are most apt to know whether what I have to say in these pages is of some lasting value.

Abbreviations in Notes

AHR	*American Historical Review*
JSH	*Journal of Southern History*
LC	Library of Congress
LLMVC	Louisiana and Lower Mississippi Valley Collection, Hill Memorial Library, Louisiana State University
LHQ	*Louisiana Historical Quarterly*
LaH	*Louisiana History*
NA	National Archives
SHC	Southern Historical Collection, University of North Carolina Library

UNCIVIL WAR

Introduction

The Problem of War and Politics in Reconstruction

On January 10, 1875, Maj. Gen. Philip H. Sheridan sat down in his room at the St. Charles Hotel in New Orleans to write a long letter to the president of the United States, Ulysses S. Grant. He had known Grant for years. Together they had fought a series of legendary battles during the American Civil War, stretching from the wild, impulsive charge up Missionary Ridge at Chattanooga, Tennessee, in 1863 that shattered Braxton Bragg's Army of Tennessee to the final engagement near Appomattox Court House, Virginia, in 1865 that compelled Robert E. Lee's Army of Northern Virginia to surrender and sealed the doom of the Confederacy. That powerful bond of trust that develops when men risk their lives and those of their soldiers together in battle had deepened in the decade since the end of the war. Grant had asked his trusted lieutenant to make a secret trip to Louisiana to report on intensely troubling developments in the state's government and politics.

Today it might seem odd for a president to ask a general to undertake a mission that, on its face, seemed more suited for the talents of a politician than a professional soldier. Part of Grant's inclination to send Sheridan stemmed from his discomfort in being surrounded in Washington by career politicians he did not believe he could trust as he did an old comrade in arms. In part, though, he sent Sheridan because they shared a bond not only from the Civil War but from Louisiana as well. Postwar events in that state played a little-known but significant role in Grant's decision to resign as commanding general of the army in 1868 and run for president. From the end of the Civil War until 1867, Sheridan had commanded occupation forces in Texas and Louisiana from his headquarters in New Orleans. In 1867, over Grant's personal protest, then-president Andrew Johnson removed Sheridan from his command for zealously enforcing the Military Reconstruction Acts, which Johnson's enemies in Congress had passed to return Confederate states to the Union. Distress with Johnson's decision to fire a Union war hero while he simultaneously doled out pardons to former Rebels had helped persuade Grant that securing "the fruits of victory" from the Civil War demanded that he run for president.

In his long letter to Grant, Sheridan laid bare the shocking conditions he found in Louisiana. Since 1865 more than 3,500 people had been killed in politically inspired violence in every corner of the state. Untold thousands more had been shot, whipped, raped, or assaulted. Most of this violence had been directed at terrorizing freed slaves, newly enfranchised by the Military Reconstruction Acts that had cost Sheridan his command, but a number of white Union army veterans and native white southerners had also died. In 1868 alone he estimated that close to 1,880 had been killed or wounded in a carnival of terror aimed at preventing Louisiana's freedmen from using their numerical majority to win the state's electoral votes for Grant and the Republicans. Of the more than 1,200 politically inspired killings since 1868, Sheridan could not find a single example that resulted in a successful prosecution for murder. The passage of time had only refined rather than diminished this tidal wave of lawlessness. Several months before Sheridan's arrival, a white supremacist militia defeated the state police and militia in bloody fighting in New Orleans and ousted the Republican governor. While federal troops restored him to office a few days later, chaos continued. Several days after Sheridan arrived in the city, white supremacists tried to overthrow the state government again, this time with a carefully orchestrated parliamentary coup in the Louisiana House that degenerated into a brawling free-for-all among the legislators. Order was not restored until federal troops marched onto the House floor armed with rifles and fixed bayonets.[1]

Had Louisiana relapsed into a kind of uncivil war, smaller in scale than the Civil War of 1861–65 but perhaps made even more vicious in its perceptible slide toward violence lacking any restraint or limits in its cruelty? Sheridan, who wrote in the blunt cadences of a practical nineteenth-century field soldier, did not actually come out and say so in his letter. Yet the historical perspective provided by the passage of more than a century and the analytical tools of contemporary political science suggest that was exactly what had happened.

The most extensive quantitative study conducted on modern war, the Correlates of War Project directed by J. David Singer, has analyzed quantifiable aspects of more than 150 civil wars over almost two centuries. In the end the project's researchers decided four essential factors determined whether they would classify a particular conflict as a civil war. First, there had to be military action involved. Second, the na-

---

1. Telegram, Maj. Gen. Philip H. Sheridan to William W. Belknap, Jan. 10, 1875, RG 94, Records of the Adjutant General's Office, 1780–1917, NA. Belknap was Grant's secretary of war at the time. Sheridan's rough estimate of the scale of violence in Louisiana has held up remarkably well under modern scrutiny. See Gilles Vandal, *Rethinking Southern Violence: Homicides in Post–Civil War Louisiana, 1866–1884* (Columbus: Ohio State University Press, 2000).

tional government had to be involved. Third, effective resistance had to occur on both sides. Lastly, at least one thousand battle deaths had to result from the conflict. By those standards Louisiana had indeed descended into another, albeit different kind, of civil war.[2]

Neither Louisiana nor the Reconstruction-era American South as a whole appear on the political scientists' approved list of civil wars, and it is not difficult to discern why. The strict criteria they developed do not count deaths attributable to political violence per se, only what they describe as "battle deaths." General Sheridan—no less than most military historians and professional soldiers since his time—took the phenomenon of "battle" very much for granted. He rarely gave much thought to whether or not a particular skirmish, raid, or ambush qualified as a battle. Even so penetrating a work as John Keegan's brilliant study *The Face of Battle* devotes almost three hundred pages tracing the development of modern battle over the last five centuries before grappling with how to define the subject of its study—and then abruptly lapses into an argument that battle is disappearing from Western history. More recently Victor Davis Hanson has argued forcefully for "the primacy of military history" across several millennia of Western culture while admittedly finding it difficult to define what factors determine what constitutes a "great battle." Small wonder then that Sheridan found himself frustrated in trying to adequately describe the situation he found in Louisiana. While the state clearly had a serious security problem, nowhere could Sheridan, an eyewitness and participant in dozens of campaigns against Rebels and Plains Indians, point to something that looked much like the decisive battles he had so often fought and won.[3]

With the perspective that time and critical distance provide, we can distinguish, as Sheridan could not, the arc of an "uncivil war" during Reconstruction by tracing it through a series of five street battles fought out between opposing forces in the Louisiana state capital of New Orleans between 1866 and 1877. Through them it is possible to grasp more clearly the intertwined relationship between force and politics in the origin, development, and final demise of the Republican-dominated state governments across the South, which briefly empowered millions of freed slaves before the long shadow of Jim Crow laws and segregation fell over the entire region.

To be sure, none of these street battles would likely qualify for inclusion on a tra-

2. J. David Singer and Melvin Small, *Resort to Arms: International and Civil War, 1816–1980* (Beverly Hills, Calif.: Sage, 1982).

3. John Keegan, *The Face of Battle* (New York: Viking, 1977), 297–98; Victor Davis Hanson, *Ripples of Battle: How Wars of the Past Still Determine How We Fight, How We Live, and How We Think* (New York: Doubleday, 2003), 15, 244–58.

ditional military historian's list of "great battles." In some cases the combatants themselves did not much look like nineteenth-century armies, even though Civil War veterans filled the cadres on both sides in every one of them. The numbers of participants involved frequently amounted to a mere fraction of the massive field armies of the famous battles of the Civil War, yet they sometimes numbered in the thousands—larger in some cases than the rebel forces that fought at such battles as Lexington, Concord, Trenton, or Kings Mountain that shaped the course of the American War of Independence a century earlier. In several of these street battles, few or no casualties have been recorded, but those who came armed and prepared to fight had no way of knowing what would happen once the action began. In part, then, this study aims to begin to rethink the meaning and nature of "battle" itself, a study perhaps made more urgent and understandable in an age where American military deployments have again become dominated by interrelated questions of military intervention and insurgencies, peacekeeping and nation building, as well as the challenge of terrorism.

THE UNIQUE ROLE OF LOUISIANA IN RECONSTRUCTION

While every ex-Confederate state experienced a surge of violence associated with racialized struggles for internal political power after the Civil War, Louisiana became a unique epicenter of violent politics. This occurred, not because Louisiana was typical of the Old South, but precisely because it was so singularly distinct in its population, its geography, and the role it played in the conduct of the Civil War. In most of the states of the former Confederacy, freed slaves formed a minority of the population. Louisiana was one of only three states where black slaves outnumbered free whites in the census of 1860. Neither black nor white Louisianians could escape the momentous political consequences of this fact once enfranchisement came.

Unlike any other southern state, antebellum Louisiana possessed a large and vibrant community of free blacks, who called themselves *gens de couleur libre* (free people of color). These people formed a distinctive caste between black slaves and free whites within Louisiana society. Heavily concentrated in the French-speaking sugar parishes of the southern part of the state and especially in New Orleans, the gens de couleur libre emerged as a people of mixed racial ancestry, the offspring of European settlers, African American slaves, and in some cases Native Americans. In addition to their unusual degree of wealth and education, they possessed a distinctive Creole culture, combining traditions derived from continental Europe, the Caribbean, and Africa. Among the most durable of those traditions was militia service, developed over a century of French and Spanish colonial rule. Even after France sold the territory of Louisiana to the United States, the gens de couleur libre retained their militia companies and repeatedly proved their worth, most famously against the British in 1815, when several battalions of black soldiers fought under Andrew Jackson's command at the battle of New Orleans. After his victory, Jackson commended their loyalty and courage in the fighting while silently ignoring the fact that their military service and formations had been technically illegal under existing federal militia laws.[4]

In addition to the cosmopolitan character of its population, Louisiana played a critical role in Reconstruction because of its strategic location along the southern end of the Mississippi River and the economic role New Orleans, the largest city in the Confederacy (population about 168,000 in 1860), played in the South's plantation economy. Before the Civil War, New Orleans was the largest southern center for the export and finance of cotton and sugar. The city's geographic position as entrepôt for the vast expanse of the Mississippi River valley had originally attracted Thomas Jefferson's desire to purchase it from the French, whom he feared might use it to dominate the interior of the continent and inhibit the expansion of the United States. That location also made New Orleans vulnerable to naval attack from an expedition sailing upriver from the Gulf of Mexico, and a prize the Union could not afford to ignore during the Civil War. When the city fell intact to Adm. David Farragut's fleet in the spring of 1862, New Orleans became not only the Union army and navy's base for the reconquest of the entire Mississippi Valley but also a laboratory for Abraham Lincoln's most important experiment in wartime reconstruction. For the next fifteen years, Louisiana became a tantalizing object of attention in the quest for a plan to restore or reconstruct the seceded states. All three of Lincoln's successors, Andrew Johnson, Ulysses S. Grant, and Rutherford B. Hayes, attached great importance to its government. Each in turn hoped that the patronage they wielded through federal customs offices overseeing New Orleans's port facilities, their influence with party officials in the new state capital established at New Orleans during the war, and their power as commander in chief of the occupying federal troops would encourage the success of their national reconstruction plans and policies.[5]

4. Charles E. A. Gayarré, *History of Louisiana*, 4 vols., 5th ed. (New Orleans: Pelican, 1974); Ira Berlin, *Slaves without Masters: The Free Negro in the Antebellum South* (New York: Pantheon, 1974), 108–33; Laura Foner, "The Free People of Color in Louisiana and St. Domingue: A Comparative Portrait of Two Three-Caste Slave Societies," *JSH* 3 (1970): 408–22; John W. Blassingame, *Black New Orleans, 1860–1880* (Chicago: University of Chicago Press, 1973); Caryn Cossé Bell, *Revolution, Romanticism, and the Afro-Creole Protest Tradition in Louisiana, 1718–1868* (Baton Rouge : Louisiana State University Press, 1997); Arnold R. Hirsch and Joseph Logsdon, *Creole New Orleans: Race and Americanization* (Baton Rouge: Louisiana State University Press, 1992); Roland C. McConnell, *Negro Troops of Antebellum Louisiana: A History of the Battalion of Free Men of Color* (Baton Rouge: Louisiana State University Press, 1968).

5. Gerald M. Capers, *Occupied City: New Orleans under the Federals, 1862–1865* (Lexington: University of Kentucky Press, 1965). The antebellum state capitol at Baton Rouge burned during the Union occupation of that city. Federal authorities established a military government for Union-controlled Louisiana at

THE PROBLEM OF THE POLITICAL HISTORY OF RECONSTRUCTION

American historians argue over when to date the start of the era known as Reconstruction. Some date the era from the end of the Civil War, a convenient chronological division, but it neglects Lincoln's wartime exertions and struggles with members of his own party in Congress over the issue. Others opt for 1860 or 1861, making the rational argument that, for the Union, waging the Civil War had always been predicated upon some form of reconstruction program. Still others have chosen January 1, 1863, the date Lincoln signed the Emancipation Proclamation, arguing that freeing the slaves formed a watershed that fundamentally changed both the war and American society. Whatever date historians pick for the beginning of Reconstruction, few can argue that a historical period came to a definitive close when the U.S. Army ended its mission to protect the last Republican state government in the South. That moment came on April 24, 1877, when newly inaugurated president Rutherford B. Hayes ordered the federal troops who had been guarding the Louisiana state capitol in New Orleans to return to their barracks. The Republican claimant for the disputed governorship, Stephen B. Packard, had been acting as chief executive since his inauguration four months earlier, but he abdicated the day the federal troops departed. He fled from a post he had resolutely maintained rightfully belonged to him, prompted by the presence of almost four thousand white supremacist militia who had occupied most of New Orleans and laid siege to his capitol, located in the French Quarter. Demanding Packard's abdication was his rival for the governorship, Francis Redding Tillou Nicholls, a former Confederate general and the self-proclaimed commander in chief of the militia besieging New Orleans. General Nicholls had carefully arranged his forces to avoid threatening federal troops while deploying them to undermine every branch of Packard's beleaguered government. President Hayes was well aware that his orders would end both a political and a military era that day, even if he did not foresee that a new one would begin in which warring memories of Reconstruction would cast a lengthening shadow.

In symmetry with this last scene of Reconstruction, featuring the intrusion of force into politics, this study begins in the spring of 1865, after another American president, Abraham Lincoln, was assassinated by a white supremacist and Confederate sympathizer, John Wilkes Booth, in an act of deliberate terrorism. This event also had its links to politics in Louisiana. Booth had plotted against Lincoln for some time, but what finally triggered his murderous fury was the president's last public address,

New Orleans in 1862, and that city remained the state capital until the Constitution of 1879 returned the seat of government to Baton Rouge.

delivered to a crowd standing below his second-story window at the White House on April 11. In his meticulously prepared speech, Lincoln proclaimed the death of the rebellious Confederacy and all its state governments. "There is no authorized organ for us to treat with," he insisted. Rather than see all political power returned to the same white electorates that had seceded from the Union in 1861, however, Lincoln called for the enfranchisement of at least some of the free blacks from Louisiana, especially those who had volunteered to fight in the Union army. Lincoln and Booth both recognized that this first public step toward black enfranchisement would unleash another revolution on southern society at least the equal of that caused by emancipation. Booth perpetrated his act of terrorism in order to forestall just such a revolution.[6]

Americans generally do not associate such naked displays of violence as occurred in Lincoln's 1865 assassination or the New Orleans coup d'état of 1877 with democratic government and free elections. Political scientists and historians have all too often mistakenly tried to make Reconstruction's origins, development, and outcome fit a model of stable, competitive party politics, articulated by the study of political parties, interest groups, voter mobilization, and election returns. In doing so they have labored to force a different historical era to conform to a paradigm of party politics in our own time that has largely been peaceful and consensual in practice. As Sheridan's letter to Grant makes abundantly clear, the politics of Reconstruction were neither peaceful nor consensual.[7]

A demonstration of how the normal American model of domestic politics fails to account for the unique character of Reconstruction politics can be found in a brief review of the political careers of the five governors who held office in Louisiana between 1865 and 1877: James M. Wells, Henry C. Warmoth, P. B. S. Pinchback, William P. Kellogg, and Stephen B. Packard. Each one of these men faced a serious threat of replacement or impeachment. Each faced either assassination attempts, death threats, or both. Each struggled against a rival state government that proclaimed its own le-

6. Abraham Lincoln quoted in James M. McPherson, *Battle Cry of Freedom: The Civil War Era* (New York: Oxford University Press, 1987), 851–52. On Lincoln's own attempt at wartime Reconstruction, see Peyton McCrary, *Abraham Lincoln and Reconstruction: The Louisiana Experiment* (Princeton, N.J.: Princeton University Press, 1978).

7. On the theory and history of partisan realignments and critical elections, see James L. Sundquist, *Dynamics of the Party System: Alignment and Realignment of Political Parties in the United States*, rev. ed. (Washington, D.C.: Brookings Institution, 1983). For a historical study of Reconstruction politics informed by the partisan-realignment theory, see Michael Perman, *The Road to Redemption: Southern Politics, 1869–1879* (Chapel Hill: University of North Carolina Press, 1984).

gitimacy while refusing to recognize his. And each had to cope with an armed attempt to overthrow his administration. None could have survived in office for long without the continued intervention of federal troops.

Only one of the five (Wells) was a native of Louisiana, yet the majority of his class and race reviled him for heading what they considered to be a puppet government established by an invading army. Only one of the five (Kellogg) finished a complete four-year term, but his tenure was interrupted in 1874 when his administration was overthrown and his state militia destroyed in a battle featuring more combatants than the skirmishes near Boston that ignited the American Revolution. While he was acting governor for only about a month, Pinchback was unique in American political history for more than a century as the only African American to have served as governor of a southern state (until Virginia elected Douglas Wilder in the 1980s). Pinchback gained office by orchestrating the impeachment of his predecessor and delivered it to his successor only after suppressing a mutiny within the state militia.[8]

While no other state's political experience during Reconstruction was as chaotic or violent as Louisiana's, several came close, and all southern states exhibited at least some of those elements so prominent in Louisiana. The extent of this violence left lasting marks. Part of Louisiana's unusual, if not exotic, subsequent political history can be traced to the fact that its military occupation, from 1862 to 1877, lasted longer than that of any other ex- Confederate state; indeed, it was the longest of its kind in American history. Not coincidentally, this era of state government backed by federal military occupation preceded one of the longest periods of unbroken one-party dominance in American history (1877–1972). Ever since Reconstruction, Louisiana's reputation for a kind of amused cynicism toward extravagant political corruption has remained without peer, even three decades after the return of a functioning two-party system.

In accounting for the unusual nature of postwar politics, it has now become common for historians to describe the era of the Civil War and Reconstruction as a "revolution," sometimes as the "Second American Revolution." Curiously, however, far less attention has been accorded to analyzing the mechanics of the counterrevolution against Reconstruction, despite the fact that theoretical studies of revolution invari-

---

8. The political history of the state government in Louisiana at this time was so byzantine that many historians might dispute the inclusion of one or more in this list of five governors. Some lists of Louisiana governors add other names, specifically those appointed by military commanders or of rival governors that different authors argue were actually elected. The five listed here were all de facto civilian governors elected or succeeding under the Constitutions of 1864 and 1868 and actively supported by federal troops between April 1865 and April 1877.

ably emphasize that the one phenomenon cannot logically exist without the other. To be sure, the use of the term "counterrevolution" itself has been complicated by its ideologically loaded use in the twentieth century, to say nothing of the empirical observation that no counterrevolution, strictly speaking, has ever fully restored an old regime. Nevertheless, it has been particularly useful to this study to begin by understanding that the structures of a centuries-old agrarian society established upon plantation slave labor broke up and then vanished on the road to total war from 1861 to 1865. When that happened, all those who saw their old positions of power and privilege likewise vanish had every incentive through the postwar struggle to rebuild a new society in the likeness of the old. If, as Prussian theorist Carl von Clasuewitz famously stated, "War is the continuation of politics by other means," then it can perhaps be said that Reconstruction politics became the continuation of civil war by other means.[9]

THE PROBLEM OF THE MILITARY HISTORY OF RECONSTRUCTION

While the principal currents in the historiography of American politics have tended to ignore or suppress aspects of Reconstruction that do not readily conform to contemporary political-science models, the military history of the era has hardly been more satisfactory. For the most part, historians have either ignored Reconstruction or treated it as though it did not profoundly affect the institutional development of the American military.

There are understandable, if not entirely satisfactory, reasons why this should be so. First of all, like American political history, much of American military history has become adamantly presentist in outlook and, therefore, highly selective in its narrative. In retrospect the growth of a powerful, efficient, and professional standing military in the course of the twentieth century tends to obscure the historic importance

9. On the Civil War and Reconstruction as a revolutionary experience, see, for example, James M. McPherson, *Abraham Lincoln and the Second American Revolution* (New York: Oxford University Press, 1991); and Eric Foner, *Reconstruction: America's Unfinished Revolution, 1863–1877* (New York: Harper and Row, 1988). For an analysis of counterrevolution in the framework of nineteenth- and twentieth-century European history, see Arno J. Mayer, *The Dynamics of Counterrevolution in Europe, 1870–1956: An Analytic Framework* (New York: Harper and Row, 1971). According to Mayer's model, the secession of the southern states in 1861 was a "preemptive counterrevolution" determined to prevent the demise of slavery foreseeable in the election of Abraham Lincoln as president. The repeated and then cresting waves of violence after 1865 would therefore be "posterior counterrevolutions," which did not completely restore the old regime (i.e., plantation slavery) but rather retrieved as much of it as was possible within the structure of a federal polity that continued to grant great latitude to state governments.

of the volunteer militias that provided the backbone of American military power until the professionals' apparent triumph in the Civil War.[10]

The fighting that took place during Reconstruction occurred almost exclusively between various combinations of these local volunteer forces engaged in an irregular, intermittent, and sometimes clandestine struggle. The forces opposed to the congressional program of reconstruction consciously avoided provoking battle with the intervening forces of the federal army. After Confederate armies surrendered in 1865, no armed group, however ardently they favored "home rule" and bitterly resented military occupation, dared to attack federal troops. After the rapid demobilization of Union army volunteers and a return to a peacetime organization, the U.S. Army adopted a constabulary role for the duration of Reconstruction. The requirements of this policing mission changed over time, but at no time did it ever engage in what its leaders would have recognized as "battle." From the standpoint of many generals within the army at the time (and most military historians since), Reconstruction represented a unique and never-to-be-repeated problem that departed from a proper focus on the fighting of big battles and the winning of extensive campaigns. The military problems of peacekeeping therefore deserved scant professional interest, even if it did, from time to time, consume their attention and embroil them in embarrassing political questions of civil-military relations.[11]

10. For an important dissenting view, see John Shy, "The American Military Experience," in *A People Numerous and Armed: Reflections on the Military Struggle for American Independence*, rev. ed. (Ann Arbor: University of Michigan Press, 1990), 267–98.

11. See, for example, Russell F. Weigley, *The American Way of War: A History of the United States Military Strategy and Policy* (Bloomington: University of Indiana Press, 1977). Weigley's *History of the United States Army* (New York: Macmillan, 1967) does include a section on Reconstruction, though only within a larger chapter that treats the post–Civil War period as one in which the army lacked a significant mission; he also skirts the creation of Reconstruction state militias as an historical experience linking black military service in the Union army to aspirations for political power after the Civil War. James E. Sefton, *The United States Army and Reconstruction* (Baton Rouge: Louisiana State University Press, 1967), provides an overview of the army's roles and missions during the period. The only monograph on the role of the military in Louisiana, Joseph Dawson, *Army Generals and Reconstruction: Louisiana, 1862–1877* (Baton Rouge: Louisiana State University Press, 1982), contains a wealth of primary-source detail from official records but never comes to grips with the central facts of Confederate veterans' determination to use force to oust Republicans from power and end the army's constabulary role of surveillance over state elections. The standard work on the history of the militia in the United States, John K. Mahon, *History of the Militia and the National Guard* (New York: Macmillan, 1983), is an uncritical chronicle of the rise of the National Guard that has little to say about either black state militias or white vigilante, paramilitary, and militia groups during Reconstruction. The latter is a particularly curious omission considering the key roles that the leaders of these forces frequently played in organizing the militia and National Guard in states "redeemed" by Conservative forces.

Historical analysis of the military dimension of Reconstruction has undoubtedly been inhibited because it followed so closely on the heels of the Civil War, which has long remained the largest and deadliest conflict in American history. The Civil War's immense scale, dramatic events, larger-than-life personalities, and stark clash of ideals all have made the military details of Reconstruction seem even smaller and less consequential by comparison. When lawlessness and violence periodically swept across the ex-Confederacy after 1865, it appeared to many, both at the time and later, to be simply repeating patterns present during the Civil War itself. It is probably also fair to say that after so much death and destruction during the four-year struggle, American society had become hardened to the recurrence of such violence, even when it took on the ugly guise of terrorism, assassination, and massacre.

Besides reappraising the nature of the violent politics of Reconstruction, then, another goal of this work is to reconceptualize both the fighting and the roles that different types of military forces played in its origins, development, and outcome. Over time the violent localized counterrevolutions against the national reconstruction program passed through three general and overlapping phases. The first phase, made infamous by the first Ku Klux Klan, was vigilante action, characterized by covert terrorist acts usually conducted by small groups operating at night, in disguise, or both. Vigilante action led by Confederate veterans, especially in the early years of Reconstruction, struck against a broad and often indiscriminate range of targets, including schools, churches, local Republican officials, and freedmen and their families. While this activity undeniably produced a wave of terror that inflicted considerable damage and doubtlessly blunted the growth and vigor of the infant southern Republican state parties, it was generally not as politically effective as has sometimes been imagined. Its ineffectiveness can be partly attributed to its indiscriminate nature. In fact such violence became so indiscreet by 1868 that it provoked countermeasures, including the recruitment of Republican-sponsored state militias and the intervention of the U.S. Army or the newly created Department of Justice. Nonetheless, vigilante action certainly damaged the growth of the Republican Party in the South. Repeated waves of terror discouraged many blacks from voting and caused a number of whites to either leave politics or the South altogether.[12]

12. There has been considerable scholarship on Reconstruction violence. While some of it is quite good, it has some significant shortcomings. First, it does not adequately trace the origins of Reconstruction violence to the Confederate military experience. Second, it overemphasizes vigilantes like the Ku Klux Klan at the expense of later white-supremacist groups (both paramilitaries and militias), which could be at least as violent and frequently more politically effective. Third, it has sometimes mistakenly imposed models of twentieth-century northern urban "race riots" onto analyses of southern "race riots" (rural as

Paramilitary action became a second and intermediate form of white supremacist violence, which first appeared in Louisiana in 1873 and in some cases reappeared intermittently even after Reconstruction's formal ending. Despite the fact that contemporary observers and many historians described them as "riots" or "outrages," connoting spontaneity, paramilitary actions had a clearer political focus than vigilante action. Paramilitary action often required extensive planning and mobilization to bring hundreds of armed men together to strike at targets chosen after careful deliberation. And unlike vigilante action, it was not covert. Paramilitary leaders were invariably well-known local leaders, often addressed by the military rank they had earned as Confederate army officers. Favored targets of paramilitary companies (variously known as White Leagues, Red Shirts, or rifle companies) tended to be local officials, black militia companies, or Republican Party political rallies. Timing of such actions was crucial, with disruption of local elections the prized goal. Organized with care and sufficient numbers, a successful paramilitary strike might end in the capitulation and dissolution of the opposition on the spot without any bloodshed. In any case an assault, sometimes followed by massacre, of local Republican officials and party leaders frequently produced one-party rule in Louisiana parishes that lasted for decades or longer because it triggered the slaughter, exile, or intimidation of the fragile first generation of leadership among the freedmen. Although they often emphatically disavowed any explicit political intent, paramilitary forces invariably acted as an armed wing of the Conservative/Democratic Party and were often one and the same.

The third and most sophisticated form of counterrevolution, carried out only in Louisiana and Arkansas but contemplated in Mississippi in 1875 and South Carolina in 1877, was the formation of a de facto white supremacist militia claiming de jure status. The aim of these forces was to overthrow the state government in the capital through an organized coup d'état. It was the number and growing sophistication of its coup attempts that eventually distinguished Louisiana's counterrevolution against Reconstruction. Even given the relatively rudimentary organization of state government in the 1870s, a successful coup attempt required extensive collusion by political and economic elites.[13]

---

well as urban) of the nineteenth century. See especially Allen W. Trelease, *White Terror: The Ku Klux Klan Conspiracy and Southern Reconstruction* (New York: Harper and Row, 1971); David M. Chalmers, *Hooded Americanism: The History of the Ku Klux Klan,* 3rd ed. (Durham, N.C.: Duke University Press, 1987); and George C. Rable, *But There Was No Peace: The Role of Violence in the Politics of Reconstruction* (Athens: University of Georgia Press, 1984).

13. The literature on the coup d'état is surprisingly thin, though stimulating. See especially Curzio Malaparte, *Technique du Coup d'Etat* (Paris: Glasset, 1931); Edward Luttwak, *Coup D'Etat: A Practical Handbook*

In the end the era of Reconstruction formed a watershed in the rise of both the professionalized standing military and the demise of traditional volunteer militias in the United States. The professional military emerged from the Civil War triumphant in its struggle for organizational primacy against the local volunteers of the antebellum era. The agonized decision of professional soldiers like Grant, Sherman, and Sheridan to support Congress over President Johnson in the struggle for Reconstruction policy profoundly affected their view of the roles they believed befitted their new status. For militias the struggles of Reconstruction represented both a last hurrah for the local volunteers and a bridge to the creation of the state-sponsored organizations of the National Guard. Leaders of the post-Reconstruction National Guard liked to portray themselves as the natural heirs of the volunteer-militia tradition, but their units emerged in the late nineteenth century as captives of political elites and economic interests that distanced themselves from the egalitarianism and democratic traditions of antebellum militias.

Finally immersion in the microhistories of these incidents of more than a century ago makes it possible to suspend the overwhelming sense of inevitability about the ultimate tragedy of Reconstruction's outcome and glimpse the historical contingency of another era. As America's earliest exercise in what could today be justifiably described as nation building, Reconstruction failed, and it failed badly. A close examination of its struggles, however, leads to an understanding that such an outcome was by no means unavoidable. The prolonged crisis of one of the most intense periods in American history could have, and indeed might have, turned out differently for all those involved.

(New York: Alfred A. Knopf, 1968), which argues for the "political neutrality" of the coup d'état in the modern era; and Eric J. Hobsbawm, "Coup d'Etat," in *Revolutionaries: Contemporary Essays* (New York: Pantheon, 1973), a blistering rejoinder to Luttwak that makes a cogent case for the reactionary orientation of those with the requisite military skills and motivations needed to launch coups.

The Politics of Louisiana Civil War Veterans in 1865

Historians of nineteenth-century America frequently marvel at how easily most Union veterans doffed their blue uniforms and resumed civilian life after the war was over. For the defeated and decimated ranks of Confederate veterans straggling back to their homes in New Orleans after the surrender of their armies, no real resumption of their antebellum lives was possible. It is worthwhile examining their contrasting experience of defeat, ruin, and failure, for it does much to illuminate the source of their emerging outlook on the issues of Reconstruction.[1]

Defeat came to Confederate soldiers from Louisiana in a variety of confusing and sometimes ambiguous ways in the first half of 1865. However it came, though, defeat left marks that would scar southern society for decades to come. For Louisianians in Robert E. Lee's and Joseph E. Johnston's armies in the eastern theater of the war, surrender came in a relatively orderly, if still discouraging, fashion. Their commanders surrendered to Union generals in the field, and each soldier received a parole pending final exchange and pardon. For those in Edmund Kirby Smith's Army of the Trans-Mississippi, demobilization in 1865 resembled the chaos of mobilization of 1861 run in reverse. At camps near the Confederate state capital in Shreveport, Smith's army disintegrated through mass desertions in which squads, companies, and sometimes entire regiments vanished overnight. Whether it came by surrender or disintegration, final defeat was emotionally crushing. It seemed to scorn the heroic sacrifices and privations of both the soldiers in the field and their families at home. The wounds of their shared experience in the war scarred them bitterly for the rest of their lives, but these shared experiences also bound them together in a fraternity against which all other distinctions of social rank, class, or culture paled in significance.

---

1. James M. McPherson, *Ordeal by Fire: The Civil War and Reconstruction* (New York: Alfred A. Knopf, 1982), 486. See also the essays in Maris A. Vinovskis, ed., *Toward a Social History of the American Civil War* (New York: Cambridge University Press, 1990). Curiously none of the essays compare and contrast the experience of Union and Confederate veterans.

An example of one of the many regiments raised in New Orleans illustrates the dimensions of the Confederate veterans' psychic trauma in 1865 and how it shattered and recreated their sense of themselves and their world. The Seventh Louisiana Volunteer Infantry Regiment was raised in the first wave of Confederate enlistments in Louisiana in the spring of 1861. Although the majority of its soldiers came mostly from New Orleans, it also had a company each from Baton Rouge and Donaldsonville, added in the excitement of the first year of war to rush full regiments of ten companies into service before what all anticipated would be a brief war ended. Altogether, the Seventh Louisiana enrolled 1,077 soldiers during the war. Among its officers were a number of the most socially prominent men in New Orleans, including Brig. Gen. Harry T. Hays and Col. Davidson B. Penn, both of whom commanded the regiment during the war and later played important roles in Louisiana Reconstruction.[2] The ranks of the regiment were filled, as were most of the New Orleans units, with clerks, day laborers, and a few farmers from the surrounding parishes. Because it recruited from urban New Orleans, the Seventh Louisiana also had a high proportion of foreign-born volunteers, mostly from Ireland, Germany, and England. Perhaps in this regard alone it bore some resemblance to Union regiments raised from major northern cities such as New York, Boston, or Philadelphia.[3]

Unlike those units, however, the Seventh Louisiana—like the rest of the Confederate army after the Conscription Act of 1862—served "for the duration of the war," a fateful decision that meant it took the field in every major battle of what became the Army of Northern Virginia from First Manassas in 1861 to Appomattox Court House in 1865, garnering a list of battlefield honors few northern regiments could match. At First Manassas, under Louisiana native son Gen. Pierre Gustave Toutant Beauregard, the Seventh Louisiana helped repulse the first Union offensive of the war. Under "Stonewall" Jackson it routed Union forces in the Shenandoah Valley in 1862 in a dazzling display of hard marching and near-reckless attacks that inspired contemporary observers to compare them with Napoleon's troops. At Antietam the regiment held its ground against McClellan's first attack of the day with great tenacity. At Gettysburg

---

2. Hays served in a Mississippi volunteer cavalry regiment during the Mexican War and was a prominent antebellum Whig lawyer in New Orleans. See Harry W. Pfanz, *Gettysburg: Culp's Hill and Cemetery Hill* (Chapel Hill: University of North Carolina Press, 1993), 236–37. Penn was a native of Lynchburg, Virginia, graduated from Virginia Military Institute with honors, and had been in the cotton-press business in New Orleans before the war. See Glenn R. Conrad, ed., *A Dictionary of Louisiana Biography*, 2 vols. (New Orleans: Louisiana Historical Association, 1988), 2:639.

3. All figures for the Seventh Louisiana are from Terry L. Jones, *Lee's Tigers: The Louisiana Infantry in the Army of Northern Virginia* (Baton Rouge: Louisiana State University Press, 1991), 240–41.

in 1863 the Seventh Louisiana and the First Louisiana Brigade under General Hays actually succeeded in taking part of Culp's Hill on the second day of the battle—the only Confederate unit to achieve its objective on that unlucky day for General Lee's army. Even after New Orleans fell to the Union in 1862 and Confederate fortunes took a turn for the worse in late 1863, the regiment refused to abandon Lee and Virginia for home. In the defensive battles of the Wilderness, Spotsylvania, and a second, if less successful, campaign in the Shenandoah Valley in 1864, it repeatedly held its ground and inflicted heavy losses on attacking Union forces. Resisting to the bitter end, the regiment took part in the very last attack made by the Army of Northern Virginia at Appomattox Court House, a desperate and nearly suicidal dawn assault on April 9, 1865, launched in the futile attempt to break out of Grant's encirclement of Lee's dwindling army.[4]

All that martial glory came at a fearful price. Of all those enlisted in the regiment, 190 were killed or mortally wounded in battle, another 68 died of disease, 1 was murdered, and 1 executed. Altogether, the regiment's war dead came to roughly one out of every four who enlisted.[5]

These numbers, of course, do not include those wounded in the fighting: amputees from shrapnel or bullet wounds in an era before antibiotics could treat gangrene, or those whose health was ruined or life shortened by exposure to the elements and the epidemics of disease that periodically raced through the camps. Nor does that toll include those captured in a conflict in which becoming a prisoner of war often proved more deadly than battle. At Rappahannock Station, Virginia, in late 1863, more than one hundred soldiers of the Seventh Louisiana fell into enemy hands after a failed attempt to hold a bridgehead against a rare Union night assault. Of those prisoners, an undetermined number later died of disease or exposure at prisoner-of-war camps in the North that winter. For fifty-three others, the stress of battle or the tug of home was simply more than they could stand. They deserted from the Confederate army, though it should be noted that some of these soldiers probably fought again with Confederate partisan groups that sprang up in and around Louisiana. Another fifty-seven men, however, turned on the Confederacy and took the oath of allegiance offered by the Union. This step earned their comrades' lifelong enmity and caused many of them to be socially shunned or forced into exile in later years. By the winter of 1865,

---

4. On Gordon's assault at Appomattox Court House, see Douglas Southall Freeman, *Lee's Lieutenants: A Study in Command*, 3 vols. (New York: Charles Scribner's Sons, 1942–44), 3:726–29. In July 1864 Lee consolidated all ten Louisiana infantry regiments in the Army of Northern Virginia into a single, understrength brigade.

5. McPherson, *Lincoln and the Second American Revolution*, 11–12.

a Louisiana officer who had known many of the regiment's members back home in New Orleans was shocked to learn that its 1,000 soldiers at First Manassas in 1861 had dwindled to fewer than 250 at Petersburg in the winter of 1865. Union captain and later Supreme Court justice Oliver Wendell Holmes spoke with justifiable pride of how his generation had been "touched with fire" in the Civil War, but when he did so he was naturally thinking of those of his generation who served in the Union army. In contrast the veterans of the Seventh Louisiana Regiment had good reason to feel not so much "touched with fire" but rather scorched, burned over, and decimated by their passage through the war.[6]

Perhaps even more forbidding to these veterans as they returned, though, was the dawning realization of just how much southern society had changed during their odyssey. For most of the antebellum commercial class of New Orleans, from which the Seventh Louisiana's officers had principally been drawn, the war was an un-qualified financial disaster, compounding the tragedy of their personal losses of friends and family. Even before the occupation of New Orleans, the Union naval blockade and the Confederate cotton embargo triggered a deep depression in the city's commerce in early 1862. It was not until after the fall of Vicksburg and the reopening of the Mississippi River to the North the following year that commerce began to pick up again. That resurgence, however, came far too late for most of the cotton factors and merchants, who had either gone bankrupt from lack of business or their outright refusal to take the required oath of allegiance. Vigorous economic growth did not re-turn to the city until 1864, but by then the dominant forces in the local economy were the military plans of the Union army rather than the cotton and sugar markets. The demise of slavery triggered a near-total collapse of trade in sugar, and while the cot-ton market improved with the quintupling of antebellum prices by the end of the war, U.S. Treasury agents held monopoly power over local markets, thanks to their au-thority to confiscate cotton suspected of belonging to the enemy. Thus when battered Confederate veterans at last returned to New Orleans, they found not only themselves penniless but also many of their enemies ensconced in their former places of wealth, influence, power, and prestige.[7]

6. Freeman, *Lee's Lieutenants*, 3:265–68; William Miller Owen, *In Camp and Battle with the Washing-ton Artillery* (Boston: Ticknor, 1885), 363; Oliver Wendell Holmes Jr., *Touched with Fire: Civil War Letters and Diary of Oliver Wendell Holmes, Jr., 1861–1864*, ed. Mark DeWolfe Howe (Cambridge, Mass.: Harvard University Press, 1946), vi.

7. Capers, *Occupied City*, 144–48. For the demise of the cotton factors, which hit the merchant class in New Orleans particularly hard, see Roger L. Ransom and Richard Sutch, *One Kind of Freedom: The Economic Consequences of Emancipation* (Cambridge: Cambridge University Press, 1977), 106–13.

Not only were their economic prospects dim, but the social order they had gone off to war to defend seemed turned on its head too. Confederate soldiers returning to New Orleans invariably remarked upon the flood tide of freedmen streaming into the city. Their perception was no illusion. Between 1860 and 1870, New Orleans experienced a 109.6 percent increase in its black population, while its white population slipped by 2.5 percent. Not only were blacks present in far greater numbers than in antebellum times, but they also had begun asserting their freedom in ways unthinkable to prewar society. Maj. William Owen of the elite Washington Artillery Battalion was surprised to discover that two of his own battalion's black body servants, who had run off during the war, not only had become Union army officers but also had already immersed themselves in local politics by the time he returned home in the fall of 1865.[8]

Among Confederate veterans from Louisiana in the summer of 1865, there was no consensus over how to deal with the issues of defeat, military occupation, and emancipation—or if even to accept them at all. Leading figures from Louisiana had been among the last Confederates to capitulate. Lt. Gen. Richard C. Taylor, son of president and Mexican War hero Zachary Taylor, surrendered his army east of the Mississippi at the end of April. The commander of the Trans-Mississippi Department, which included all of Louisiana west of the Mississippi, Gen. Edmund Kirby Smith, refused to surrender until May 25, 1865. He harbored the forlorn hope that Jefferson Davis could escape from the Confederate capital in Richmond to Texas and then rally the Southwest to guerrilla warfare. Davis's ignominious capture in Georgia dashed those last hopes of avoiding the finality of defeat. Even so, an influential nucleus of white Louisianians rejected any future back inside a United States of America now dominated by hated Yankees. Led by both of the Confederate governors of the state, Thomas Overton Moore and Henry Watkins Allen, hundreds of prominent Louisianians as well as thousands of other Confederates voluntarily left their homes for exile in Mexico.[9]

Some motivation for this flight of the state's elite resided in uneasiness over

8. See Ransom and Sutch, *One Kind of Freedom*, 63, table 4.1; Owen, *Washington Artillery*, 22.

9. The Confederate surrender in Louisiana was quite confused. Gen. Edmund Kirby Smith sent Maj. Gen. Simon B. Buckner to New Orleans to negotiate the surrender while he left for Galveston, Texas. Smith did not initial the final terms of surrender until June 2, 1865. See John D. Winters, *The Civil War in Louisiana* (Baton Rouge: Louisiana State University Press, 1963), 426. See also McPherson, *Ordeal by Fire*, 465. For the last-ditch effort to reorganize Confederate resistance in the southwestern United States and Mexico, see Wallace P. Reed, "Last Forlorn Hope of the Confederacy," *Southern Historical Society Papers* 30 (1902): 117–21.

whether the North would exact vengeance upon Confederate leaders. The actions of a number of the exiles, however, belie their frequently repeated assertion that "the wealth and intelligence" of the South had accepted the war's twin verdicts of unconditional surrender and emancipation. Some Confederate officers, including Maj. Gen. J. B. Magruder, immediately took commissions in Maximilian's army. Many of the planters among the expatriates, encouraged by the friendly attitudes of Napoleon III and his Hapsburg puppet, Maximilian, nourished hopes of resurrecting a plantation society, complete with legalized African slavery, south of the border. Still other planters, mindful of Mexican instability and the proximity of the Union army, looked even farther south for refuge. Through the summer and fall of 1865, planters' letters and diaries debated the prospects for establishing a Confederate colony in Brazil, where land was plentiful and slavery's future seemingly secure. Many more Confederate veterans who remained in Louisiana at the end of the war might have joined the exiles, but the total collapse of the southern economy left them without the necessary capital to do so.[10]

GOVERNOR WELLS'S APPEAL TO THE CONFEDERATE VETERAN VOTE

Fear of the political clout of Confederate veterans was an important factor in Gov. James Madison Wells's course of action after his inauguration in March 1865. A wealthy planter from Rapides Parish along the Red River between Alexandria and Shreveport, a Conservative Unionist, and an organizer of a Unionist partisan outfit led by his own son during the war, Wells could hardly be described in 1865 as a Confederate sympathizer, but neither was he a likely candidate to champion ideas like black suffrage and land confiscation then brewing in the North. In the 1864 election organized under Lincoln's "Ten Percent Plan" for wartime reconstruction, Wells won as lieutenant governor on the Free State ticket under Michael Hahn principally as a bid to appeal to those Whig planters and merchants who had been cool to secession in 1861. Throughout the war these Conservative Unionists tantalized Lincoln with the prospect of a voluntary restoration of seceded states, but the hope always proved

---

10. Freeman, *Lee's Lieutenants*, 3:779. Desire to emigrate to a country where slavery was not in question appeared throughout the ranks of the Confederate army, especially after the possibility of defeat loomed larger in 1863. See, for example, Elijah P. Petty to Margaret E. Petty, Aug. 17, Sept. 11, 1863, in Petty, *Journey to Pleasant Hill: The Civil War Letters of Captain Elijah P. Petty*, ed. Norman D. Brown (San Antonio: University of Texas Institute of Texas Cultures, 1982). Petty was a captain in a Texas regiment that fought in Louisiana from 1862 to 1865. He was killed at the battle of Pleasant Hill in 1864. After Appomattox, Maj. William Owen and several of his comrades from the Washington Artillery discussed emigration to Brazil with General Lee, who advised against it. See Owen, *Washington Artillery*, 396.

greater than the reality. Congress refused to seat the Free State representatives elected in 1864, and recognition of Louisiana's government remained an unsettled issue at the time of Lincoln's assassination. When Governor Hahn accepted election by the legislature to the U.S. Senate in early 1865, Wells assumed the governor's office and, much to the surprise of Republicans in New Orleans, immediately began taking steps transparently aimed at appeasing Confederate veteran voters.[11]

In his first actions as governor, Wells tried to bolster his authority over the state and the capital city of New Orleans. Within days of his inauguration on March 5, Wells wrote Lincoln asking the president to appoint him military governor of the state; he renewed that request once Andrew Johnson was sworn in.[12] In New Orleans he appointed one of his friends, Hugh Kennedy, as mayor of the city and then began a wholesale purge of Unionist officeholders appointed by Hahn and Gen. Nathaniel P. Banks.[13] Kennedy took his cue from Wells by cutting the size of the city's police department from 450 to 400 officers and replaced many of the remaining force with Confederate veterans, some still clad in their gray uniforms.

Wells's attempts to appease Confederate veterans even before the surrender of all Rebel forces ran into immediate opposition from the Union army's proconsul in Louisiana. General Banks, still military commander of Louisiana despite the fiasco he had made of the campaign up the Red River in 1864, retaliated by ordering Kennedy physically removed from his office. He justified the expulsion on the grounds that Kennedy had been a Confederate officeholder and had not been formally pardoned.[14] In Kennedy's place Banks picked Col. S. M. Quincy, a native of Boston, an ardent abolitionist, supporter of black suffrage, and the commander of the most prominent black regiment in New Orleans. The general picked this staunch Yankee to strike a nerve

11. For a contemporary expression of fear of an alliance of Maximilian and ex-Confederates in Mexico, see William Cornell Jewett to Andrew Johnson, July 30, 1865, Andrew Johnson Papers, LC. An overview of Wells's antebellum wealth is found in Joseph Karl Menn, *The Large Slaveholders of Louisiana—1860* (New Orleans: Pelican, 1964), 335–36. On Wells's Civil War activities, see Walter M. Lowrey, "The Political Career of James Madison Wells," *LHQ* 31 (Oct. 1948): 995–1123. The Confederate government in Shreveport reviled Wells. Richard Taylor's troops ransacked and then burned his plantation during the Red River campaign of 1864. See Winters, *Civil War in Louisiana*, 373; and Dawson, *Army Generals and Reconstruction*, 29.

12. Gilles Vandal, *The New Orleans Riot of 1866: Anatomy of a Tragedy* (Lafayette: Center for Louisiana Studies, University of Southwestern Louisiana, 1983), 61.

13. J. Madison Wells to Andrew Johnson, May 22, 1865, Johnson Papers. General Banks appointed Maj. Stephen Hoyt acting mayor in 1864. Wells replaced Hoyt with Kennedy in March 1865, just after his inauguration.

14. For Wells's eyewitness description of Kennedy's ouster, see J. Madison Wells to Andrew Johnson, May 5, 1865, Johnson Papers.

with the patrician southern planter.[15] Enraged at this affront to his authority and dignity, Wells immediately embarked for Washington to personally confer with Johnson about Reconstruction policy.

Wells's meeting with Andrew Johnson at the White House on May 25, 1865, had a momentous influence on the course of presidential Reconstruction. At first glance it might appear that the two men had little in common. Wells represented the wealth and self-assured aristocracy of Whig sugar planters from the Deep South. Johnson, by contrast, came from the hill country of Tennessee and had scrambled up the slope of life, the entire way resenting the wealth and self-assurance that Wells represented. Nonetheless, in their public lives the two men shared similar wartime experiences, and from their later correspondence it is clear that they shared similar views on Reconstruction policy at the end of the war. Both publicly opposed secession in the feverish days of 1861. Both held Unionist office, at considerable personal danger to themselves and their families, in slave states during the war. Both opposed black suffrage, a position they concealed from their temporary allies in the Republican Party in 1865. While no written record remains of their talks in Washington, the likelihood that Wells and Johnson came to a significant understanding during this meeting is suggested both by the fact that Johnson issued his Proclamation on Pardon and Amnesty just four days after the meeting and that the policy he enunciated neatly dovetailed with Wells's already expressed strategy of appeasing the ex-Confederate vote in Louisiana. After their May conference, Wells wrote frequently to Johnson, keeping him informed of developments in New Orleans and peppering him with requests and demands to override rulings of the local military commanders in charge of the occupation. Johnson's responses were invariably solicitous, and it soon became apparent to contemporaries that the president intended to make the Wells administration in Louisiana a showcase for his policy of reconstruction by restoration.[16]

Upon returning to New Orleans, Wells accelerated the implementation of his political strategy. But by this time the War Department in Washington had already recalled his antagonist, General Banks. In his stead Ulysses S. Grant, the army's commanding general, appointed Maj. Gen. E. R. S. Canby, a professional soldier, who Wells and Johnson both hoped would prove more in tune with Johnson's policies than

---

15. For a list of officers of the regiment, see War Department, *Official Army Register of the Volunteer Force of the United States Army for the Years 1861, '62, '63, '64, '65*, 8 vols. (Washington, D.C.: Government Printing Office, 1865), 8:246. A number of them (e.g., Maj. Francis E. Dumas, Capt. James Ingraham, Lt. Jules Mallet, and Lt. Emile Detiege) became Republican politicians and militia officers during Reconstruction.

16. William McFeely, *Yankee Stepfather: General O. O. Howard and the Freedmen* (New Haven, Conn.: Yale University Press, 1968), 166–89.

Banks, a political general from Massachusetts. Following the dictates of Johnson's Proclamation of Pardon and Amnesty, Wells announced a new registration of voters and set a date for a statewide election of offices on November 6, 1865. On July 1 he reinstalled Hugh Kennedy as mayor of New Orleans.[17] Within weeks Governor Wells and Mayor Kennedy had persuaded Johnson to remove the assistant superintendent of the Freedmen's Bureau for Louisiana, Thomas Conway, who openly supported black suffrage and refused to permit New Orleans police to arrest "negro vagrants" and assign them labor contracts with planters looking for cheap labor.[18] Johnson pressured Maj. Gen. O. O. Howard, superintendent of the Freedmen's Bureau, to transfer Conway and then replace him with an ally in the bureau, Joseph S. Fullerton. In the final six weeks before the state elections, Fullerton reversed all of Conway's policies that Wells had found offensive. For good measure Fullerton confided to ex-general Taylor that he would strictly prohibit bureau agents from attending black political gatherings in the future. He hastened to add that he also intended to embark on a massive program to restore land titles to all Confederates who would apply for amnesty under Johnson's program.[19]

Wells also pressed Johnson repeatedly to use the army to conscript black labor to repair levees along the Mississippi, which had suffered from neglect and damage during the war and demanded attention before the best alluvial plantations in the state could be returned to profitable cultivation.[20] Again Johnson complied, ordering Secretary of War Edwin Stanton to make the necessary arrangements with local army commanders. At about the same time, Johnson directed the military to stem the influx of blacks into southern cities like New Orleans and deactivate all black Union regiments recruited during the war as quickly as possible.[21]

In retrospect it is clear that the Wells-Johnson alliance in the summer of 1865 was already founded on a shared desire to restore the status quo antebellum, minus the formalities of slavery, rather than to reconstruct southern society along the lines of the free-labor ideology predominant in the Republican Party of the North. Social restoration in the South dictated that civil and military authorities should discourage

17. J. Madison Wells to Andrew Johnson, July 3, 1865, Johnson Papers.

18. McFeely, *Yankee Stepfather*, 172. For Wells's views on black labor and complaints about Conway, see J. Madison Wells to Andrew Johnson, July 29, 1865, Johnson Papers.

19. Joseph S. Fullerton, *Report of the Administration of Freedmen's Affairs in Louisiana* (Washington, D.C.: Government Printing Office, 1865), 3–6; McFeely, *Yankee Stepfather*, 177.

20. J. Madison Wells and Hugh Kennedy to Andrew Johnson, May 27, 1865, Johnson Papers; J. Madison Wells to Andrew Johnson, July 5, 1865, ibid.

21. McFeely, *Yankee Stepfather*, 173.

ex-slaves from migrating from rural plantations to New Orleans by means of the va-grancy laws that Conway had opposed. Economic restoration entailed not only im-mobilizing black labor on plantations but also a swift restoration of land titles to planters, thwarting hopes of northern Radical Republicans and southern freedmen for an extensive land redistribution upon which a new class of black and white yeo-man farmers might arise. Finally, political restoration demanded that all ex-Confed-erates (excepting perhaps only the most important political and military leaders, in-cluding Jefferson Davis and Robert E. Lee) be speedily pardoned, restored in their voting rights, and authorized to hold political office. By this program of closely inter-related policies, Wells and Johnson hoped to quickly restore confidence among white southerners that the outcome of the Civil War would alter neither their traditional way of life in general nor the racial verities of antebellum society in particular.

This strategy appeared to pay important political dividends for Wells and Johnson in the fall of 1865. In October Wells received nominations for Louisiana governor from both the Conservative Unionists and the National Democrats, who fused their tickets for governor and lieutenant governor under the banner of the National Dem-ocratic Party. Free from the taint of either Confederate service or an explicit advocacy of black suffrage, Wells held what seemed to be the decisive middle ground on elec-tion day. With the incumbent governor eager to swiftly remove all disabilities threat-ening Confederate veterans, support for a brazen Conservative write-in campaign to reelect Confederate governor Allen, who was then editor of a newspaper for exiles in Mexico City, waned. Without black votes, no Republican candidate stood a chance of winning, and therefore—as we shall see—Louisiana Republicans chose to field no challenger at all in November. When the returns were announced, Governor Wells had indeed won a commanding victory over ex-governor Allen, by a vote of 21,000 to 5,000, and thereby seemed firmly in control of the future of Reconstruction in Louisiana. That appearance would prove illusory. Events would show that Confeder-ate veterans, rather than Wells, had done the manipulation in the 1865 election. Events would also find Louisiana Republicans equally adept at electoral politics, for they discovered a way for the potential weight of black political votes to be felt, even if they had been excluded from Wells's election.

BLACK AND WHITE UNION VETERANS RESIST THE RESTORATION
OF THE OLD REGIME

Governor Wells's strenuous efforts to restore the old regime in Louisiana did not go unnoticed or unopposed by Union army veterans in New Orleans. Perhaps as many as five thousand white Union veterans, many from abolitionist backgrounds in New

England, chose to remain in Louisiana at the end of the war, most settling in and around New Orleans. Some, like Col. Henry C. Warmoth, had already established thriving business and law practices in the city before the end of the war through contacts they had established while serving in the wartime occupation forces. Others, including William Pitt Kellogg, who had been a cavalry colonel, and Stephen B. Packard, a former captain, made smooth transitions from wartime military duties to federal patronage jobs with the U.S. Custom House on Canal Street. Still other northerners, like Capt. Marshal Harvey Twitchell, bought plantations in the rural parishes, convinced that they could translate their experience with free-labor agriculture in the North into profit in the South.[22]

While these nonnative white veterans—who came to be known as "carpetbaggers"—represented an important source of wealth and organizational talent for the Republican Party in Louisiana, it was already clear by 1865 that they would never have the votes to win the state on their own. Unlike such Upper South states as Tennessee, North Carolina, or Arkansas, Louisiana possessed no region where native white Unionists approached a majority of the white population. Most white Radicals, led by men such as Benjamin Flanders (a schoolteacher) and Thomas J. Durant (a lawyer), resided in New Orleans and represented a tiny slice of the 1860 electorate—too small to even permit the Republicans to consider fielding a slate of candidates in that year. Thus, perhaps more quickly than in any other state of the former Confederacy, the nascent white Republican leadership in Louisiana turned to the prospect of black suffrage to secure their political future.

If there were to be black voters in Louisiana, they would doubtlessly come first from the ranks of black Union army veterans. Louisiana contributed more black soldiers and more black officers to the Union cause than any other state, North or South.[23] Of the more than 178,000 black soldiers who served in the Union army,

22. Henry Clay Warmoth, *War, Politics, and Reconstruction: Stormy Days in Louisiana* (New York: Macmillan, 1930), 30; Ted Tunnell, *Crucible of Reconstruction: War, Radicalism, and Race in Louisiana, 1862–1877* (Baton Rouge: Louisiana State University Press, 1984).

23. Details on the creation of black military units in the Union army can be found in Ira Berlin et al., eds., *Freedom: A Documentary History of Emancipation, 1861–1867: Selected from the Holdings of the National Archives of the United States. Series 2: The Black Military Experience* (Cambridge: Cambridge University Press, 1982), 1–34. Two-thirds of all commissioned black officers in the Union army came from the three black regiments from New Orleans, all mustered in to service by Maj. Gen. Benjamin Butler in late 1862. Generally, black regiments organized as U.S. Colored Troops (USCT) after 1863 had white officers, with the exception of an occasional black chaplain or surgeon. As the war became more bitter and costly in the winter of 1864–65 (and as white enlistments began to expire in larger numbers), some halting steps were taken to offer more commissions to blacks like Maj. Martin Delaney of the 104th USCT, who proposed using all-

24,052 came from Louisiana. From the beginning of the military occupation of New Orleans in 1862, Union commanders inevitably if often reluctantly turned to of black volunteers, both free and slave, to serve as military laborers, militia troops, and finally soldiers. In May 1863, black troops from the First and Third Louisiana Guards (later the Seventy-Third and Seventy-Fifth U.S. Colored Troops) participated in the assault on Port Hudson, a Confederate citadel on the Mississippi that ranked only behind Vicksburg in its strategic command of the river. A curious northern press, noting that it was the first large-scale use of black soldiers in the war, hailed their example as a great success. The publicity encouraged General Banks to spur recruitment of blacks and to create the "Corps d'Afrique," composed of infantry, artillery, cavalry, and engineers. Banks's campaign up the Red River in 1864, while a disappointment to Lincoln and Grant, further encouraged that trend. By impressing able-bodied male slaves into newly formed regiments and sending the remainder to contraband camps, the Union army helped drain the plantation labor force supporting cotton production in areas still under Confederate control. By the end of the war, nearly 31 percent of all black men of military age in the state had served with the Union forces.[24]

Nineteenth-century social historians stress that military life in the army was the first introduction many blacks had into the world of free labor. Black soldiers, even when paid less than their white counterparts, received bounties as well as regular pay; went to schools run by Yankee missionaries set up in army camps near New Orleans; and began to think and act as wage earners in a market economy by the time their terms of service expired. What must be stressed here, however, is that military service was also a profoundly politicizing experience for black soldiers, radically altering their perceptions of themselves and their expectations of the larger society around them.

The key to the political future of black Louisiana lay with the gens de couleur libre in New Orleans. Numbering almost thirteen thousand in 1860, this community of free blacks represented a peculiar institution within the peculiar institution of slavery. Unlike the plantation slaves of largely unmixed African descent in the rural parishes, the gens de couleur libre were mulattos of mixed African and European descent who were as often than not literate, educated, propertied, and, in a few cases, slaveholders themselves. During the secession crisis of 1861, they formed three militia regiments in New Orleans for defense against the expected Yankee invasion. But

---

black units to conduct guerrilla raids behind Confederate lines. The war ended before his regiment saw action.

24. Ira Berlin et al., eds., *Slave No More: Three Essays on Emancipation and the Civil War* (Cambridge: Cambridge University Press, 1992), 203 (table 1).

when Admiral Farragut and General Butler arrived in the city in April 1862, they abruptly switched sides and offered their services to the Union army. Among the officers of these regiments were Maj. Francis E. Dumas, Capt. P. B. S. Pinchback, Capt. James Ingraham, and Capt. C. C. Antoine, who would all come to play leading roles in black politics in New Orleans after 1865.

Governor Wells's announcement of a new registration of white voters for the November elections launched both black and white Unionists on a search for some way to block the resurgence of Confederate veterans back into political power. Some Radical Republicans, led by T. J. Durant, had argued as early as 1863 that by seceding, Louisiana and the other Confederate states had committed what they called "state suicide," and therefore could not be fully restored to the Union by executive action alone. As early as 1864 Durant had advised Secretary of the Treasury Salmon P. Chase that "Congress should assume control of the whole matter and fix on an immutable basis the civil and political status of the population of African descent, before any state shall be readmitted to the Union."[25] Durant suggested that these conquered states ought to revert to territories, whose reorganization and readmission to the Union would be overseen by Congress, as specified in the Constitution, rather than the president. By late 1865 this plan gathered momentum, for it afforded Republicans in Congress the opportunity to block the Johnson-Wells plan of antebellum restoration by requiring black suffrage as a condition of congressional representation.[26]

On June 10, 1865, Durant chaired the first meeting of the biracial Universal Suffrage Movement in New Orleans, during which the group adopted a resolution supporting his territorial plan of reconstruction. Then they approved steps to exert pressure to block the Johnson-Wells restoration program. They sent an appeal to friendly Republican congressmen in Washington asking that Louisiana's representatives not be recognized or admitted to Congress, proposing instead that Louisiana be treated as a territory, and calling for an election to choose delegates for a state territorial convention in September, well in advance of the Wells-ordered state election in November. This election, in which blacks would be encouraged to cast ballots along with whites, would name delegates to a statewide convention that in turn could petition Congress for admission to statehood in the same manner that territories had historically followed.[27]

25. T. J. Durant to S. P. Chase, Feb. 21, 1864, Salmon P. Chase Papers, LC.

26. Some congressmen in 1865, of course, demanded additional measures besides black suffrage. Among these were more stringent loyalty oaths than had been demanded by Johnson, land confiscation, and Confederate disfranchisement.

27. Vandal, *New Orleans Riot of 1866*, 70. Although its results were never recognized, this was the first

Events moved rapidly in the fall, resulting in an undermining of Wells's claim to lead the sole legitimate government of the state. On September 16, after feverish organizing, especially on the part of the gens de couleur libre in New Orleans, the election for the state convention took place. Turnout was light by antebellum standards (only about three thousand ballots cast) but respectable enough to give notice that the radicals would not acquiesce in Wells's plan. Nine days later 111 elected delegates assembled in Economy Hall in New Orleans. In addition to adopting resolutions that signaled their radical leanings, they ingeniously decided to hold the election for a territorial delegate to Congress on the same day—November 6—that Wells had designated as the election day for new statewide offices under Johnson's restoration policy. Discarding the Universal Suffrage banner, they embraced the title of the National Republican Party and, by a narrow vote, chose Colonel Warmoth as their party's nominee for territorial delegate.[28]

Thus there was not one but two separate and mutually hostile elections in Louisiana on November 6, 1865, and proponents of each denied the legitimacy of the other. In Wells's election only whites eligible under the terms of the 1864 Constitution and ex-Confederates who had taken Johnson's amnesty could cast ballots. Because the Unionist constitution had not accepted black suffrage, only white men could register to vote, which was precisely the population that in 1861 had supported secession and fought in the Confederate army. In contrast the territorial election organized by Republicans remained theoretically open to both blacks and whites, but Confederate veterans soon realized that a vote in the territorial election was a vote against the Johnson-Wells restoration. Accordingly they stayed away from the territorial polls and in some cases tried to prevent Republicans from voting. Despite the lack of organization and scarcity of polling places outside the New Orleans–area parishes, the outcome of what most ex-Confederates regarded as an illegitimate election was a rebuke to Johnson and Wells. In his own election, run with such machinery of the state bureaucracy as existed at the time, Wells polled about 21,000 votes. In contrast Warmoth—whose supporters managed to establish polls in only ten parishes around New Orleans, drew a total of 19,105 votes—nearly as many as Wells had in the "official" election. An analysis of the vote reveals that about 2,500 of Warmoth's votes came from whites (who could have voted in the Wells election), with the remainder (roughly 16,500) cast by blacks and mulattos denied ballots by the Wells government.

---

southern election in which blacks were encouraged and authorized to vote. Since blacks formed such a tiny minority of the population in northern states, it was also probably the first election held in U.S. history in which black voters composed a majority.

28. Ibid., 77.

For Republican leaders in Congress searching for a strategy to thwart Johnson's restoration-without-reconstruction program and anxious to assess how southern blacks might vote, the territorial elections in Louisiana produced gratifying results. They warmly greeted Warmoth's arrival in Washington, particularly those in the radical wing of the party. Although congressional Republicans eventually declined to grant him official membership in the House, they could not resist granting Warmoth his own seat on the floor of the House of Representatives, if only to snub the representatives chosen in Wells's election, who did not gain official admission to the floor and had to follow proceedings from the gallery.[29]

THE ARMY AND THE PROBLEMS OF MILITARY OCCUPATION

The looming struggle between the president and Congress for control over Reconstruction policy caught the army's leading generals off guard. Having devoted four years to the epic pursuit of victory over Rebel armies, ranking generals like Grant, Sherman, and Sheridan seemed oblivious to the complications that an occupation mission in the postwar South might present. Part of the explanation for why the challenges of Reconstruction seem to have surprised the generals lay in their preoccupation with what seemed to them to be more pressing matters at the time. These issues included ensuring that the vast expanse of the Confederacy west of the Mississippi surrendered, pressuring the French to leave Mexico, and demobilizing the one million volunteers of the Union army and replacing them with a much smaller peacetime professional force. All three of these missions seemed critical to completing the final phase of the Civil War. While the army accomplished them with greater ease than might have been imagined possible, this achievement came at the cost of pursuing more-effective occupation policies.

To accomplish the first two goals, Grant dispatched Sheridan to Texas with fifty thousand troops and orders to hunt down Smith's Rebel army in May 1865, bluntly informing him: "if Smith holds out, without even an ostensible Government to receive orders from, . . . he and his men are not entitled to the considerations due to an acknowledged belligerent. Theirs are the conditions of outlaws making war against the only Government having an existance over the territory where war is being waged."[30]

Characteristically Sheridan attacked his new mission with the ferocious zeal that

29. Warmoth, *War, Politics, and Reconstruction*, 45.

30. U. S. Grant to P. H. Sheridan, May 17, 1865, in Ulysses S. Grant, *The Papers of Ulysses S. Grant*, ed. John Y. Simon, 18 vols. (Carbondale: Southern Illinois University Press, 1988), 15:43–44. Grant was a notoriously poor speller his whole life but nevertheless a highly effective writer. His written messages are presented unaltered and uncorrected throughout this work to preserve his distinctive style.

had made him one of Grant's favorite subordinates. In June Sheridan arrived in New Orleans to establish his headquarters, but for the next year he spent most of his time on the Texas border. He had sized up the situation on the border quickly and reported to Grant that French-backed imperialist troops and the remnants of Smith's army seemed intent on forming an alliance south of the border. His scouts had sighted columns of Rebels crossing the Rio Grande at Matamoras, accompanied by senior Confederate officials laden down by wagon trains of weapons.

Sheridan artlessly linked the two threats in an attempt to encourage Washington to expand the Civil War into Mexico. In June he informed Grant's chief of staff, John A. Rawlins, that "I have always believed that Maximilians advent into Mexico was a part of the rebellion."[31] Tired of chasing the last Confederate stragglers across the continent, the general wanted to make a quick end of it: "[T]here is no use to beat around the bush in this mexican matter," he wrote Grant later that month. "We should give a permanent government to that republic. Our work in crushing the rebellion will not be done until this takes place. The advent of Maximilian was a portion of the rebellion and his fall should belong to its history."[32]

In July Sheridan plied Washington with fresh details from the Texas border, warning that Maximilian had made "an agreement with the rebels for the colonization of Tehuantepec and Chiapas," which he colorfully described as a "Brazilian scheme," suggesting that the Confederate exiles wanted to establish safe havens for plantation slavery.[33] It was not until April 1866 that the French excursion into Mexico began to falter, after Napoleon III announced his intention to withdraw all of his troops. Even then Sheridan remained distrustful of whether the French would keep their word and abandon Mexico and Maximilian.

While Sheridan focused on Mexico, Grant wrestled in Washington with demobilization and reorganizing a peacetime army. Union volunteers had enlisted for fixed terms of service or for the duration of the war, "if sooner." Most chafed to return to civil life as quickly as possible, heedless of all rationales advanced by their generals to keep at least some of them in uniform after Lee's surrender at Appomattox. At its greatest strength in early 1865, the Union army had surpassed one million soldiers in uniform.[34] Within months, this force, the largest field army in the world in the century between Waterloo and the Marne, melted away. After the magnificent parades at the Grand Review in Washington, most of the volunteer regiments simply stacked

31. Sheridan to Rawlins, June 4, 1865, ibid., 15:129.
32. Sheridan to Rawlins, June 29, 1865, ibid., 15:259.
33. Sheridan to Grant, Aug. 1, 1865, ibid., 15:260–61.
34. Weigley, *United States Army*, 569.

their arms, received their pay at a final muster, changed clothes, and left for home. By November 1865 just 182,784 soldiers remained on active duty; by July 1866 even this truncated force had dwindled to fewer than 40,000 men. The speed and scale of this wholesale decline in the volunteer army would perceptibly affect the course of Reconstruction in Louisiana.[35]

In general, white troops had served longer than black troops during the war, thus demobilization schedules for 1865 dictated that white regiments mustered out of federal service before black regiments. This was naturally viewed in the North as a fair policy to adopt for an army of citizen-soldiers who had suffered through the long years of war, low pay, and military discipline. In practice, though, it could not help but complicate the problems of race relations within the southern states, where the sight of black men in blue uniforms served as a constant reminder of Confederate defeat and black emancipation.[36]

Thus, even before the end of 1865, careful observers could predict that serious trouble was brewing in Louisiana. A large and restless population of Confederate veterans had returned to the state and had overwhelmingly sought to restore the world they had known before the war. The largest population of black veterans in the South, encouraged by a nucleus of white Union veterans who stayed in New Orleans after the war, demanded a fundamental, perhaps even revolutionary, change in the franchise that would reward those who had proven their loyalty to the Union by fighting for it. The leaders of the postwar army, absorbed with the complicated details of demobilization, reorganization, and unresolved international tensions with Mexico, found themselves distracted from the vital role of military occupation and political reconstruction. Together, these problems comprised a recipe for a shocking massacre that would focus national attention on Louisiana and the dispute over Reconstruction in the following year.

35. U. S. Grant to W. H. Seward, Nov. 10, 1865, in Grant, *Papers*, 15:413; Weigley, *United States Army*, 262.

36. Mary Francis Berry, *Military Necessity and Civil Right Policy: Black Citizenship and the Constitution, 1861–1868* (Port Washington, N.Y.: Kennikat, 1977).

❧ 2 ❧

The Street Battle of 1866
A Massacre of Union Veterans

Political initiative quickly passed from Governor Wells with the election of Louisiana's new state legislature in 1865, which became known as the "Rebel Legislature" because so many Confederate veterans held seats in the assembly. Despite Wells's repeated assurances to President Johnson that their reliability was beyond question, legislative leaders wasted no time demonstrating their determination to undermine the policies of both men and restore the antebellum political order.

GOVERNOR WELLS VERSUS THE REBEL LEGISLATURE

The new legislators immediately tried to cast off Governor Wells. After the election Wells called the newly elected lawmakers into a special session at the end of November 1865 to deal with the state's dire finances. They responded by ignoring his appeal for action and then spent the session scheming to jettison the governor and the constitution imposed on the state by the Union army in 1864. To rid themselves of Wells, legislators at first proposed a motion to elect him U.S. senator. Had he accepted their offer, it would have propelled a former Confederate officeholder, Lt. Gov. Albert Voorhies, into the governor's chair. When Wells refused their nomination, Rebel legislators shifted course and embarked on a lengthy debate over the legality of the 1864 Constitution, seemingly oblivious to the fact that their own claim to office stemmed from that document. Some wanted to proclaim it a legal nullity because only a fraction of the state's voters had approved its creation. Others preferred to skip nullification and proposed calling a new constitutional convention. Concerned that jettisoning a constitution that had been endorsed by Lincoln might be badly interpreted by Republicans in Congress, Andrew Johnson personally warned leaders of the Rebel Legislature of the political indelicacy of taking such a step, and they let that proposal die without action.[1]

---

1. Gilles Vandal has substantiated the influence of Confederate veterans in the 1865–66 Louisiana legislature. See *New Orleans Riot of 1866*, 98.

31

While neither of these attempts to run roughshod over Wells succeeded, they foreshadowed a looming chasm between the governor and the Confederate veterans who had elected him. When the legislature reconvened for its regular session in December 1865, it passed a series of bills regulating plantation labor. State senator Duncan F. Kenner, who had formerly been Louisiana's wealthiest slaveholder and the personal envoy of Jefferson Davis to the European powers in the last days of the Confederacy, sponsored all four bills. They ostensibly dealt with vagrancy, punishment for those helping laborers escape from their employers, "enticement" (the crime of hiring workers away from their previous employers), and defining agricultural labor contracts. But they were actually an attempt to supplant the institution of chattel slavery with a form of state-sponsored serfdom. While northern opinion popularly regarded these proposals as another of the "Black Codes" that sprang from all southern legislatures during presidential Reconstruction, Kenner's bills discretely refrained from mentioning the race of their intended targets of regulation. Wells reluctantly signed the first three bills but not the last, explaining in his pocket-veto message that it construed the former slaves' new status so narrowly that it violated the Thirteenth Amendment, which had been passed by the U.S. Congress while many of Louisiana's current legislators had still been serving in the Confederate army.[2]

More disputes followed, mostly centered on economic issues. Emancipation of Louisiana's slaves had slashed the total taxable wealth of the state by more than half. Three years of war within the state's borders had crippled cotton and sugar production, Louisiana's principal sources of income. In addition, the Unionist government in New Orleans had collected no taxes from any of the parishes under Confederate control after 1862. As a result the state treasury was empty and services nonexistent. The funding solution that the Rebel Legislature enacted was simple, though cleverly crafted to shift the burden of state government off those who had supported the Confederate cause and onto those who had not. A bill passed to suspend tax collection for the years 1862–65 until at least 1867. Current expenses would be met in the coming year from a new bond issue, triggering an enormous rise in the state's indebtedness. Lawmakers also deemed a number of capital improvements, such as railroads, canals, and ferries, critical to economic revival and granted charters to private corporations. Prominent Confederate generals, including Richard Taylor (New Basin Canal), E. Kirby Smith and Simon B. Buckner (Southern Telegraph Company), and

---

2. On Kenner's career as a Confederate diplomat during the last months of the war, see McPherson, *Battle Cry*, 837–38. For an explanation of the role of the Black Codes in the transition from plantation gang labor to sharecropping in the post–Civil War South, see Ransom and Sutch, *One Kind of Freedom*, 67.

James Longstreet (Texas and Pacific Railroad), headed every one of these enterprises. Disturbed by the prospect of letting Confederate property holders escape back taxes, Wells reluctantly approved the bond issue and charter grants but vetoed the suspension of wartime tax repayment.[3]

The final break between the governor and the Rebel Legislature came in a dispute over a bill for new city elections in New Orleans and Orleans Parish, which surrounded the city. Lawmakers realized that these offices and their patronage positions, when added to their electoral sweep in November 1865, would speed the removal from power of the remaining prominent wartime Unionists in the state. Sensitive to his need to hold on to control of New Orleans, Wells vetoed the bill. Undaunted, the Rebel Legislature overrode his veto on February 15, 1866, forcing a new election.[4]

The New Orleans municipal election held on March 12 was not particularly violent by later standards in Reconstruction, though it did not pass without contention. Local newspapers reported numerous threats of intimidation at the polls, though only one murder. Unionists proved as eager to bend the rules as Rebels. Mayor Kennedy reportedly fired policemen who refused to support Well's Conservative Unionist ticket. Unionist politicians, eager to sway the city's labor vote, tried to spend $26,000 on public-works projects in the last month before the election. Their efforts did not pay off. Confederate veterans, under the banner of the Conservative Party, swept in to office. New Orleans's new mayor, John T. Monroe, had held the same position under the Confederate government until General Butler removed him for refusing to swear the oath of allegiance to the Union in 1862. And on the New Orleans City Council, Conservatives won a commanding twenty-one seats to the Conservative Unionists' ten.[5]

Analysis of the Conservatives' Civil War backgrounds reveals that New Orleans's new city government was as overwhelmingly Confederate as the Rebel Legislature. In all, 88 percent of Conservative candidates for city council were former Confederate soldiers or officeholders; none had served with Union forces. Conservative Unionist candidates represented a wider spectrum of allegiances. Seventeen percent of them had been Confederate soldiers, but the party also ran a number of Union veterans as well as a few who had actually served on both sides. In May Harry Hays, the former commander of a Louisiana brigade under General Lee, led another slate of Confederate veterans to victory in the Orleans Parish elections and became the new sheriff.

3. Winters, *Civil War in Louisiana*, 429; Joe Gray Taylor, *Louisiana Reconstructed, 1863–1877* (Baton Rouge: Louisiana State University Press, 1974), 81, 86–87.

4. *Louisiana House Journal*, Feb. 13–15, 1866, 44–50.

5. *New Orleans Times*, Mar. 10, 1866, 1.

General Hays's bravery under fire during the war made him a popular figure among Louisiana Confederates. After the surrender he enhanced this reputation by founding the Hays's Brigade Benevolent Association, which offered aid to sick and wounded veterans who had served under his command.[6]

The Confederate veterans now in charge of New Orleans moved quickly to consolidate their control over all patronage positions. Mayor Monroe's new police chief, former Confederate colonel Thomas E. Adams, raised a new police force by the end of May. He later admitted under oath to a U.S. Army military commission that at least two-thirds of his 550 officers were Confederate veterans. Confederate soldiers who had returned penniless and unemployed to the city after the war greatly appreciated these appointments. Pay for the new positions was eighty dollars per month, at a time when Union soldiers received only thirteen dollars per month, and many Rebel soldiers had received nothing but near-worthless Confederate currency in the last year of the war. Competition for the appointments proved intense. Of the 12,600 qualified voters in New Orleans in 1866, nearly 4,000 men, or about one in three, applied for the force.[7]

The rapidity with which Confederate veterans returned to power just months after losing the war dismayed Louisiana Republicans and forced them to question how to stem this political onslaught. "The Johnny rebels are in great glee in anticipation of having the City Hall," wrote one New Orleans observer to Henry Warmoth in Washington. "[They have] cleaned out all of those whose sympathies and assistance have been given to the U.S. Government." By early 1866 Warmoth and T. J. Durant had exchanged letters expressing their fear that Johnson's political strategy of mollifying southern Democrats had succeeded. They worried that Congress would refuse to enact black suffrage and that even the proposed Civil Rights Bill of 1866 had so many loopholes that ex-Confederate states would easily find ways to circumvent it.[8]

After severing his ties to the Rebel Legislature by vetoing the New Orleans elections, Governor Wells reversed political course and sought an alliance with his former opponents—Louisiana Republicans. In March 1866 he promised Warmoth that,

6. Vandal, *New Orleans Riot of 1866*, 119 (table IV.2). Vandal's quantitative research is detailed, but he draws different conclusions from that research than does this author. Confederate veterans from Hays's Brigade, Gibson's Brigade, Washington Artillery Battalion, and Fenner's Battery all formed charitable organizations in New Orleans after the war. An indication of the importance of the Hays's Brigade Relief Society in the city's post–Civil War society is found in William Harper Forman Jr., "William P. Harper in War and Reconstruction," *LaH* 13 (1972): 69.

7. Vandal, *New Orleans Riot of 1866*, 120, 204–5, 208–9.

8. G. W. Stauffer to H. C. Warmoth, Feb. 6, 1866, Henry C. Warmoth Papers, SHC.

"By the Eternal, he intended to beat the rebels and keep them out of power, if in doing so he destroyed the state government and produced anarchy for twenty years." He announced that he would support reconvening the convention of 1864, at which he intended to work to disfranchise Rebel voters and petition for black suffrage.[9]

Not all of Wells's new allies favored his strategy. Some Republicans wanted to see the Rebels disfranchised but remained uncertain whether the time had really come for black suffrage. One of the delegates to the new convention, John P. Henderson Jr., had advised General Banks in December 1865 that "the loyal voters of the south are not yet prepared for political equality of the negro with the white man." Other Republicans, black and white, opposed Wells's plan to reconvene the constitutional convention. Some white radicals like Warmoth and Durant argued that the Confederates states had committed "state suicide" by seceding, insisting that only Congress could revive them through its constitutional power to admit territories to the Union. Black sentiment, reflected in the editorials of the *New Orleans Tribune*, demanded equality and immediate enfranchisement but argued that only a constitutional amendment from Congress could put those issues safely beyond the grasp of southern states.[10]

Governor Wells, however, was in no mood by the spring of 1866 to wait for help from Washington. He seized upon a provision in the 1864 Constitution that permitted the state convention to reconvene by a call from its president. A preliminary meeting on June 26 revealed that there was no quorum of convention delegates and that the original president, Judge Edmund H. Durrell, refused to participate. Wells called for an election of new delegates in September, citing the absence of delegates from many parishes that had previously been under Confederate administration. At the same time, he endorsed a second attempt to convene the convention for July 30. He hoped that the new president pro tem, Louisiana Supreme Court associate justice Rufus K. Howell, might somehow produce a quorum of delegates in the interim.[11]

By challenging the very existence of the Rebel Legislature, Wells knew he would make political enemies, but he may not have anticipated that chief among them would be Andrew Johnson. When the legislature began considering the bill for New Orleans elections in January 1866, Wells had warned the president not to support the measure. Johnson blithely replied that he had no objections to local elections, provided

---

9. H. C. Warmoth Diary, Mar. 22, 1866, ibid.; Taylor, *Louisiana Reconstructed*, 104.

10. John P. Henderson Jr. quoted in Vandal, *New Orleans Riot of 1866*, 112. Henderson was one of the three white convention delegates who died in the street battle of July 30. Warmoth, *War, Politics, and Reconstruction*, 43–45; McFeely, *Yankee Stepfather*, 282.

11. Taylor, *Louisiana Reconstructed*, 105; Vandal, *New Orleans Riot of 1866*, 163.

that only "loyal men" were elected and they required no military interference. Whether Johnson realized that he had begun to cut out the ground from under one of his showcase southern loyalist governors is not clear, but soon enough he stopped confiding in Wells and started listening to the Rebel Legislature's leaders. His new confidantes in New Orleans included Mayor Monroe, Lieutenant Governor Voorhies, and Atty. Gen. Andrew S. Herron, who had all held Confederate office. On July 13 Voorhies and Herron warned Johnson of the danger of permitting a new convention to meet, claiming that "the revolution to be inaugurated here forms part of a program of the Radical Revolutionists at Washington—it becomes a question of prudence not to treat this matter too lightly, but taking things at the court, to prepare for all possible emergencies." They informed the president that Herron planned to petition the state district court in New Orleans to declare the new convention illegal and issue an injunction forbidding it to meet.[12]

As the dispute escalated, both sides put pressure on the army general in charge of Louisiana, who found himself unwillingly drawn into the local political dispute. With General Sheridan gone to Texas to oversee the standoff along the Mexican border, the ranking officer present in New Orleans in mid-July 1866 was Maj. Gen. Absalom Baird, military commander for the state. Baird had arrived in his position through a circuitous route typifying the muddled condition of military commands during the army's postwar demobilization. In August 1865 he accepted an appointment as assistant superintendent of the Freedman's Bureau for Louisiana after President Johnson removed T. W. Conway, the Baptist minister who refused to support administration policies. In contrast to Conway, Baird was a West Point graduate and a professional soldier who had served on the staff of the Army of the Potomac and rose to command a division under Sherman in the campaigns of 1864 and 1865. Johnson apparently thought that professional soldiers would make more pliant administrators than civilians under peacetime conditions. There were dozens of Union generals available for these sorts of nonmilitary duties, and many willingly took such assignments because their positions as generals in the volunteer army expired when their commands mustered out of service. They would then revert to their lower regular-army rank, a change portending a loss of pay, privileges, and prestige. General Baird's subsequent pro-

12. Wells to Johnson, Jan. 29, 1866, Andrew Johnson Papers, LC; *New Orleans Tribune*, Mar. 11, 1866, 1. Herron raised and commanded Company B, 7th Louisiana Infantry in 1861. The company was organized from the Baton Rouge Fencibles of East Baton Rouge Parish, one of the antebellum militia companies that forced the surrender of the federal arsenal at Baton Rouge on January 10, 1861, *before* Louisiana passed its ordinance of secession. Winters, *Civil War in Louisiana*, 9; Jones, *Lee's Tigers*, 240–41; Albert Voorhies to John A. Rozier, July 13, 1866, Johnson Papers; Dawson, *Army Generals and Reconstruction*, 38.

nouncements suggest that he desperately tried to avoid the sort of entanglements with local politics that had cost his predecessor his job.[13]

Many generals found the rapid demobilization of the army unsettling and did not handle the conflicting missions of the peacetime military well. While Baird was replacing Conway in the Louisiana Freedmen's Bureau, Sheridan became displeased with his own subordinate, Gen. E. R. S. Canby, the military commander of the state after Johnson recalled General Banks. Sheridan accused Canby of devoting too much time to civil affairs and too little to maintaining the military readiness of the regiments under his command. In return Canby complained to Sheridan that he lacked sufficient troops to suppress lawlessness in the rural parishes. By May 1866 Sheridan eased Canby out of command, permitting him to request a transfer "on the score of health." In his place Sheridan accepted his former subordinate, Baird, whose appointment on May 28, 1866, effectively consolidated command of federal troops in Louisiana with the state office of the Freedman's Bureau.[14]

On July 25 Mayor Monroe wrote to General Baird to inform him that he intended to arrest the new convention delegates if they tried to assemble, claiming that they threatened to "subvert the present municipal and State government." This was an interesting position for a leader of a party that had only recently debated calling a new constitutional convention themselves on the grounds that the current constitution lacked legitimacy. Monroe informed Baird that he intended to break up the new convention but before taking action wanted to know whether or not the group was convening with the general's official "approbation."[15]

Baird's reply reveals the army's dilemma in executing a policy openly disputed by the president and Congress. Striking an almost farcical pose of neutrality, the general denied that the new convention was meeting with his "approbation." He disingenuously claimed that "the military commanders, since I have been in the State, have held themselves strictly aloof from all interference with the political movements of the citizens of Louisiana," as though a massive military occupation since 1862 and the army's vigorous sponsorship of the 1864 Constitution did not constitute political "interference" of the highest order. He then tried to straddle the issue of the new convention by lecturing Monroe that it was not his duty as mayor to decide whether or not a new state convention was legal. He insisted that if the "legal branch of the United States government" decided to recognize the new convention, Monroe should protect it. If

13. Dawson, *Army Generals and Reconstruction*, 27, 37.

14. Ibid., 34, 35.

15. John T. Monroe to Absalom Baird, July 26, 1866, in U.S. House, *New Orleans Riots,* 39th Cong., 2nd sess., 1867, H. Exec. Doc. 68, 6–7.

not, he should regard it as nothing more than "a piece of harmless pleasantry" and ignore it. What Baird wanted most of all was "the maintenance of perfect order and the suppression of violence." Should the mayor require military assistance to maintain that peace, he would gladly provide all the forces required.[16]

Baird's declaration of political neutrality did not satisfy the leaders of the Rebel Legislature. On Saturday, July 28, 1866, Lieutenant Governor Voorhies and Attorney General Herron dispatched a telegram directly to President Johnson asking him to intervene. They complained that the Radicals had held a mass rally supporting the new convention on the previous night in which, they claimed, Radical leaders made "Violent and incendiary speeches," "negroes [were] called to arm themselves," and speakers "bitterly denounced" Johnson himself. They asked the president whether he would allow the military to "interfere" with their attempt to use the courts to stop a new convention from meeting.[17]

Alarmed by the deteriorating political situation in New Orleans, Johnson shot back a stern reply. "The military will be expected to sustain, and not to obstruct or interfere with the proceedings of the courts," he firmly insisted. He also fired off a harshly worded telegram to Governor Wells demanding to know "by what authority" he had authorized a new convention to meet. Wells responded promptly but deftly sidestepped the thrust of Johnson's inquiry by noting that, technically, he had not authorized a new convention, the president pro tem of the convention had. His role was merely responding to the convention president's call for new elections to fill vacancies left because some delegates had failed to appear and other parishes, having now returned to pro-Union government, required new elections to select their delegates. After meeting on Saturday with Voorhies and Monroe, who showed him Johnson's telegram, General Baird immediately wired Secretary of War Stanton to explain the situation and plead for explicit guidance on how to proceed. Baird waited in vain over the next two days for a reply; none came.[18]

By late in the day Saturday, it had become apparent to everyone involved in New Orleans—the general, the convention supporters, and the rebel legislators—that the new convention would attempt to meet the following Monday. The main questions were whether or not it would be broken up and how that might be accomplished. That

16. Baird to Monroe, July 26, 1866, in ibid., 7.

17. Telegram, Albert Voorhies and Andrew J. Herron to Andrew Johnson, July 28, 1866, in ibid., 4.

18. Telegram, Andrew Johnson to Albert Voorhies and Andrew J. Herron, July 28, 1866, in ibid., 4; Telegram, Andrew Johnson to J. Madison Wells, July 28, 1866, in ibid., 4; Telegram, J. Madison Wells to Andrew Johnson, July 28, 1866, in ibid., 4; Telegram, Absalom Baird to Edwin M. Stanton, July 28, 1866, in ibid., 4–5.

weekend, all three sides prepared themselves for the possibility of a violent confrontation.

Leaders of the Rebel Legislature later claimed that Radicals incited violence by their speeches at a mass rally for their supporters on Friday night, July 27. At that meeting nearly fifteen hundred people assembled to hear a platform of speakers endorse the new convention and black suffrage. Newspaper accounts, regardless of their political outlook, agreed that the great majority of the crowd was black. Dr. A. P. Dostie, a white dentist who was a colleague of T. J. Durant and a longtime resident of the city, was the most passionate speaker. In his speech Dostie endorsed the call for a new convention and the ultimate goal of black suffrage in Louisiana. He also reminded his audience that white vigilantes had recently killed black Union veterans and civilians in Memphis. For that reason he warned them to defend themselves and prepare for violence. A torchlight procession followed the rally late into the night and ended in turmoil, with several people killed.[19]

On Saturday night the leaders of the Rebel Legislature and the city government, along with fifteen of the city's leading merchants, assembled hastily in what resembled a council of war. The officials present were Mayor Monroe, Chief of Police Adams, City Atty. H. D. Ogden, Orleans Parish Sheriff Hays, General Taylor, and a former Union army officer, Maj. Gen. F. J. Herron. All the principal state officers, led by Lieutenant Governor Voorhies and the Attorney General Herron, were present too, with the notable exception of Governor Wells. Voorhies and Monroe began by reviewing their meeting with General Baird and their telegrams to President Johnson. Herron emphasized the link between the struggle over the convention in New Orleans and the struggle between Congress and the president over Reconstruction policy in Washington. He warned of the danger of violence, which all who spoke agreed would damage their cause. After a general discussion the group decided that the best way to proceed was to permit the convention to meet, to order Sheriff Hays and his posse to arrest the delegates, and then to turn the matter over to a grand jury. Monroe's private secretary noted, however, that "if a riot does break out, and the United States government wants it quelled, all that is necessary for them to do is to open the gunshops and arm the confederate soldiers."[20]

Chief Adams and Sheriff Hays did not wait for the "gunshops" to open on Monday to begin preparing their forces for battle. After the Radicals' mass rally on Friday,

19. No transcript of Dostie's speech survives. Dostie was mortally wounded in the street battle of July 30, and all accounts of his remarks were posthumous and partisan. See Rable, *There Was No Peace*, 49. On the Memphis street battle, see McFeely, *Yankee Stepfather*, 274–81.

20. Unnamed secretary quoted in Vandal, *New Orleans Riot of 1866*, 166–70.

two-thirds of the city police force had remained on continuous duty during the next two nights. Mayor Monroe ordered all police to spend Sunday night at their precinct stationhouses so that the maximum possible force would be available Monday morning. While gathered in their precincts, many of the police discussed the coming convention with one another and decided to buy handguns when the stores opened Monday morning. Prior to that weekend, New Orleans police had only been armed with nightsticks, but many now decided that they needed firearms as well. No record exists that the mayor or the police chief did anything to discourage or forbid the police from carrying guns on Monday, but neither did they issue firearms or an edict encouraging the police to arm themselves. Precinct captains organized their officers into squads and gave specific orders that the city's general alarm by the fire department would signal a general convergence on the Mechanics' Institute, at the corner of Dryades and Canal streets, where the convention would meet. In order to prevent confusion in case of a fight, the department decreed a uniform of white shirtsleeves and a white handkerchief tied around the neck for a hastily deputized force recruited to support regular police and firemen.[21]

While awaiting Stanton's reply to his request for guidance, Baird completed his own plans to prepare federal troops for action. On Sunday he confined the First U.S. Infantry Regiment and the Eighty-First U.S. Infantry Regiment to their quarters at Jackson Barracks, three miles downriver from Canal Street, and ordered their officers to be prepared to move immediately if called out on Monday. He also arranged for a boat to standby at the Jackson Barracks landing to be prepared to move the troops. At the wharf in New Orleans, he ordered a tug prepared to shuttle messages between his headquarters at Carondolet Street and Jackson Barracks. By Monday morning he was confident that he had prepared for any eventuality.[22]

THE STREET BATTLE OF JULY 30, 1866

The morning of Monday, July 30, 1866, dawned hot and muggy in New Orleans, suggesting that it would be another broiling hot summer day. Mayor Monroe's proclamation, printed in all the city newspapers except the *New Orleans Tribune*, declared the new convention illegal and warned the public to stay away from the Mechanics' Institute. At 9:00 A.M., however, a crowd that eventually grew to three or four hundred began assembling on the street in front of the building in a rally for black suffrage. Most of the crowd were black, but some white convention delegates and sup-

---

21. Ibid., 169; Taylor, *Louisiana Reconstructed*, 108.
22. Dawson, *Army Generals and Reconstruction*, 38.

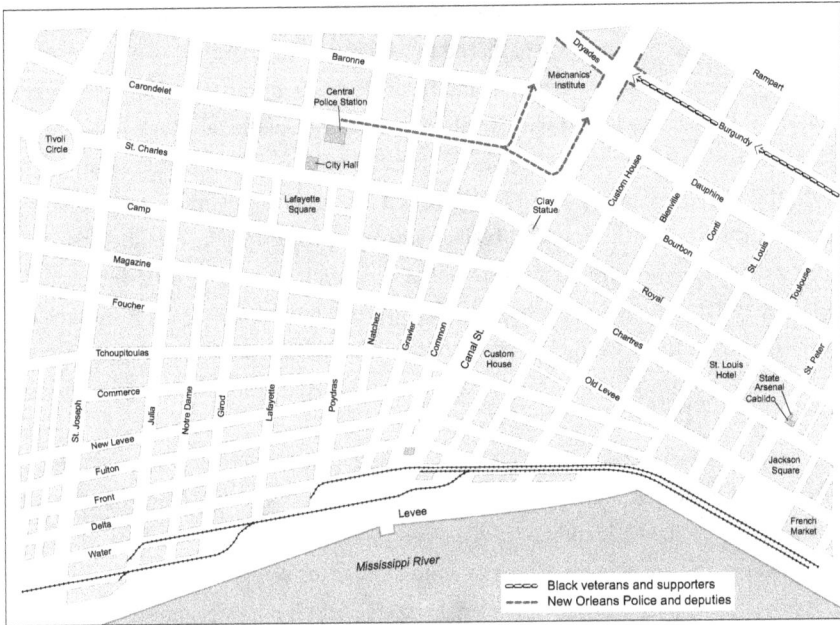

The Street Battle of 1866

porters also appeared. At 10:00 A.M. the convention organizers, fearing the worst, held a preliminary meeting at the hall to arrange for bail bonds in case Sheriff Hays arrested them, agreeing that they would offer no resistance to the police or the sheriff. When noon came, President Pro Tem Rufus Howell called the new convention to order and Reverend Horton gave an invocation. Unable to muster a quorum, Howell decided to adjourn for an hour, vaguely hoping that the sergeant at arms could round up more delegates. Had the leaders of the Rebel Legislature calmly considered Howell's parliamentary predicament, they might have been tempted to simply let the new convention expire without their intervention.[23]

Legislative leaders, however, had prepared their troops for a battle, and they were already losing control of the situation. Mayor Monroe and Chief Adams lined the streets outside the Mechanics' Institute with hundreds of police and temporarily deputized officers. Sheriff Hays's posse was also present, and all city police and fire precinct houses were on alert to march to the sound of the gunfire. The dry tinder of a mass of threatened Confederate veterans required only a spark to ignite it.

The spark came in the form of a march by about two hundred black Union veterans. That morning they had formed in the lower city to parade in column from the

23. Taylor, *Louisiana Reconstructed*, 109.

Third District, across the entire French Quarter, then cross Canal Street to the Mechanics' Institute. The column gathered followers and momentum as it marched. In a scene harkening back to the first American Revolution, this march of the Second American Revolution led off with an all-black Yankee Doodle tableau consisting of a flag bearer, a drummer, and a fife player. The flag bearer was Lt. L. A. Thibaut, a former officer in the Seventy-Third U.S. Colored Troops (USCT) and a veteran of Port Hudson, the first battle in which black regiments had fought in a deliberate attack during the Civil War. Some of the veterans carried sticks and canes with them for self-defense, and a few carried privately owned pistols. From reading the local newspapers, they knew there would almost certainly be massive white resistance to the new convention, but they did not intend to be intimidated or turned away from making the march.[24]

Tensions rose between the black marchers and white onlookers as the column approached the Mechanics' Institute at about 12:30 P.M. Along the way one spectator hurled an insult at the marchers, and a black marcher broke ranks and knocked him down. The gathering crowds of hostile whites and black veterans then exchanged several pistol shots near Dryades and Canal streets, but no one was apparently hit, and the marchers crossed over Canal Street toward the entrance to the Mechanics' Institute. As they approached the hall, they intermingled with the black supporters who had gathered outside the front doors.[25]

Also waiting, though, was a growing assembly of perhaps as many as fifteen hundred white civilians and police near the hall and lining the streets. Just as the column reached the front doors of the Mechanics' Institute, enraged whites threw a volley of bricks at the marchers. The marchers threw them back, the two crowds exchanged pistol shots, and a wild melee erupted on the street. As the tumult grew, police commanders sounded the general alarm and ordered their men to rush the marchers. Policemen knocked down a number of blacks, shooting some dead on the spot.[26]

Inside the Mechanics' Institute, a sudden crush of bodies trying to squeeze through the doorways surprised the leaders of the convention. In addition to 30 or 40 white delegates and officials, nearly 150 black spectators stood in the galleries of the hall awaiting the start of the proceedings. Convention leaders shouted for the people in

---

24. Testimony, George Foster, in House, *New Orleans Riots*, 188. Foster identified the marchers as "colored men," members of the "1st and 2d Louisiana, three years." U.S. Army records indicate that Thibaut participated in the assault on Port Hudson in May 1863 but was dismissed during Banks's purge of black officers on August 26, 1863. See War Department, *Official Army Register*, 8:247.

25. Rable, *There Was No Peace*, 51.

26. Ibid., 52.

the hall to lie down on the floor until federal troops arrived. With police right on the heels of the fleeing marchers, a few black defenders inside the hall pushed back the doors and frantically barricaded tables and chairs against them to keep out their attackers. Repeatedly the police fired volleys of shots through the doors and then tried to batter them down from outside. Repeatedly the defenders took cover from the hail of bullets and then buttressed the impromptu barricade with their own bodies and furniture from inside the hall to keep the police out.

While police battered down the doors, convention supporters inside and outside the building attempted to flee. Police and vigilantes immediately captured, beat, or shot those who leaped from the second-story windows of the hall. Dr. Horton, the white minister who had given the invocation, tried to wave a white flag of surrender through the doors only to be shot in reply. Those who had gathered outside the hall tried to escape, but squads of police and whites from the crowd ran them down. One observer "saw policemen shoot two negroes dead, who had been knocked down by rocks. I saw a policeman followed by hundreds of infuriated men and boys . . . beat a poor old negro over the head and shoulders until he fell and was then pitched upon by the rabble and kicked and stamped until they themselves were ashamed." Fire companies, summoned by the general alarm, joined in the fray; indiscriminately swinging oversized hydrant wrenches at individuals the police had wrestled to the ground or were marching off to jail.[27]

Inside the hall the officers finally prevailed and broke down the doors. Members of the convention shouted to the police that they would not resist arrest, but their cries went unheeded. The police singled out well-known white leaders for special attention. Dr. Dostie, the inflammatory speaker at the previous Friday night rally, was shot five or six times and then run through with a sword. He died several days later. John Henderson, the delegate who had been ambivalent about black suffrage, was mortally wounded. Police dragged Michael Hahn, Wells's predecessor as governor, from the hall. Vigilantes periodically beat him senseless and screamed for the police to kill him. Badly injured, Governor Hahn survived the battle but was crippled for the rest of his life.[28]

Most of the victims of the fighting, however, were black, not white. After the police forced in the doors, black convention supporters fled in all directions away from the site of the carnage, trailed by impromptu squads of white pursuers. General Taylor later recalled seeing one black man racing down Canal Street chased by an armed

27. H. C. Warmoth Diary, July 30, 1866.
28. Taylor, *Louisiana Reconstructed,* 110; Rable, *There Was No Peace,* 54.

white boy who appeared to be no more than fifteen years old. Henry Warmoth, who left the hall just minutes before the fighting started, watched the massacre in horror from the vantage point of the balcony of a friend's house at 150 Canal Street. He later recalled that he "saw policemen and citizens deploying across the end of Dryades and firing briskly. The fire was kept up for two hours and a half." The final toll of dead and wounded remains uncertain, but the army surgeon detailed to write the official report counted 38 dead and 184 wounded in the fighting. The actual number was almost certainly higher since many of the families of those involved wanted to bury their dead and treat their wounded in secrecy, out of fear of what added publicity might bring. Police hauled off almost two hundred people, some of whom were severely wounded, to the city jail, which the army's surgeon described as "more like a slaughter-pen for animals than a receptacle for human beings."[29]

General Baird summoned his troops from Jackson Barracks as soon as an aide notified him of what was happening. His troops arrived at the Mechanics' Institute about 3:00 P.M., but by then fighting in the immediate vicinity of the hall had passed its crescendo. Baird declared martial law in the city, which put a curfew into effect and made it easier for his soldiers to clear the streets, and appointed a military governor. He also mobilized all of his available forces, consisting of two infantry regiments, a cavalry squadron, and an artillery battery, to occupy the city, but there were no more major incidents that night. General Sheridan returned to New Orleans from Texas a few days later after receiving word of the fighting by telegram. Upon his arrival he confirmed Baird's order for martial law despite protests from Lieutenant Governor Voorhies, Attorney General Herron, and Mayor Monroe, who claimed that the New Orleans police did not need the army's aid to keep order. Sheridan also appointed a military commission of three generals to investigate the incident. On August 2, 1866, he sent a telegram to General Grant with his first impressions: "The more information I obtain of the affair of the 30th in this city the more revolting it becomes. It was no riot; it was an absolute massacre by the police which was not excelled in murderous cruelty by that of Fort Pillow. It was a murder which the mayor and police of this city perpetrated without the shadow of a necessity; furthermore, I believe it was premeditated, and every indication points to this."[30]

Not formally counted among the casualties of this street battle, but mortally

29. Richard Taylor, *Destruction and Reconstruction: Personal Experiences of the Late War*, ed. Charles P. Roland (Waltham, Mass: Blaisdell, 1968), 248–49; H. C. Warmoth Diary, July 30, 1866; Testimony, Surgeon A. Hartsuff, in House, *New Orleans Riots*, 32–36.

30. Dawson, *Army Generals and Reconstruction*, 40; Telegram, P. H. Sheridan to U. S. Grant, Aug. 2, 1866, in House, *New Orleans Riots*, 11.

wounded just the same, was President Johnson's plan to restore the ex-Confederate states to the Union by executive order. Through most of 1865 and 1866, moderate northern Republicans, who held the balance of power in Congress, had watched the growing tensions between the president and the radical wing of their party, looking for some sign to judge whether or not his plan would work. The deaths of so many loyal Unionists, white and black, at the hands of Confederate veterans barely a year after Appomattox represented all the proof most of them needed that Johnson's policy was an utter failure.

That fall Johnson stumped the country in his "Swing around the Circle," a whistle-stop campaign of the country in which he railed against Radicals in Congress and desperately defended his southern policy. With an entourage of Civil War heroes, including General Grant and Admiral Farragut, uncomfortably in tow, he made history by becoming the first president to campaign for his party in the midterm elections of November 1866. In his speech at St. Louis he openly blamed Radicals in Congress for the violence in New Orleans and accused them of conspiring with local Republicans to bring on a massacre to justify passing harsher Reconstruction measures. Grant, who had never felt comfortable around politicians but accompanied the president out of respect for the dignity of the office, found himself appalled by Johnson's bombastic harangues. "I look upon them as a National disgrace," he secretly wrote to his wife, Julia. He concocted an excuse to leave the tour, and as 1866 waned, Grant distanced himself from support for Johnson and his policies. At the same time, he secretly confided his concerns to his most important and loyal officers, Sherman and Sheridan, and began to build bridges to Republicans in Congress.[31]

In November 1866 Republicans made history of their own with a dramatic landslide victory that gave them veto-proof majorities in both houses of Congress. Within months they would exercise their new mandate by overturning Johnson's provisional state governments in favor of direct military rule and laying the foundation for Radical Reconstruction.

THE CIVIL WAR ORIGINS OF RECONSTRUCTION VIOLENCE

Following in the footsteps of the participants themselves, historians have waged a long struggle to apportion blame for the vigilante violence that burst into national prominence in New Orleans in 1866. Volleys of charges and denials have been periodically exchanged, arguing that one side or the other conspired to exploit violence

31. Foner, *Reconstruction*, 264–67; U. S. Grant to Julia Dent Grant, Sept. 9, 1866, in Grant, *Papers*, 16:308.

to serve their own political ends. All such attempts to prove that an actual conspiracy existed on one side or the other, based on the emotionally infused and ferociously partisan testimony of eyewitnesses, have been inconclusive.

In his fiery stump speeches in the fall of 1866, Andrew Johnson thundered that responsibility for the bloodshed in New Orleans fell squarely on what he described as a "Radical conspiracy" in Congress. A generation later the scholarly white-supremacist historians of the Dunning school of Reconstruction history upheld his view. As they correctly point out, congressional Republicans did have much to gain from violence against southern Unionists at the polls in 1866, and they exploited to the fullest the opportunity that the massacre in New Orleans provided. The damaging disclosure that Secretary Stanton had failed to answer General Baird's urgent plea for guidance less than forty-eight hours before the convention met led Dunning and his followers to point accusing fingers at the congressional Republicans' most important ally in the Cabinet. Stanton's failure to act, they argue, left blood on his hands and those of his collaborators.

There is no question that Stanton bitterly opposed Johnson's policy of restoration. In the inquiries that followed, Johnson discovered that his secretary of war, perhaps deliberately, received but did not act upon General Baird's urgent telegram. Eventually the distrust between the two widened, and Johnson suspended Stanton from office in 1867, an impolitic move that triggered the first impeachment trial of a U.S. president.

The difficulty with the "Radical conspiracy" line of reasoning, however, lies in the assumption that Stanton and the Radicals could actually conjure up a confrontation in New Orleans or subsequently manipulate it from Washington. As Sheridan's investigation revealed, Baird tried to prepare for the possibility of violence but made several crucial blunders that helped bring on the massacre in New Orleans, not by design, but by negligence. Even after the warning provided by a similarly violent incident in Memphis in May, Baird decided to keep most federal troops three miles downriver at Jackson Barracks rather than in the city itself. This was a tactical mistake that he tried to justify by claiming, first, that it lowered the public profile of the army and enhanced the perceived authority of a weak state government. The practical effect of his decision was that no federal troops intervened at the Mechanics' Institute to separate crowds of police from marchers and prevent the slaughter that followed. Had they been present, as they would be during later confrontations in New Orleans, there might have been no fight and, more than likely, no massacre. Second, and underscoring just how incredibly detached from the inflammatory local political situation he had been, Baird told the military commission that he had mistakenly thought that the convention was scheduled to meet on the evening of July 30 rather than at noon.[32]

In retrospect the lengthy transcript of the military commission reveals that the army had done little to prepare to carry out policing functions, or what today would be termed "peacekeeping operations" in support of a postwar military occupation. An unstated premise of the military investigation seemed to be to gloss over the full extent of the army's mistakes and try to shift blame elsewhere. Sheridan's military commission cross-examined dozens of witnesses in a futile attempt to pin responsibility on known Confederate veteran organizations. When Baird testified, however, his fellow officers permitted him to enter a lengthy and self-exculpatory statement into the record. They then promptly dismissed him without a serious cross-examination of his own actions.

Baird was held responsible by his military superiors, however, in a certain American military tradition that continues to this day. Shortly after the commission finished its work, the general quietly took an extended leave of absence and left New Orleans. On September 1, 1866, Baird surrendered his commission as a volunteer major general and reverted to his regular-army rank of lieutenant colonel. This steep reduction in rank signaled a loss of prestige even more palpable than pay or responsibilities. Baird retired from the army in 1888, twenty-two years after the street battle in New Orleans, but never regained the rank he had held in 1866. Several weeks after Baird's departure, Sheridan appointed the head of the military commission, Maj. Gen. Joseph A. Mower, as the new military commander and head of the Freedmen's Bureau for Louisiana. The serious mistakes of the military command in New Orleans, which Baird's superiors demonstrated they understood perfectly well when they cashiered him, reveal that a "Radical conspiracy" to engineer a politically useful massacre was not only farfetched but also demonstrably beyond the capacities of those who would have had to help execute such a scheme.[33]

Not to be outdone in the hunt for conspiracies, other historians have suggested that the powerful New Orleans white elite deliberately planned a slaughter at the Mechanics' Institute to destroy the movement for black enfranchisement in Louisiana. Foremost among those historical revisionists suggesting such a cabal was W. E. B. Du Bois in his groundbreaking work, *Black Reconstruction*. More recently Eric Foner has suggested that the city police "conspired" to disperse the convention. Du Bois and Foner certainly had plenty of empirical evidence to suspect that a murderous conspir-

32. Testimony, Maj. Gen. Absalom Baird, in House, *New Orleans Riots*, 11.

33. Dawson, *Army Generals and Reconstruction*, 42–43.

acy had been hatched; Sheridan mentioned that very opinion in his initial telegram to Grant. Sheridan, however, was not present at the scene, and his own military commission had not yet even begun its investigation when he wrote his message to Grant. Additionally, later accounts of the leaders of the Rebel Legislature remain highly suspicious. Several leaders present at the Saturday night council of war later gave sworn testimony that was either false or evasive. Mayor Monroe had reputedly been the mastermind behind several Know-Nothing-inspired street fights in New Orleans in the 1850s and became notorious for preferring expulsion from the city to taking a Union oath of allegiance in 1862. In his memoirs Confederate general Richard Taylor claims that the violence he personally witnessed on Canal Street caught him by surprise, but he neglects to mention that he had been present at the Saturday night meeting with the Rebel legislators before the convention met that discussed that possibility in detail.[34]

Unquestionably the Rebel Legislature's leaders had taken steps over the preceding weekend to prepare the New Orleans police for action. The army's inquiry at the time and the more recent scholarship of Gilles Vandal, however, have clearly established that while the white elite present at the Saturday night meeting tried to prepare for the possibility of violence, they knew that the stakes were high and that any misstep on their part would discredit them and endanger President Johnson's effort to keep Reconstruction out of the hands of Congress. They had a vested interest in avoiding that outcome. By the end of the meeting, a consensus emerged that they should assemble a powerful police force at the Mechanics' Institute, not to ignite, but rather to control any turmoil.[35]

Instead of continuing down a road of charges and countercharges over the elusive *motives* of the participants, it is more analytically fruitful to seek out the origin of the *behavior* of vigilante violence evident in the New Orleans street battle of 1866. Here it would appear that General Sheridan was precisely, if perhaps unwittingly, on the right track when he informed General Grant that the event "was an absolute massacre by the police, which was not excelled in murderous cruelty by that of Fort Pillow."[36] Historians repeatedly quote Sheridan's dramatic words, yet their meaning remains unexamined. Why did the street battle of New Orleans remind a Civil War general of a Civil War battle?

34. W. E. B. Du Bois, *Black Reconstruction in American* (New York: Harcourt, Brace, 1935), 464–65; Foner, *Reconstruction*, 263; James G. Hollandsworth, *An Absolute Massacre: The New Orleans Race Riot of July 30, 1866* (Baton Rouge: Louisiana State University Press, 2001); Taylor, *Destruction and Reconstruction*, 249.

35. Testimony, Maj. Gen. F. J. Herron, in House, *New Orleans Riots*, 56–57. Herron was a former Union army general and a most unlikely candidate to join in a "Rebel conspiracy."

36. Telegram, P. H. Sheridan to U. S. Grant, Aug. 2, 1866, in ibid., 11.

The battle at Fort Pillow in 1864 remains one of the most controversial episodes of the Civil War. In his exhaustive opus on the history of American slavery, *Roll, Jordan, Roll,* Eugene Genovese describes the encounters between former slaves and former masters as "the moment of truth," a singular historical watershed in which each saw the other and their relationship in an entirely new light. Surprisingly Genovese neglects the evidence that many of these "moments of truth" came in pitched combat between black Union and white Confederate soldiers. Before the end of the war, the effects of such encounters radiated back from racialized battlefields through every level of southern society.[37]

Fort Pillow was the most infamous of many such militarized "moments of truth" between former slaves and former masters during the Civil War. In April 1864 a Confederate force of 1,200 led by Maj. Gen. Nathan Bedford Forrest, a prewar Memphis slave trader and the postwar imperial wizard of the Ku Klux Klan, attacked Fort Pillow, situated along the banks of the Mississippi, and slaughtered most of its 561 defenders. The fort's garrison consisted of recently freed black slaves in combat for the first time and white Tennesseeans, many of whom were Confederate deserters. After his forces surrounded the fort, Forrest demanded the garrison's surrender. In reply came a string of audible taunts. The commander of the Union troops tried to stall for more time, but Forrest cut short his truce and ordered an all-out attack. As they swarmed over the Union parapets, Confederate soldiers cried out "No quarter!" and executed their surrendering enemies, white as well as black, sometimes after chasing them all the way down to the river. According to some witnesses, the decision to take no prisoners was Forrest's own, a charge he and his supporters hotly denied. According to others, the decision to take no prisoners was made by Forrest's soldiers themselves, and the general intervened to stop them after the fort fell and he realized that he had lost control over his men. Atrocity stories circulated later claiming that the Rebels also executed black women and children found within the fort and buried some of their wounded prisoners alive.[38]

Fort Pillow was no isolated incident. It was like the tip of an iceberg, the most visible event of a mostly submerged pattern of burgeoning interracial vigilante violence within the war. Throughout 1863 and 1864, as it began to dawn on Rebel troops that

---

37. Eugene D. Genovese, *Roll, Jordan, Roll: The World the Slaves Made* (New York: Vintage, 1972), 97–98.

38. Albert Castel, "The Fort Pillow Massacre: A Fresh Examination of the Evidence," *Civil War History* 4 (1958): 37–50. New evidence of a massacre, culled entirely from contemporary diaries and letters, is found in John Cimprich and Robert C. Mainfort Jr., "Fort Pillow Revisited: New Evidence about an Old Controversy," *Civil War History* 28 (1982): 296–306.

they could lose the war and they began encountering armed ex-slaves, an intense rededication to the creation of a white southern nation swept like wildfire through the Confederate armies. One manifestation of this closing of the ranks, involving civilians as well as soldiers, was an outpouring of evangelical Protestantism in camp-meeting revivals and elaborate funerals to fallen Confederate heroes, such as the one held for Gen. "Stonewall" Jackson after his death at Chancellorsville in May 1863. Another indicator was an upshot in the number of public military executions for desertion. Execution for desertion in the Confederate army was a highly ritualized and profoundly cathartic ceremony that honored the devotion of those who stood by the St. Andrew's Cross by inflicting the ultimate dishonor on those who did not. This new spirit also manifested itself in a widespread determination to take no black prisoners of war.[39]

In a host of minor battles, raids, skirmishes, and chance encounters in the lower Mississippi valley in 1863, Confederate soldiers began to show their determination to fight under the "Black Flag" whenever they faced black troops. Many of these Confederates came from Louisiana, where the Union army had begun to raise large numbers of black troops in occupied territory. At Port Hudson (May 27, 1863) Confederate defenders refused a traditional white flag of truce requested by two black regiments to recover their dead and wounded after a failed assault. At Milliken's Bend (June 7, 1863) black recruits, many of whom were so new they still had no uniforms, held off an attack by superior Confederate forces until overwhelmed. Witnesses later reported finding a number of dead black soldiers lining their trenches in poses and with wounds that suggested execution-style slayings. At a raid on a Union encampment at Goodrich's Landing (June 22, 1863), the Confederate commander reported the wholesale capture and reenslavement of two thousand freedmen, "with the exception of those captured in arms." When informed of reports that Gen. Richard Taylor, the overall Confederate commander of troops in all of these actions, might have taken some black prisoners alive, Gen. E. Kirby Smith ordered Taylor to remind his

39. New research has uncovered a number of interracial atrocities during the Civil War. See especially Gregory J. W. Urwin, ed., *Black Flag over Dixie: Racial Atrocities and Reprisals in the Civil War* (Carbondale: Southern Illinois University Press, 2004). On the intense wave of evangelization in the Confederate army, see especially Drew Gilpin Faust, "Christian Soldiers: The Meaning of Revivalism in the Confederate Army," *JSH* 53 (Feb. 1987): 66–90. On executions within the Confederate army, see Jack A. Bunch, *Military Justice in the Confederate States Armies* (Shippensburg, Pa.: White Mane, 2000). For specific examples of Confederate executions, see Freeman, *Lee's Lieutenants*, 3:219, which recounts an 1863 mass execution of North Carolina deserters in the wake of the failed Gettysburg campaign; and William J. Seymour, *The Civil War Memoirs of Captain William J. Seymour: Reminiscences of a Louisiana Tiger*, ed. Terry L. Jones (Baton Rouge: Louisiana State University Press, 1991), 100–101, an eyewitness account of a deserter's execution after the battle of the Wilderness in 1864.

officers of "the propriety of giving no quarter to armed negroes and their officers. In this way we may be relieved from a disagreeable dilemma."[40]

The general's "disagreeable dilemma" sprang from the problem Confederate leaders confronted in responding to Lincoln's decision to emancipate and arm the slaves. Confederate soldiers knew that Jefferson Davis had equivocated over the use of black troops by the Yankees. He had at first condemned it as a barbaric act of uncivilized war and then backtracked for fear of Lincoln's promise of retaliation against Confederate prisoners of war. On the battlefield Rebel soldiers devised their own informal rules for dealing with the harsh new realities they now faced. In 1864 the issue burst into the realm of public opinion with sensational newspaper reports of Confederate massacres against black troops at the battles of Fort Pillow, Poison Springs, and the Crater. By the time of this last battle—a spectacular attempt to mine the Confederate trenches at Petersburg followed by a massed Union assault utilizing black regiments on July 30, 1864—the cycle of reprisals showed fresh signs of escalation. Black soldiers apparently began refusing to take Confederate prisoners in retaliation for their own ill treatment. Said one of their abolitionist officers: "The darkies fought ferociously. . . . If they murder prisoners, as I hear they did, . . . they can hardly be blamed."[41]

The end of the Civil War interrupted the cyclic escalation of atrocities on the new interracial battlefield, but it did not halt the underlying impulses. Like Fort Pillow, the street battle of New Orleans was only the tip of the iceberg, the most visible manifestation of a much broader pattern of vigilante violence across racial lines. Throughout the South the appearance of vigilantes and militia companies drawn from among Confederate veterans accompanied the revival of the political fortunes of these men in 1865 and 1866. In cities like New Orleans and Memphis, it coalesced in the form of police forces composed of Confederate veterans determined to reassert close control over the influx of black migrants trying to escape the constrictions of everyday plantation life. In rural areas, such as Mississippi, the militia was different in form, if not necessarily function. Provisional governor William L. Sharkey appointed new state militia officers, over the objections of the local federal commander, and mus-

---

40. For contemporary Confederate eyewitness advocacy on "flying the Black Flag," see Petty, *Journey to Pleasant Hill*, 206, 223. On the evolving attitudes within the Confederate high command to the practice of "no quarter" being offered to black soldiers, see Lt. Gen. E. Kirby Smith to Maj. Gen. Richard Taylor, June 13, 1863, in War Department, *The War of the Rebellion: A Compilation of the Official Records of the Union and Confederate Armies*, 128 vols. (Washington, D.C.: Government Printing Office, 1880–1901), ser. 2, 6:21–22. For a discussion of Taylor's role, see T. Michael Parrish, *Richard Taylor: Soldier Prince of Dixie* (Chapel Hill: University of North Carolina Press, 1992), 288–94.

41. Capt. Charles Francis Adams Jr. quoted in McPherson, *Battle Cry*, 795.

tered militia companies composed of Confederate veterans in the "Black Belt" counties. Carl Schurz, a prominent German American leader and former Union army general, while making an inspection tour of the state warned that this new force represented nothing less than "the restoration of the old patrol system which was one of the characteristic features of the regime of slavery."[42]

By no means were all of these militias inspired solely by Conservative and Democratic elites. Many had been organized "from the bottom up," that is, out of the ranks of veteran enlisted men and their company officers desperately fearful of the chaos and anarchy that reigned over much of the South after the collapse of Confederate authority in 1865. Compounding the general breakdown of civil society was a new wave of fear—bordering on genuine hysteria among whites—that the freedmen would rise up at Christmas in 1865 and massacre their former masters and all the whites they could reach.[43] Similar panics broke out at Christmas in 1866 and 1867. Each time there were renewed calls to muster local militia companies and vigilantes. These repeated cycles of insurrection hysteria and vigilante response help explain how later white supremacist movements like the White Leagues expanded so rapidly during the 1870s, when violent campaigns attended electoral campaigns to overthrow the remaining southern Republican state governments.

Neither the fierce racial prides nor the murderous racial hatreds that exploded in the street battle of New Orleans in 1866 originated in Reconstruction's looming political struggles over black enfranchisement, as many historians have tried to insist ever since. Their origins must instead be traced to the vast popular mobilization that took place on both sides of the racial divide during the Civil War. Honing those prides and hatreds to a fevered pitch demanded years of discipline, dedication, heroism, leadership, privation, and self-sacrifice that Civil War armies, alone of all the cultural institutions of nineteenth-century America, could provide.

---

42. Rable, *There Was No Peace*, 28; U.S. Senate, *Reports of Generals Grant and Schurz*, 39th Cong., 1st sess., 1865, S. Exec. Doc. 2, 36.

43. Dan T. Carter, "The Anatomy of Fear: The Christmas Day Insurrection Scare of 1865," *JSH* 42 (Aug. 1976): 351–57. Carter has found evidence in at least sixty southern counties in 1865 of a belief that the ex-slaves would revolt. These fears appeared to be heightened by the Morant Bay Affair in Jamaica, where ex-slaves actually did stage an unsuccessful insurrection in 1865. Wells appointed Col. Louis Bush, formerly of the Fourth Louisiana Cavalry (CSA), to be head of the state militia, but state records do not reveal what actions—if any—he took while in office. See Warmoth, *Letter*, 66. Bush had led counterinsurgency campaigns against runaway slaves and Confederate deserters within Confederate Louisiana during the Civil War. The governor may have had these qualities in mind when he appointed Bush as his adjutant general. See Winters, *Civil War in Louisiana*, 383.

❧ 3 ❧

The Street Battle of 1872
Carpetbaggers under Siege

Angry reaction to the New Orleans street battle of 1866 fueled a decisive turn in federal policy toward the ex-Confederate states. Less than four months after the slaughter at the Mechanics' Institute, the Republican landslide in the 1866 midterm elections decisively shifted momentum on Reconstruction policy from the White House to Congress. Within a year military government rather than military occupation defined the political landscape of southern states. This unprecedented expansion of military power over every function of civil government not only made Radical Reconstruction of the rebel states possible but also profoundly shaped the character of the new state governments themselves. The repeated use of the U.S. Army as a peacekeeping force to defend southern Republican administrations became infamous to its opponents as "bayonet rule." The New Orleans street battle of 1872, an outgrowth of a long struggle for power between factions within the Louisiana Republican Party, exposed the critical role the army's presence played in the survival of Republican governments in the South. At the same time, it demonstrated the substantial progress, however uneven, southern Republicans had made toward creating security forces of their own.

SHERIDAN AND MILITARY DICTATORSHIP, 1867–68

The Military Reconstruction Acts reflected such an unusual amalgam of egalitarian free-soil idealism and naked partisan opportunism that a whole spectrum of interpretations has been projected onto the meaning of their passage. Congress passed three such measures in the spring and summer of 1867. The original Military Reconstruction Act, enacted on March 2, 1867, by the lame-duck session of the Thirty-Ninth Congress, declared Johnson's restoration state governments to be merely "provisional" and completely subordinate to military oversight. It divided ten southern states—those of the Confederacy minus Tennessee—into five military districts, each commanded by a major general appointed by the commanding general of the army

53

rather than the president.[1] Each measure passed over the veto of an increasingly desperate Andrew Johnson. "No master ever had so absolute control over the slaves as this bill gives to the military officers over both white and colored persons," he complained in his bitter veto message to Congress.[2]

The generals' authority ranged over all aspects of state government. District commanders had the power to remove any local official, elected or appointed, from office on their sole discretion. They could close civil or criminal courts if they desired or simply remand court cases to general courts-martial (whose presiding members these same generals appointed), or to lesser military courts, such as the provost-martial courts that the army established in occupied areas during the Civil War.[3]

Under the terms of the act, an end to military rule and readmission to the Union would occur once a state completed a complicated sequence of requirements. Each state had to hold a new constitutional convention, with delegates elected on the basis of universal male suffrage. Once the convention approved a new constitution, the military government would organize and conduct a constitutional referendum that required the approval of a majority of the state's voters. Only then could new elections be held for state offices. After the new legislature convened and ratified the Fourteenth Amendment, Congress would indicate its approval by voting to readmit its representatives and senators. This endorsement would mark the state's readmission to the Union and a formal end to military rule.[4]

Some state legislatures tried to thwart the First Military Reconstruction Act by refusing to convene constitutional conventions or to ratify the Fourteenth Amendment. The lower chamber of Louisiana's Rebel Legislature, for example, indicated its displeasure by voting 100-0 against the Fourteenth Amendment. The incoming Fortieth Congress remedied this potential roadblock. On March 23, 1867, it passed the Second Military Reconstruction Act. This law ordered the military rather than the states to conduct voter registration for delegates to the new constitutional conventions. It also decreed the disfranchisement of Confederate officials, generals, and all those who had resigned from federal office to join the rebellion. This provision did not, as has sometimes been portrayed, disfranchise all Confederate veterans. Supporters intended se-

---

1. Congress excluded Tennessee because its state legislature passed the Fourteenth Amendment in 1866. Moderate Republicans insisted on this exception as an alternative to military Reconstruction. No other ex-Confederate state legislature chose to follow Tennessee's lead. See Foner, *Reconstruction*, 276–77.

2. For the complete text of Johnson's veto message, see James D. Richardson, ed., *A Compilation of the Messages and Papers of the Presidents, 1789–1897*, 10 vols. (Washington, D.C., 1896–97), 6:472–502.

3. Sefton, *Army and Reconstruction*, 109–17.

4. Taylor, *Louisiana Reconstructed*, 129.

lective disfranchisement to block the old class of southern leaders from seizing the reigns of power again while nurturing a new class of political leaders willing to accept black enfranchisement.[5]

In July 1867 Congress passed the Third Military Reconstruction Act to thwart Johnson's attempt to encourage his attorney general, Henry Stanbery, to issue legal guidance to the district commanders that construed the first two acts as narrowly as possible. This measure directed military commanders to report directly to the commanding general of the army rather than to the secretary of war or the president. It authorized them to deny the vote to anyone, regardless of whether or not that person had previously taken a loyalty oath or already received a presidential pardon. In reviewing the list of eligible voters in each state, Congress empowered the generals to add or subtract names from the lists at their sole discretion.[6]

The provisions of the Military Reconstruction Acts made generals into virtual dictators of conquered territories. And none was better prepared to play that role in 1867 than Maj. Gen. Philip H. Sheridan. Long afterward, partisan opponents of congressional Reconstruction and some historians portrayed him as swayed by a devotion to Radical politics. More likely Sheridan's motives for his actions during Reconstruction sprang from his harsh experiences with Confederate civilians and guerrillas during the Civil War and his determination to carry out the intent of enacted law and the orders he received from Grant. The personal tone of his correspondence with the general in chief in 1866 and 1867 suggests that he worried that permitting an unrepentant South to resume the status quo antebellum might lose "the fruits of victory" for the Union and ignite another civil war, one in which a massacre like the 1866 New Orleans street battle would be merely an ugly preview.[7]

Sheridan's dislike for Rebels emerged in the bitter campaign he waged against Confederate partisans in Virginia's Shenandoah Valley in the fall of 1864. Frustrated in his drive to destroy Lee's army before Richmond, Grant had placed Sheridan at the head of the newly created Army of the Shenandoah, with blunt orders to turn the val-

5. Lowrey, "Political Career of James Madison Wells," 1086.

6. Taylor, *Louisiana Reconstructed*, 131.

7. William B. Hesseltine suggests that Sheridan was "the most objectionable [of all the military governors], in the Democratic-Conservative view." *Ulysses S. Grant: Politician* (New York: Dodd, Mead, 1935), 83–84. More recent accounts by military historians Joseph Dawson and Roy Morris also insist that Sheridan was a "Radical." This author has yet to find a single quotation attributed to Sheridan in which he personally advocated black enfranchisement and civil rights, either in public or in private correspondence. Dawson, *Army Generals and Reconstruction*, 36; Roy Morris Jr., *Sheridan: The Life and Wars of General Phil Sheridan* (New York: Crown, 1992).

ley into "a barren waste."[8] Sheridan responded with raids that littered the countryside with burning barns, with livestock confiscations, and with summary hangings aimed at breaking the resistance of the hostile civilian populace who harbored the guerrillas. The campaign became, literally and figuratively, a smashing success, permanently pacifying the Shenandoah Valley and ending its role as the granary of the Lee's army. At the same time, Sheridan's extension of the Union war effort directly to southern civilians and his blunt pronouncements created a legacy of bitterness lasting for generations.[9]

While he burned no barns and conducted no summary executions in New Orleans, the Military Reconstruction Acts in some ways made Sheridan an even more powerful figure in postwar Louisiana than he had been in wartime Virginia. After a trip to Washington in January 1867 for confidential talks with Grant, Sheridan returned to New Orleans reinvigorated by the certainty that the measures he saw fit to impose would be fully supported. Neither general kept a record of what they said to each other in confidence, indicative of just how tense Grant's relations with President Johnson had grown. Sheridan's barrage of decrees just after the passage of the First Military Reconstruction Act suggests that Grant had discussed his knowledge of congressional Republicans' plans for a new method of reconstruction and that he encouraged Sheridan to be prepared to implement it.[10]

Sheridan began his reign in the spring of 1867 by demanding an end to lawlessness and a strict adherence to congressional legislation, from the Civil Rights Bill of 1866 to the Military Reconstruction Acts. In his first action he removed the officials he held responsible for the massacre at the Mechanics' Institute in 1866. Among the dismissed were Mayor Monroe, who had authority over the police; Attorney General Herron, who had refused to prosecute anyone for murder; and Judge Edmund Abell, who refused to permit trials of any of the police.[11] In May, after a dispute broke out between the Rebel Legislature and Governor Wells over patronage on the state levee board, Sheridan removed Wells, insisting that he had become "an impediment" to Reconstruction. There had long been bad feelings between the two, and Sheridan had expressed his personal view to Grant that Wells was a coward because he had stayed inside his house while the 1866 street battle raged.[12] Annoyed at continuing frictions

8. McPherson, *Battle Cry*, 778.

9. John L. Heatwole, *The Burning: Sheridan in the Shenandoah Valley* (Charlottesville, Va.: Rockbridge, 1998). See also Virgil Carrington Jones, *Gray Ghosts and Rebel Raiders* (New York: Henry Holt, 1956).

10. Dawson, *Army Generals and Reconstruction*, 42.

11. P. H. Sheridan to U. S. Grant, Apr. 19, 1867, in U.S. Senate, *Military Letters, Orders, and Telegrams*, 40th Cong., 1st sess., 1867, S. Exec. Doc. 14, 201.

12. Taylor, *Louisiana Reconstructed*, 140.

with the New Orleans city government, he eventually removed all twenty-two members of the Board of Aldermen and the city police chief. In their place he appointed his own slate of officials, including a few black men, who apparently became the first blacks to hold office in Louisiana.

Sheridan took other actions that drew applause from Radical Republicans, though that was probably not his intention. Ever since the Union army had decided to recruit black soldiers, free blacks had agitated for full access to public services in New Orleans. Under wartime occupation, tensions grew with the company operating New Orleans's trolley lines, which insisted that blacks continue to ride in segregated cars marked with a star, or "star cars." When Mayor Monroe and the Rebel Legislature came to power, the city police began enforcing the trolley company's policy of segregated cars. After Mayor Monroe's expulsion, the head of the trolley company appealed directly for Sheridan's help to enforce racial separation. The general flatly refused on the grounds that the Civil Rights Act of 1866 banned such segregation. "Erase your stars and make all your buses open to all," he ordered.[13] The trolley company meekly complied. After the local commander in Texas requested that Sheridan approve the assignment of blacks to jury pools in that state, he not only agreed but ordered a similar decree for Louisiana as well.[14] In June 1867 the general intervened in the city's public works by voiding $100,000 worth of state contracts to pave New Orleans's wretched streets, which he claimed had been fraudulently negotiated.[15]

At the same time he bulldozed aside the wreckage of Louisiana's old regime, Sheridan opened the way for a new one. On March 9, 1867, he canceled New Orleans's city elections and informed Louisiana that there would be no more local elections until all the requirements of the Military Reconstruction Acts had been fulfilled; in the interim he would appoint any officials required, and they would serve at his pleasure.[16] Across the state he established parish election boards and ordered registrations of black and white voters for the new constitutional convention to be held that fall. Sheridan tried to ensure equal access to registration for the freedmen by appointing at least one former Union army officer to each board, but he probably fell short of this

---

13. Sheridan quoted in Jean-Charles Houzeau, *My Passage at the New Orleans "Tribune': A Memoir of the Civil War Era.*, ed. David C. Rankin, trans. Gerard F. Denault (Baton Rouge: Louisiana State University Press, 1984), 119–20; P. H. Sheridan to U. S. Grant, May 11, 1867, in Senate, *Military Letters, Orders, and Telegrams*, 206; Roger A. Fischer, "A Pioneer Protest: The New Orleans Street Car Controversy of 1867," *Journal of Negro History* 53 (July 1968): 228–29.

14. Sefton, *Army and Reconstruction*, 148.

15. Special Orders No. 122, Dept. of the Gulf, Aug. 21, 1867, RG 94, Records of the Adjutant General's Office, NA.

16. General Orders No. 13, Dept. of the Gulf, Mar. 9, 1867, ibid.

goal, particularly in some of the more remote upcountry parishes. It is also probable that some white Confederate veterans did not register, even though entitled to do so. Sheridan's officials may have intimidated some, but they probably heeded Democratic leaders' calls to boycott the election in an attempt to forestall a new constitution and black political power. However imperfect the implementation, by September 1867 Sheridan's registrars had enrolled more than 78,000 black and 48,000 white voters for the election of delegates to the constitutional convention. The convention convened at the Mechanics' Institute in New Orleans from November 1867 through March 1868. The location of the convention doubtlessly reminded delegates of the high cost at which black enfranchisement had been purchased.[17]

Sheridan did not remain in New Orleans long enough to see Republican dreams for a new constitution and universal male suffrage reach fruition. Increasingly frustrated by watching Congress override his vetoes, Andrew Johnson turned his wrath on the Republicans' agents of change—the secretary of war and the commanding generals of the military districts. Secretary Stanton, whom Johnson had suspected of conspiring with the Radicals ever since the fiasco over General Baird's telegram just before the massacre of 1866, was the first to go, suspended on August 1, 1867.[18] On August 17 Johnson ordered Grant to remove Sheridan from his command. Grant protested the firing, both in writing and in person at an unpleasant interview at the White House, but Johnson dug in his heels and demanded Sheridan's ouster. On the nineteenth Grant relented, breaking the news to his old friend and arranging a transfer to the Great Plains, where "Little Phil" could fight Indians instead of Rebels.[19]

WARMOTH AND THE CARPETBAGGER DICTATORSHIP, 1868–72

The principal beneficiary of Sheridan's stern military dictatorship over Louisiana was a practically unknown ex-Union colonel from Illinois, Henry Clay Warmoth, who was just twenty-five years old in 1867. He was destined to be the most controversial governor in all Louisiana history—with the possible exception of Huey Long, who studied Warmoth's methods and reputedly admired him for his ruthlessness.[20] Tall, good-looking, and a charismatic speaker, Warmoth campaigned openly and enthusiastically for black votes in 1868. On the stump he advocated full political and civil equality for the freedmen, denouncing the slaveholding class for leading Louisiana into a devas-

17. Donald W. Davis, "Ratification of the Constitution of 1868—Record of Votes," *LaH* 6 (Summer 1965), 301–5.

18. Sefton, *Army and Reconstruction*, 154.

19. Ibid., 156.

20. T. Harry Williams, *Huey Long* (New York: Alfred A. Knopf, 1969), 184–85.

tating civil war and then trying to reassert its tyrannical rule with the Black Codes. Genteel southern white society was shocked by the message and the manner in which this alien Yankee presented himself, but their shock compounded when their former slaves delivered the state to him by a solid majority in the first election under the new constitution in April 1868. Warmoth's rise to power was meteoric, and though his reign over Louisiana lasted only four years, his name became synonymous in the southern folklore of Reconstruction with demagoguery, corruption, and tyrannical personal rule. Modern scholars of the era have questioned just how corrupt and tyrannical the carpetbaggers really were, but few disagree that Warmoth sought to concentrate unprecedented political power in his own hands.

Warmoth's unlikely career in Louisiana politics was a byproduct of the upheaval of the Civil War. Born in Illinois, he became a country lawyer in central Missouri at eighteen by lying about his age to a local circuit judge. When the Democratic leadership in that state moved toward secession in late 1860, Warmoth organized a Unionist militia company. In 1861 he became commander of the Thirty-Second Missouri Infantry Regiment and fought at the battle of Wilson's Creek, which kept Missouri in the Union. In early 1863 Warmoth's regiment joined Maj. Gen. John McClernand's command, then preparing for the long-awaited campaign against Vicksburg. McClernand was an Illinois politician rather than a professional soldier and owed his commission to his connections to another Illinois politician, Abraham Lincoln. During the preparation for the campaign, Warmoth became McClernand's aide and something of a protégé. In May 1863 Warmoth was wounded during the first failed assault on Vicksburg's defenses, a minor event in the overall scheme of the campaign, but one bound to cause recriminations within the Union high command at a fearful time of stalemate on all battlefronts. While convalescing, Warmoth gave a Chicago newspaper interview that Grant interpreted as casting aspersions on his conduct of the campaign. Grant summarily dismissed him.[21]

What happened next was testimony not only to the sort of boldness Warmoth would demonstrate in Louisiana but also to his uncanny ability to insinuate himself with influential people. As he would later tell the tale, rather than accept Grant's humiliating dismissal, Warmoth traveled to Washington and presented himself at the White House to discuss his case with President Lincoln in person. Standing in a long line of favor seekers, he watched silently as the master politician dispatched petitioners with avuncular nods and evasive replies in response to pointed pleas for po-

21. Joseph Holt, [Judge Advocate General's Office], to Abraham Lincoln, Sept. 1, 1863, Warmoth Papers, SHC.

litical jobs and military commissions. When his own turn came, Warmoth did not wait to be dismissed like the others but burst out: "Mr. President, I cannot wait until the war is over for my vindication. I must have justice now. I cannot stand being put off!" Startled and possibly impressed by the young man's obvious self-confidence, Lincoln turned his case over to a War Department staff officer for review. A short time later Warmoth returned to his regiment with his old rank restored. In late 1863 he vindicated himself in combat by leading his regiment in the successful Union attack on Lookout Mountain near Chattanooga that shattered the Confederate Army of Tennessee.[22]

That winter Warmoth visited his mentor, General McClernand, whom Grant had also fired. McClernand was now attached to General Banks's command, headquartered in New Orleans and preparing for the campaign up the Red River against Shreveport, the Confederate capital of Louisiana. McClernand offered his protégé another staff job, which Warmoth promptly accepted but whose eyes were already on greater things. While attending a Union military ball in New Orleans in early 1864 sponsored by General and Mrs. Banks, Warmoth danced with the general's wife and so charmed her that she persuaded her husband to offer the young colonel an appointment in the New Orleans military provost court. Thereafter New Orleans became his base of power.[23]

From 1865 to 1868 Warmoth steadily made himself into the indispensable man in the infant Republican Party in New Orleans while enriching himself in private legal practice. After the war he used his extensive personal contacts in the army to pursue lucrative settlements in some of the thousands of legal suits that sprang from the contested ownership of cotton in Louisiana and Texas. In May 1865, even before the end of hostilities, he was already busy politicking and giving speeches favoring "political equality" and "small farms" for the freedmen, a position that identified him with the Radicals rather than Conservative Unionists like Governor Wells. His election as territorial delegate in November 1865 and subsequent trip to Washington allowed him to cultivate a growing network of influential friends in high places.[24]

In Washington Representative-in-waiting Warmoth frequented dinners and parties held by notable Republicans like Salmon P. Chase, now chief justice of the Supreme Court, and Benjamin Butler, a bad Civil War general but a formidable Mas-

22. Grant, *Papers*, 8:480–82n. For Warmoth's version of his conversation with Lincoln, see *War, Politics, and Reconstruction*, 20.

23. Nathaniel P. Banks to John A. McClernand, May 31, 1864, Warmoth Papers, SHC; Richard Nelson Current, *Those Terrible Carpetbaggers: A Reinterpretation* (New York: Oxford University Press, 1988), 10.

24. Benjamin F. Flanders to H. C. Warmoth, Nov. 23, 1865, Warmoth Papers, SHC.

sachusetts politician. Warmoth also managed to enhance his reputation socially. For a time he escorted Mary Harlan, daughter of an Iowa senator and the future wife of Robert Todd Lincoln. In his official capacity as Louisiana's representative, Warmoth launched a concerted campaign to discredit Governor Wells and the Rebel Legislature, which constantly kept his name in the newspapers back in New Orleans. Although congressional Republicans never granted him the seat he hoped to gain in the House, they provided him with numerous contacts he later employed to great effect.[25]

With the failure of his attempt to win a territorial seat in Congress, Warmoth returned to New Orleans. His political prospects had suddenly dimmed, and his law practice suffered in his absence. Identification with northern Radicals lost him clients and made political enemies in the South. At one point he was indicted in Texas on charges of embezzling $27,000 in cotton, though the courts eventually cleared him of wrongdoing. With the Rebel Legislature ascendant, his prospects looked bleak by the spring of 1866.[26]

Enactment of military rule reversed Warmoth's political fortunes, and he threw himself into organizing new voters in the river parishes, where a high black turnout could be anticipated. In 1867 the Louisiana chapter of the Grand Army of the Republic, the Union veterans organization, elected him state commander, boosting his recognition among Republicans by linking his name to Union victory, Union military service, and Union principles. Elected to the new constitutional convention of 1867–68, he helped craft many of the most progressive features of the resulting document, including civil rights, equal access to public accommodations, and state support for public schools. He also played a somewhat more shadowy role in persuading the convention to drop the proposed minimum age for governor from thirty-five to twenty-five, which conveniently made him eligible to run for the office in 1868.[27]

Warmoth's notorious reputation for corruption preceded his elevation to the governorship and demands careful scrutiny, not only because that reputation took on legendary proportions that still color critical estimates of his accomplishments but also because most charges of corruption—if that indeed is what it was—against the carpetbaggers tend to ignore the rough qualities of nineteenth-century American politics in general and the unique dilemmas that southern Republican politicians in particular faced when they came to power in a sea of nearly uniform native white hostility. At the time, Warmoth scarcely bothered to refute the accusations made

25. Warmoth, *Letter.*

26. T. J. Durant to H. C. Warmoth, Mar. 2, 1866, Warmoth Papers, SHC.

27. N. P. Chipman [adjutant general, Grand Army of the Republic] to H. C. Warmoth, Feb. 4, 1868, ibid.

against him. When a northern newspaper reporter confronted him with allegations that the legislature he controlled was thoroughly corrupt, he shot back a defiant reply: "These much abused members of the Louisiana legislature are at all events as good as the people they represent. Why, damn it, everybody is demoralized down here. Corruption is the fashion."[28]

Within days of his election as territorial representative, rumors flew that Warmoth had bought the nomination. Stories circulated that impoverished freedmen voting in the territorial election had been required to contribute a half dollar each for the privilege of letting Colonel Warmoth represent them in Congress. He insisted that the contributions were entirely voluntary and intended to help defray his unofficial expenses in Washington.[29] When Republicans met on January 14, 1868, to nominate a ticket for the upcoming election for governor and other state officers, Warmoth ran second on the first ballot to Maj. F. E. Dumas (the wealthy gens de couleur libre planter who had organized black troops for General Butler) by a vote of 41–37, with three minor candidates scattering seven votes. After a recess for a round of intense bartering, the delegates returned and nominated Warmoth over Dumas by a margin of just two votes (45–43). Miffed at his rejection, Dumas refused Warmoth's offer of the lieutenant governor's spot on the ticket, which then went to Oscar J. Dunn, another black Union veteran and prominent convention delegate from New Orleans. The next day the *New Orleans Times*, a Democratic newspaper, ran a story claiming that Warmoth bought the votes he needed to put his nomination over the top.[30] The *New Orleans Tribune*, the journal of the free-black community and many rural freedmen, picked up the story and announced a campaign advocating a new ticket that would be headed by a Conservative Unionist planter, James G. Taliaferro, and Major Dumas. The *Tribune*'s editorial line split the Republican Party and provoked internal dissent at the paper. Belgian-born editor Jean-Charles Houzeau disagreed with the Roudanez brothers, the newspaper's gens de couleur libre owners, and counseled against a schism in the first federally recognized election for black Louisianians. The Roudanez brothers retorted that Warmoth's chicanery could not escape unpunished. Houzeau disagreed and resigned, depriving the Radicals of their most effective and eloquent voice in Louisiana.[31]

When quiet appeals to the Roudanez brothers failed to bring them around, Warmoth resorted to harsher measures to instill party discipline. With the help of the con-

---

28. Warmoth quoted in Taylor, *Louisiana Reconstructed*, 201.

29. T. J. Durant to H. C. Warmoth, Feb. 9, 1868, Warmoth Papers, SHC.

30. *New Orleans Times*, Jan. 15, 1868, 1.

31. Houzeau, *My Passage*, 149–50; T. J. Durant to H. C. Warmoth, Mar. 5, 1868, Warmoth Papers, SHC.

gressional clerk in Washington, Edward McPherson, whom he had met while seeking his territorial seat, Warmoth got the *Tribune's* federal printing contract for Louisiana cancelled in February 1868, crippling the newspaper's revenue and forcing its closure the following April.[32] Among the first acts that Warmoth signed as governor was a bill establishing a state printing commission, which designated the governor as chairman.[33] The new contract for state printer went to the *New Orleans Republican*, a newly created company in which Governor Warmoth owned 250 out of 1,100 total shares outstanding. Over the next three years, the state printing commission supported between thirty-five and forty printers across Louisiana, costing the state some $1.5 million. Some of these companies were in parishes that previously had no newspaper at all, and close political supporters of the governor ran many of them.[34]

Governor Warmoth also took a keen personal interest in the transportation infrastructure and public finances of his adopted state. Because much of New Orleans lay below the flood level of the Mississippi River, the city required constant maintenance work on canals and drainage ditches to prevent the buildup of sewage, which was thought to give rise to periodic epidemics of yellow fever. After numerous delays the new legislature passed a bill awarding lucrative contracts to perform the required work. Records subsequently revealed that Governor Warmoth had not disclosed his own $100,000 stake in shares of the Mississippi and Mexican Gulf Ship Canal Company, which acquired an exclusive subcontract from the state-designated contractor, the New Orleans and Ship Island Company.[35]

The legislature also approved huge increases in the contingency indebtedness of the state in order to finance railroads between New Orleans, Houston, and Jackson, Mississippi. Conservatives and Republicans alike wanted railroad construction to develop new markets and draw much needed new business into the state. Although many of the proposed lines never materialized (which relieved the state of its contingent indebtedness), the mere rumor of such deals usually touched off frenzies of speculative bidding in shares of the firms involved and inflated the value of the state-

---

32. The precise circumstances of Warmoth's nomination remain clouded with uncertainty. See Current, *Those Terrible Carpetbaggers*, 77; Taylor, *Louisiana Reconstructed*, 156; and Foner, *Reconstruction*, 332. Current mentions Edward McPherson's role in killing the state printing contract. Taylor emphasizes Warmoth's vengeance. Foner suggests that Dumas may have been unpopular among the freedmen because he had formerly been a large slaveholder.

33. *Acts of the State of Louisiana* (New Orleans, 1868), Act 8.

34. Ella Lonn, *Reconstruction in Louisiana after 1868* (New York: G. P. Putnam's Sons, 1918), 87; Francis Byers Harris, "Henry Clay Warmoth, Reconstruction Governor of Louisiana," *LHQ* 30 (Apr. 1947): 555.

35. Taylor, *Louisiana Reconstructed*, 188; Lonn, *Reconstruction in Louisiana*, 33–34.

issued bonds that provided operating capital. Like many other wealthy men in New Orleans, Governor Warmoth bought stock in the New Orleans, Jackson, and Great Northern Railroad on insider knowledge that the legislature (which he controlled) would pass state-backed bonds, causing the value of these shares to soar.[36] Rumors in New Orleans claimed that each member of the legislature got five hundred dollars to vote for the bill; P. B. S. Pinchback, the black political leader, supposedly got one thousand dollars for his efforts; and according to one state official, "Warmoth got one hundred thousand dollars for his influence on the Jackson Railroad job."[37]

The litany of charges against Louisiana's first Republican governor portrayed him as a kind of human vulture preying on the body of an innocent Louisiana, beaten down by the cruel hardships of civil war and Sheridan's merciless military tyranny. The reality is somewhat different. Without question Warmoth personally profited from his years as governor. He departed office with a fortune large enough to buy half-interest in a large plantation of sugar cane and orange groves downriver from New Orleans near Pointe la Hache, which made him a wealthy man for the rest of his life. He certainly profited from what would today be regarded as conflicts of interest and insider trading by investing in enterprises whose success he could manipulate through his official position. Such conflicts, however unsavory they may strike contemporary observers, were not illegal in nineteenth-century Louisiana, or for that matter in the rest of the United States. At the time, enthusiasm for northern capital investment in the South crossed all party and racial lines. Economic historians studying the era routinely lament that the carpetbaggers did not attract even more capital investment to a region that chronically lagged the rest of the nation in financial wherewithal and would continue to do so well into the next century.[38]

On the more serious accusation of trading votes for bribes, Warmoth was frequently charged but never convicted, either in a court of law or by any solid evidence in the docket of historians. Part of the difficulty for historians examining such allegations stems from the fact that Louisiana had no laws against "the crime of bribery," as Warmoth pointedly reminded his critics.[39] The easy exchange of money for votes

36. Warmoth's critics failed to point out that the president and major shareholder of the New Orleans, Jackson, and Great Northern was Confederate war hero Gen. Pierre Gustave Toutant Beauregard, who was a close confidant of the new governor early in his administration. See P. G. T. Beauregard to H. C. Warmoth, Feb. 13, 1869, Warmoth Papers, SHC.

37. Richard Henry Dana [quoting T. W. Conway] to H. C. Warmoth, Aug. 25, 1870, ibid.; Taylor, *Louisiana Reconstructed*, 192.

38. Gavin Wright, *Old South, New South: Revolutions in the Southern Economy since the Civil War* (New York: Basic Books, 1986), 62–64.

39. Henry C. Warmoth, "Governor's Message," in *Louisiana Legislative Documents, 1870* (New Orleans,

had long been an entrenched practice among the cartel of planters and merchants who dominated antebellum Louisiana. Warmoth himself publicly proposed making bribery of state officials a crime, only to see the bills invariably die in legislative committee. What was new in Louisiana politics during Reconstruction was not bribery per se, rather the outcry over it. The sudden ascendancy of a new class of politicians composed of alien Yankee carpetbaggers and recently enfranchised blacks interrupted the previously submerged flow of influence peddling, thrusting the exchange of money for political power into an unaccustomed limelight.

Warmoth steadfastly denied dealing in bribes while in office and for the rest of his life. If he actually did participate in bribery, he proved marvelously adept at hiding the evidence from the public in his day and the searches of historians ever since. In one particularly sensational incident, a state legislator denounced Warmoth in public for offering him a bribe, which was supposed to buy his vote for a certain candidate in a special legislative election for lieutenant governor in 1871. The money was to have been deposited in a safe-deposit box in a New Orleans bank. After breaking with Warmoth, the legislator publicly exposed the deal and sued to have the box opened to prove the governor's corruption. When the bank president opened the box, it contained a signed copy of the legislator's agreement to sell his vote, but no money—thus proving only that the legislator had been willing to sell his vote, not that Warmoth had actually bought it.[40]

At the end of the day, the stream of corruption charges leveled against Warmoth and other Louisiana carpetbaggers were the stuff of political campaign fodder. They ultimately served only to obscure more fundamental objections to his tenure in office: first, that he had come to power on the strength of black votes and, second, that he was determined from the moment he entered office to defend his position from the real possibility of violent overthrow. In his inaugural address in the summer of 1868, Warmoth declared that Louisiana stood "amid the ruins of the old regime" and pledged to fight against the return to the sort of violence he had personally witnessed during the New Orleans street battle of 1866.[41] Over the next two years, he and Republican legislators erected a barricade of laws designed to defend the fledgling postwar government from attacks of violence and electoral fraud. Warmoth's political opponents charged that these so-called "obnoxious laws" made him a virtual dictator over the state. The charge, while perhaps not literally true, highlighted the real fear

---

1871), 10; Warmoth, "Governor's Message," in *Louisiana Legislative Documents, 1871* (New Orleans, 1872), 20.

40. Althea D. Pitre, "The Collapse of the Warmoth Regime, 1870–1872," *LaH* 6 (Spring 1965): 170.

41. Warmoth, *War, Politics, and Reconstruction*, 49–50.

among many whites that Republicans would defend black enfranchisement through a more powerful and centralized government than Louisiana had ever known.

The first of the "obnoxious laws" enacted by the Republicans took control of the New Orleans police from the hands of Mayor Monroe's Confederate veterans and replaced it with a state police force under the governor's personal command. The Metropolitan Police Act of 1868 merged the police departments in Orleans and the adjoining parishes of Jefferson and St. Bernard into a single force directed by a five-member board appointed by the governor. Added legislation stripped police power from the mayor of New Orleans but decreed that the Metropolitans' budget be paid through local assessments. Warmoth rewarded his constituents and extended the reach of his patronage by making the Metropolitans a racially mixed force from the top down. Of the five available board positions, he appointed three blacks and two whites and also named his lieutenant governor, Oscar Dunn, ex officio president. In October 1868, just before the national election, the Metropolitans employed a force consisting of 130 black and 243 white policemen, closely reflecting the demographic profile of the city (38 percent black and 62 percent white, according to the 1868 voter registration). Despite repeated accusations to the contrary, the Metropolitans were never an all black or even a majority black force at any time in their existence.[42]

The Metropolitan Police got off to a difficult start. In their first test of strength, they abysmally failed to prevent white vigilantes from disrupting Republican voter turnout for the fall presidential elections. The Knights of the White Camellia, the local Democratic Party, and a number of other Conservative political clubs took to the streets of New Orleans by the thousands in torch-lit political rallies that frequently degenerated into what the local white press indelicately termed "negro hunts." The Knights, led by Col. Alcibiades De Blanc, former commander of the Confederate Eighth Louisiana and a planter in St. Mary Parish, were closely modeled upon the Ku Klux Klan's masks, secret oaths, and quasi-Masonic rituals. Both because of its secrecy and rapid disintegration after the election, little is known about the organization other than its dedication to white supremacy and determination to prevent blacks from voting for Grant in the fall presidential election.[43]

---

42. A breakdown of the 1868 voter registration by race and ward in the city of New Orleans is found in "Report of the Board of Registration to the General Assembly of Louisiana, Session of 1869," in *Louisiana Legislative Documents, 1868* (New Orleans 1869), 17. For numbers of white and black officers in the metropolitan police force, see "Annual Report of the Board of Metropolitan Police," in *Louisiana Legislative Documents, 1869* (New Orleans, 1870). For a recent history of the Metropolitans as a police force, see Dennis C. Rousey, *Policing the Southern City: New Orleans, 1805–1889* (Baton Rouge: Louisiana State University Press, 1996), 126–58.

43. O. O. Howard, "Report of Major General O. O. Howard, Commissioner of Bureau of Refugees,

In addition to the challenge of order in the streets, the Metropolitans faced a barrage of lawsuits in the courts from local municipal authorities challenging their jurisdiction, constitutionality, and funding authority. During the force's first year of existence, several municipalities contained in the Metropolitan Police District sued to overturn the enacting legislation and tried to withhold their assessments until the Louisiana Supreme Court heard their cases. Lack of funds hobbled the Republicans' attempts to arm, uniform, and train an effective force at the outset. Because the Metropolitans had no issued firearms and were still relatively few in number, Warmoth had to appeal to federal authorities for help during the 1868 fall elections, during which another wave of vigilante violence engulfed the state. In a desperate telegram to President Johnson, the governor requested a stockpile of federal arms and an overturn of the ban against southern militias, a precautionary measure within the Reconstruction acts. Johnson demurred and told him to ask the local army commander, Maj. Gen. Lovell H. Rousseau, for assistance. Rousseau, a Democratic politician from Kentucky and Johnson's handpicked successor to General Sheridan, suggested that a large black turnout would only result in a needless statewide bloodbath. Rather than offer troops, he asked Warmoth to urge the freedmen to stay home on election day. Grant's position as the Republican candidate for president made the possibility of a direct appeal to the War Department not only awkward but also potentially impolitic. Seeing no practical way out of his dilemma, Warmoth reluctantly agreed to discourage freedmen participation, and the state went for Horatio Seymour and the Democratic ticket by a large margin.[44]

Discouraged but not intimidated, Warmoth struck back by strengthening the Metropolitans. After his first superintendent proved ineffectual, Warmoth replaced him with Algernon S. Badger in 1870. Colonel Badger was a Massachusetts-born carpetbagger and a veteran of the Sixth Massachusetts Infantry, one of the first volunteer units to come to the defense of Lincoln's beleaguered Washington in 1861. He came to New Orleans as a lieutenant in the Twenty-Sixth Massachusetts Infantry with General Butler and eventually commanded the First Louisiana Cavalry (USA). After the war he worked as a clerk in the Fourth District Recorders Court until his appointment in October 1868 as a captain in the Metropolitans.[45] Badger labored vigorously to expand and improve the effectiveness of the Metropolitans. By the end of 1870, the force had risen to 709 officers and included a river fleet of five boats, a special sanitary com-

---

Freedmen, and Deserted Lands," in U.S. House, *Report of the Secretary of War, 1868*, 40th Cong., 3rd sess., 1868, H. Exec. Doc. 1.

44. Dawson, *Army Generals and Reconstruction*, 84.

45. Glenn R. Conrad, ed., *A Dictionary of Louisiana Biography*, 2 vols. (New Orleans: Louisiana Historical Association, 1988), 1:28–29.

pany, a telegraph corps, and a contingent of mounted officers. Badger also increased the pay of patrolmen to one thousand dollars per year, even though a chronic lack of funds meant that they were sometimes paid in depressed state-issued warrants rather than U.S. currency. The annual reports of the Metropolitans clearly indicate that they spent most of their time doing routine police work. In times of crisis, however, they proved to be a reliable nucleus for a state militia force upon which beleaguered Republicans might depend.[46]

While Warmoth must have been heartened by the steady progress that Superintendent Badger made with the Metropolitans, several factors propelled him toward the creation of a volunteer state militia. The U.S. Army had provided no help in the federal election crisis of 1868. Unlike Sheridan, Rousseau proved unsympathetic to Louisiana Republicans. Additionally, by 1870 the army, now under the command of Gen. William T. Sherman, whom Grant promoted to commanding general when he himself became president in 1869, underwent another round of force reductions, dropping its total strength from about fifty-three thousand in 1868 to twenty-eight thousand in 1870. The decline in numbers forced the closure of most minor army posts in Louisiana's rural parishes. This development must have been particular troubling to Warmoth since parishes bordering on the Red River had proven especially susceptible to the violence that impaired Republican voter turnout in 1868. These parishes were also too remote from New Orleans to be effectively aided by the Metropolitans in a local crisis. Complicating matters, legal challenges to the Metropolitans' novel jurisdiction suggested that further geographical expansions to their territory would prove difficult. Warmoth was almost certainly aware that Republican governors in Arkansas, Tennessee, and North Carolina had successfully used locally raised militias to root out and suppress vigilante political violence in 1868 and 1869. In 1870 he encouraged the legislature to pass the second of the "obnoxious laws," this time a militia act designed to raise a statewide and biracial force, the Louisiana State Militia.[47]

Warmoth's creation of the new militia demonstrated his acute understanding of the subtleties of a political system rooted in political patronage balanced against the need to raise an effective and reliable local defense force. To head the militia he turned to one of the rising stars of the Republican Party in Louisiana, ex-Confederate general James Longstreet. As one of Lee's corps commanders in the Army of Northern Vir-

---

46. "Annual Report of the Board of Metropolitan Police," 7.

47. W. P. Kellogg to H. C. Warmoth, July 21, 1868, Warmoth Papers, SHC; *Acts of the State of Louisiana* (New Orleans, 1871), Act 75 (164–88).

ginia, Longstreet was famed among Confederate veterans. During the war he had become personally acquainted with many of the members of the two Louisiana brigades serving in Virginia. In 1866 he went into the cotton business in partnership with the three Owen brothers, all veterans of the Washington Artillery and prominent members of the Whig mercantile community in New Orleans that had initially been cool to secession. In 1867 Longstreet wrote a series of much-discussed letters published in the *New Orleans Times* while Congress debated passage of the original Military Reconstruction Act. Longstreet argued that the Confederacy had lost the conflict "by the hazards of revolution," and the time had now come for all southerners to accept the new political realities of black emancipation and enfranchisement. Warmoth's appointment of the former general held out the distinct possibility of splitting the façade of hostile white solidarity to the Republican government and adding a native white wing to his existing coalition of carpetbaggers and blacks.[48]

While Longstreet's military reputation played an important role in his selection, other factors entered in as well. Grant's election in 1868 was an important victory for all southern Republicans, but it posed a delicate dilemma for Warmoth personally. Grant had relieved Warmoth at Vicksburg in 1863, and the latter's close association with a parade of political generals during the Civil War did not portend a good working relationship with the new occupant of the White House. Longstreet, however, had been one of Grant's closest personal friends for years. Both men were graduates of West Point and had served together in the Mexican War. In November 1865 Grant personally recommended Longstreet for a presidential pardon. In 1868 Longstreet publicly endorsed his old friend for president. Grant rewarded Longstreet's loyalty with a patronage job as deputy customs collector at the U.S. Custom House on lower Canal Street in 1869.[49] Warmoth undoubtedly hoped that Longstreet's personal connections to the president would smooth over his own rocky relationship with Grant.

While complete muster rolls of the militia have long since vanished, the fragmentary information that remains in Longstreet's annual reports demonstrates that he and Warmoth made substantial progress toward creating a carefully crafted vol-

48. *New Orleans Times*, Mar. 19, Apr. 7, 1867; William L. Richter, "Longstreet: From Rebel to Scalawag," *LaH* 11 (Summer 1970): 215–30. Longstreet's relationship with Grant thrived on a variety of levels. In New Orleans he was in business with Col. James F. Casey, Grant's brother-in-law, in an enterprise to build the Texas and Pacific Transcontinental Railroad by way of New Orleans, Houston, Monterey, and Mazatlan, and they unsuccessfully attempted to get Grant to lend his support to the project. Casey became an official in the U.S. Customs House in New Orleans after Grant became president. James Longstreet to Ulysses S. Grant, Apr. 10, 1867, in Grant, *Papers*, 17:116–17 n.

49. U. S. Grant to A. Johnson, Nov. 7, 1865, in ibid., 15:401–2.

unteer militia force capable of defending the state government from attack. They also saw the militia as expanding and solidifying Republican political patronage.[50] An examination of the backgrounds of the major commanders of the Louisiana State Militia reveals that they uncannily mirrored the coalition of political forces Warmoth hoped to weld into a political machine to dominate Louisiana (see appendix 1, table 1.1).

Longstreet divided the militia into two divisions, the first commanded by Maj. Gen. Hugh J. Campbell of New Orleans, and the second by Brig. Gen. J. Frank Pargoud from northeastern Louisiana. Campbell was a Union officer in the Eighteenth Iowa Infantry and served as chief clerk of the 1867 constitutional convention. In 1868 he was elected state senator from Orleans Parish and became a staunch member of Warmoth's legislative faction.[51] Pargoud, about whom much less is known, resided in Monroe in Ouachita Parish and had been a Confederate colonel of cavalry.[52] The brigade commanders in the First Division were Brig. Gen. A. P. "Penn" Mason and Brig. Gen. A. E. Barbour, both of New Orleans. Mason had been an officer on General Lee's staff and was closely associated with the white Whig mercantile community in New Orleans.[53] Barbour was a free-black Union veteran, a Republican state senator from Orleans Parish, and a Warmoth faction supporter. He became, by Warmoth's appointment, one of the first commissioned militia generals of African descent in American history.[54]

Regimental and unit commanders of the militia were an equally diverse lot. Col. William M. Owen, Longstreet's business partner in the cotton trading firm of Long-

50. The author's inquiries at the archives at Louisiana State University at Baton Rouge and at the Louisiana National Guard Headquarters at Jackson Barracks have not recovered any original muster rolls for the Louisiana State Militia from Reconstruction. The Louisiana adjutant general's *Annual Reports* are themselves incomplete and are available only for the years 1870–74. Interview, chief archivist, Louisiana and Lower Mississippi Valley Collections, LSU Libraries, Louisiana State University, Aug. 2, 1994. Contemporary reports suggest that officials in the last Republican administration during Reconstruction deliberately burned records in early 1877 to prevent them from being seized by Conservatives. See "Old State Documents," *New Orleans Daily Picayune*, May 15, 1877, 1.

51. Howard J. Jones, "Biographical Sketches of Members of the 1868 Louisiana State Senate," *LaH* 19 (1978): 90–91.

52. Booth, *Records of Louisiana Confederate Soldiers*.

53. Warmoth, *War, Politics, and Reconstruction*, 100.

54. The highest-ranking black officers in the Union army during the Civil War were Maj. F. E. Dumas in Louisiana and Maj. Martin Delaney in South Carolina. See Berlin et al., *Slave No More*, 211–14. A small number of blacks also held commissions as colonels and generals in the Reconstruction militia of South Carolina by 1877, including well-known politicians Robert Smalls and Prince Rivers. See Joel Williamson, *After Slavery: The Negro in South Carolina during Reconstruction* (Chapel Hill: University of North Carolina Press, 1965), 261–62.

street, Owen, and Company, and a veteran of the elite Confederate Washington Artillery, commanded the First Regiment.[55] Col. Charles W. Squires, another veteran of the Washington Artillery, organized and led the First Louisiana Field Artillery Regiment.[56] Col. James B. Lewis commanded the Second Regiment. Lewis had served as a captain in the First Louisiana Native Guards during the Civil War, resigning during Banks's purge of black officers in 1864. He was a captain in the Metropolitan Police, but he broke with Warmoth to join the Custom House faction during the 1872 crisis.[57] The Third Regiment was the gens de couleur libre New Orleans regiment, commanded by Col. James H. Ingraham, a Republican state representative from New Orleans between 1868 and 1874. Ingraham had also been a captain in the First Louisiana Native Guards and served as chairman of the Republican nominating committee in 1868, which picked Warmoth for governor. Despite this association, he belonged to the Custom House faction in 1871 and 1872.[58] Col. Napoleon Underwood of East Baton Rouge Parish mustered six companies into the Fourth Regiment in 1870, but practically no other trace remains of this unit, which never mobilized for any conflict and appears to have been a force that existed only on paper. The Fifth Regiment was organized by Maj. George H. Braughn and was also an incomplete organization, with only five companies mustered. Although born in Cincinnati, Braughn was a longtime resident of New Orleans and a Confederate captain in the Crescent Regiment until paroled at New Iberia in 1865. He was a Democratic state senator from Orleans Parish from 1868 to 1872 and later a Democratic state judge.[59]

The militia also contained three smaller unattached elements in 1871. Henry Street commanded the separate formation of the City Guards Company of New Orleans. Street had organized and commanded the Seventy-Seventh USCT (formerly the Fifth Infantry Regiment, Corps d'Afrique) in the Civil War, served as inspector general under Longstreet from 1870 to 1872, and eventually became adjutant general of the militia in November 1872.[60] Capt. H. E. Shropshire of New Orleans organized

55. Owen, *Washington Artillery.*

56. "Muster-Roll of the Washington Artillery of the Army of Northern Virginia from May 27, 1861, to April 8, 1865," in ibid., 437.

57. Eric Foner, *Freedom's Lawmakers: A Directory of Black Office Holders during Reconstruction,* rev. ed. (Baton Rouge: Louisiana State University Press, 1996), 132–33.

58. War Department, *Official Army Register,* 8:246; Charles Vincent, *Black Legislators in Louisiana during Reconstruction* (Baton Rouge: Louisiana State University Press, 1976), 49.

59. Jones, "Biographical Sketches," 100–102.

60. War Department, *Official Army Register,* 8:253; Louisiana Adjutant General's Office, *Annual Report, 1873,* 1–11.

and commanded the lone cavalry company in the militia. He later became a member of the White Leagues in 1874.[61] The last independent militia unit raised in 1871 was a single black company organized by Capt. William Ward at Colfax. Ward was a black Republican state representative from 1870 to 1872 for Grant Parish, which was created in 1869 out of parts of three adjoining parishes. Ward was a sergeant in the USCT and moved to Grant Parish after the close of the Civil War. Apparently Warmoth and Longstreet planned a complete Sixth Regiment, perhaps embracing a number of the Red River parishes, because the Colfax militia company appears under that heading in the 1871 Annual Report. No other companies mustered, however, and no regimental commander was ever named. Ward and members of the Colfax militia became involved in the battle of Colfax on Easter Day 1873, the deadliest battle of Reconstruction.[62]

The Louisiana State Militia's organization in 1871 suggests several conclusions about the character of Republican state government militias during Reconstruction. First of all, despite efforts by Warmoth and Longstreet, it remained firmly rooted in New Orleans throughout its existence. Of the fifty companies mustered before 1872, thirty-nine (78 percent) came from that city alone, which contained just 25 percent of the state's population. Only five other parishes (Lafourche, Plaquemines, East Baton Rouge, Grant, and Ouachita) formally mustered any militia companies at all, and of these eleven units, only one (from Grant Parish) took part in a significant action during Reconstruction—and that (as we shall see) was an unqualified disaster. Thus the Louisiana State Militia remained—despite its boosters' best hopes and its detractors' worst fears—a force that never had much success in reaching out from its cosmopolitan base into the plantation belt, where it might have played a greater role in securing Republicans' embattled parish-level political organizations.

While the militia's geographical range remained limited, the political and ethnic composition of its leadership did reflect Warmoth's ambition to forge a broader southern Republican Party. Despite the imagery conjured up by a generation of historians devoted to demonizing the "negro militia" of Reconstruction, the Louisiana State Militia in 1871 was led mostly by white men and contained a surprisingly large number of Confederate veterans. Ex-Rebel officers, whose wartime service records could

61. "List of Those Who Took Part in the Battle of 14th September, 1874," in Stuart Omer Landry, *The Battle of Liberty Place: The Overthrow of Carpet-Bag Rule in New Orleans—September 14, 1874* (New Orleans: Pelican, 1955), 239. Shropshire's name does not appear in the National Archives' card file of Confederate veterans.

62. Manie White Johnson, "The Colfax Riot of April 1873," *LHQ* 13 (July 1930): 391–427. The battle at Colfax will be covered in more detail in chapter 5.

only be described as exemplary, filled many of its active leadership positions during Warmoth's term. If the Civil War service records of the militiamen mustered into service matched that of their company commanders (a reasonable assumption, given the common recruiting patterns of the era), the "Radical militia" of Louisiana in 1871 was as much Confederate as it was Union by background. In his first annual report, General Longstreet claimed that nearly "one half of our force is composed of officers and soldiers who were in the military service of the Southern States during the late civil conflict."[63] Few of these southern white men could even be properly termed "scalawags," though some militia officers, like Longstreet himself, did hold political patronage positions under the Republicans and joined the Republican Party. But others were Democrats, like Major Braughn, who held office as a Democrat during Reconstruction, and W. J. Behan, the lieutenant colonel of the militia artillery elected Democratic mayor of New Orleans in the 1880s.[64]

To be sure, the Louisiana State Militia also included carpetbaggers and blacks. Of those for whom information is available, white militia officers of northern origin tended to have demonstrated an ideological devotion to the radical wing of the Republican Party, either by their service with black regiments in the Civil War (like Colonel Street) or by their political activity during the recent constitutional convention (like General Campbell). Black officers in the Louisiana State Militia tended to be veterans of the Louisiana Native Guards, which fought for the Union during the Port Hudson and Red River campaigns. Apparently Banks's prejudice against such men (forcing most to either resign or be dismissed in 1863) did not permanently sour them on either the Republican Party or voluntary military service. For a time Jordan Noble, the renowned drummer boy of the free men of color battalion in the 1815 battle of New Orleans and one of the original organizers of the Louisiana Native Guards, appeared on the rolls as a field-grade staff officer, probably for the prestige his name carried in the free-black community.[65]

While promotion in the Union army for black officers had been virtually closed

63. Louisiana Adjutant General's Office, *Annual Report, 1870*, 3.

64. Otis Singletary insists that the "overwhelming majority of Negro militiamen seem to have been recruited from the plantations," which was manifestly untrue for militia units from Louisiana. *Negro Militia and Reconstruction* (Austin: University of Texas Press, 1957), 110. Joseph Dawson erroneously describes Louisiana's Reconstruction militia as "composed almost entirely of blacks." *Army Generals and Reconstruction*, 106. On W. J. Behan's unusual political career, see Joy J. Jackson, *New Orleans in the Gilded Age: Politics and Urban Progress, 1880–1896* (Baton Rouge: Louisiana State University Press, 1969), 77–78.

65. Mary F. Berry, "Negro Troops in Blue and Gray: The Louisiana Native Guards, 1861–1863," *LaH* 8 (Spring 1967): 165–67; Louisiana Adjutant General's Office, *Annual Report, 1871*, 5.

above the rank of captain, the Louisiana State Militia was considerably more open to black military talent. In addition to a brigadier general and a regimental commander, Warmoth signed commissions for at least seven black field-grade officers and as many captains and lieutenants as their mustered companies entitled them to fill.[66]

Reconstruction Louisiana's militia units were racially segregated, just as the U.S. Army remained until 1948, but they nevertheless incorporated several distinct advances over the army in terms of racial equity and mobility. From the beginning, advancement to higher rank, while influenced by the politics of patronage, was open to black officers. Part of this new vertical mobility stemmed from social patterns of recruitment in which black militia officers raised their own companies and held a formal election of officers before the entire unit was offered for state service. In contrast the U.S. Colored Troops raised units primarily by a federally appointed cadre of white officers who then enlisted their regiments' black soldiers.[67] In Warmoth's militia there was no difference in pay, uniforms, or equipment between black and white troops as there had often been for the first regiments of the USCT. Nor did Warmoth's government assign black militia units the menial fatigue duties that often characterized black military service during the Civil War. Another unique advance was the mandatory state oath introduced by General Longstreet in 1870, which obliged all members of the militia to, at least in theory, embrace the Republicans' egalitarian creed:

> You, each and all of you, do solemnly swear (or affirm) that you accept the civil and political equality of all men, and agree not to attempt to deprive any person or persons on account of race, color, or previous condition of any political or civil right, privilege or immunity enjoyed by any other class of men. That you will support the constitution and laws of the United States and the constitution and laws of this State, and that you will faithfully and impartially discharge all the duties incumbent on you as non-commissioned officers and soldiers of the Louisiana State Militia, and that you will obey the orders of the Governor of the State, and other officers appointed over you . . . SO HELP YOU GOD.[68]

Despite the impressive strides Longstreet made in molding the militia into a politically reliable and militarily effective force, it remained throughout its existence a

66. Maj. Octave Rey, Maj. C. W. Ringgold, Maj. George Y. Kelso, Maj. R. S. Isabelle, Maj. J. B. Noble, Maj. J. J. Mallet, and Surgeon J. T. Jackson. See Louisiana Adjutant General's Office, *Annual Report, 1871*, 10, 13.

67. Berlin et al., *Slave No More*, 211–14.

68. General Orders No. 39, July 20, 1870, in Louisiana Adjutant General's Office, *Annual Report, 1870*, 39–40.

chronically weak organization. Maintaining a militia that was both effective and in-expensive exposed Louisiana Republican leaders to the classic dilemma of the American tradition of voluntary military service. Part-time forces required regularly paid drill periods if they were expected to muster in times of crisis. In Reconstruction-era Louisiana, though, the state paid for time in drill and on active duty in depreciated state-issued warrants rather than hard currency, which discouraged recruitment, retention, and training, as Longstreet and his successors annually reminded the governor. Whole units sometimes failed to muster for state-mandated inspections. Armories were often makeshift affairs in rooms of commercial buildings that lacked secure protection from either mass break-ins or petty theft. It took years to provide the entire militia with new uniforms, a fault not remedied until Governor Kellogg later found himself faced with a serious challenge and instituted a crash effort to improve his forces.

The quality of weapons improved steadily between 1870 and 1874, due largely to the efforts of Longstreet and Henry Street in obtaining federal grants and purchases of the latest models of weaponry available, but delays continued in issuing them to existing formations. In June 1870, not long after receiving his commission from Warmoth, Longstreet left New Orleans to lobby the Grant administration for support. While in Washington, Longstreet visited with the president, the secretary of war, and various staff officers in the War Department. Grant promised Longstreet he would "do all that can be done under the law" to lend his support. He asked the War Department to donate twenty-five hundred surplus Enfields and loan two thousand more from the federal arsenal in Baton Rouge. Longstreet also decided to purchase two batteries of cannon immediately and later added two new Gatling guns, perhaps foreseeing that the new weapons might prove useful for crowd control in New Orleans. Some of the wealthier militia companies apparently purchased Winchester rifles, which had a much higher rate of fire than Enfield rifled muskets, with their own funds between 1870 and 1872.[69] Longstreet would have liked to equip the entire militia with Winchesters, but only a part of Warmoth's most trusted force, the Metropolitans, received new weapons before the crisis of 1872.

In addition to creating a new state police force and militia, Conservatives became incensed by the Registration and Election laws Warmoth shepherded through the state legislature in 1870. The Registration Law allowed the governor to appoint his own candidates for voter registrar in each of the parishes. Recalling how General

69. General Orders No. 4, June 14, 1870, in ibid., 50; James Longstreet to H. C. Warmoth, June 30, 1870, Henry C. Warmoth Papers, LLMVC.

Sheridan's tight reign over voter turnout had frustrated their chances in the new elections of 1868, Conservative leaders expressed horror at the possibility that Warmoth would use his impressive powers of persuasion to make sure his registrars signed up every potential Republican and discouraged every potential Democrat. Even more depressing to them was the Election Law of 1870, which established the state Returning Board to validate parish returns at the state level. With his own fears of a return to the massive violence of 1866 and 1868, Warmoth wanted the Returning Board of five members (all appointed by him) empowered to adjust or strike down parish vote totals in cases of suspected fraud or violence. Conservatives smoldered in outrage at the idea that the Republican governor might try to steal the next election from them, their only justification being that they had tried to steal the presidential election of 1868 from the Republicans.

THE FRACTURING OF THE LOUISIANA REPUBLICAN PARTY

Warmoth's command over the Metropolitans, the state militia, the registration of voters, and the Returning Board seemed to make for an iron grip over Louisiana affairs. The results of the midterm elections of November 1870 confirmed the governor's mastery. In addition to the Republican candidates sweeping all five of the U.S. House races, Benjamin Flanders won the mayor's office in New Orleans for the party, easing fears about their hold over the state capital. Black candidates across the state also won an impressive number of local and state offices, including 36 out of 110 seats in the House. All these accomplishments signaled a bright future for the Republican Party in the state, particularly since the election had been so quiet that the Returning Board did not feel compelled to throw out a single parish vote total for fraud or violence. Four constitutional amendments proposed by the legislature also passed easily. The one that attracted the most attention affected the young governor personally, for it repealed the constitutional ban on the chief executive's reelection to office.[70]

Warmoth modestly claimed in his memoirs that the people of Louisiana demanded this amendment to the constitution, but his rivals, both in and out of the Republican Party, saw through him. Conservative political leaders in the state had always regarded Warmoth as an alien interloper and a "usurper" propped up only by federal military intervention. But now some Republican leaders began to see his growing power as a threat to their own aspirations. Opposition against him within the party coalesced in the so-called Custom House Ring, which broke with the governor

---

70. See Appendix C, "Black Members of the 1870–1872 House of Representatives," in Vincent, *Black Legislators*, 114; Taylor, *Louisiana Reconstructed*, 186; Current, *Those Terrible Carpetbaggers*, 247.

in 1871 by seizing control of the Republican state convention while Warmoth conva-
lesced from a foot injury in Pass Christian, Mississippi. The Ring was a group of carpetbaggers whose power derived from their power over federal patronage positions.
Their headquarters was in the U.S. Custom House in New Orleans, from which they
oversaw customs collections on the city's Mississippi port facilities. Because the security of their jobs depended solely upon the continued support of the federal government, they remained largely immune to the effects of social ostracism from whites
as well as the pressures of the locally based patronage machine Warmoth built. The
head of the Custom House Ring was the U.S. marshal for New Orleans, Capt. Stephen
B. Packard, originally from Maine. Packard's brother, Christopher, was a Republican
state senator, but Marshal Packard preferred to manipulate the Ring behind the
scenes. His principal allies were James Casey, the customs collector of the Port of New
Orleans who had obtained his office from his brother-in-law, President Grant, and Oscar J. Dunn, the black lieutenant governor and president of the state senate.

Dunn and a faction of black legislators grew unhappy with Warmoth early in his
administration. The governor earned their enmity by vetoing a civil rights bill passed
by the legislature of 1868 with Dunn's sponsorship. In his veto message Warmoth argued that the new constitution already protected civil rights, but behind closed doors
he told his fellow Republicans that he thought the cause of civil rights in Louisiana
could be better advanced indirectly through the governor's appointive and administrative powers rather than seeking out legal confrontations with truculent white
southerners.[71] Although the governor did allow a similar civil rights bill to become law
without his signature in 1869, this did not assuage Dunn. Warmoth argued that under his administration New Orleans had the best civil rights record of any southern
city during Reconstruction. He continued to use his police powers to keep the city
trolley system desegregated after Sheridan's military decree in 1867. And his superintendent of education, T. W. Conway, was quietly but effectively desegregating the New
Orleans public school system one school at a time, the only place during Reconstruction that public schools had been desegregated.[72] At first Dunn did not openly

71. *Official Journal of the Proceedings of the House of Representatives of the State of Louisiana at the Session Begun and Held in New Orleans, June 29, 1868* (New Orleans, 1868), 246.

72. Louis R. Harlan, "Desegregation in New Orleans Public Schools during Reconstruction," *AHR* 67 (Apr. 1962): 663–75. Some of the new state constitutions of Reconstruction had language that theoretically prohibited discrimination in public schooling or called for equal access to public education. New Or-
leans was the only major school system in which integration was practiced as a matter of policy. T. W. Conway was the same official in charge of the Freedmen's Bureau in Louisiana before being fired by President
Johnson in 1865 (see chapter 1).

break with Warmoth, but neither was he impressed by the governor's transparent attempts to woo the white business community. By 1870 Dunn shifted his allegiance to the leaders of the Custom House. There the impasse probably would have remained had it not been for Dunn's untimely death on November 22, 1871, and the ensuing scramble for the mantle of black political leadership in Louisiana.

Dunn's death handed Warmoth an opportunity to pick his own candidate for lieutenant governor. He offered the position to P. B. S. Pinchback, a black carpetbagger whose political acumen rivaled Warmoth's skills. Born to a wealthy white Mississippi planter and a mother of mixed ancestry, Pinchback was schooled in Cincinnati and onboard Mississippi steamboats, where he excelled at poker and other confidence games in which he and several companions regularly fleeced rich travelers. After the Union army occupied New Orleans, he made his way to the city and served for a time as captain of his own company in Banks's Corps d'Afrique. In 1867 he was a delegate to the new constitutional convention, then ran for state senator from Orleans Parish in 1868. Although he lost the initial count, the state senate voted to seat Pinchback after he convinced the legislature's electoral review committee that his Conservative opponent, E. L. Jewell, had won by fraud.[73] Warmoth appeared to admire Pinchback's political artistry but did not trust him in the least. Years later he recalled that Pinchback was "a restless, ambitious man . . . [who] had more than once arrayed himself against me. He was a free lance and dangerous and had to be reckoned with at all times."[74]

Like Warmoth, Pinchback sought indirect approaches when confronted with racially sensitive political issues. This produced the charge by his own grandson, Harlem Renaissance writer Jean Toomer, that Pinchback was nothing more than an opportunist who used his "taint of negro blood" to further a lucrative career.[75] While he certainly seemed to relish the games of patronage politics, Pinchback also managed to bargain for the creation of Southern University, which continued to give thousands of black Louisianians a chance for higher education after Reconstruction. His black political opponents, who sometimes styled themselves as "pure Radicals," castigated him for his deal making with white politicians. Pinchback frequently pointed out that his ideologically pure challengers had relatively little to show for their eschewal of his pragmatism.[76]

---

73. Howard Jones describes Pinchback's controversial seating as a state senator. "Biographical Sketches," 69–70. Jewell did not forget his defeat and eventually became one of the Republicans' bitterest foes in New Orleans as editor of the *Commercial Bulletin*, which regularly trumpeted a fierce and denigrating view of all carpetbaggers and black politicians.

74. Warmoth, *War, Politics, and Reconstruction*, 120.

75. Jean Toomer, *Cane*, 3rd ed. (New York: Harper and Row, 1969).

76. James Haskins, *P. B. S. Pinchback* (New York: Macmillan, 1973); Taylor, *Louisiana Reconstructed*, 221.

To confirm Pinchback as his lieutenant governor, Warmoth ordered the Louisiana Senate into extra session, a move his Custom House and Democratic opponents vehemently denounced as unconstitutional. Nevertheless, the Senate convened on December 6 and nominated Pinchback and Theodore V. Coupland for its president. Coupland was a carpetbagger who had been major of the First Texas Cavalry (USA) from 1862 to 1865. Elected state senator from Orleans Parish in 1868, he was a deputy customs collector and the Custom House Ring's candidate.[77] On the first ballot the candidates tied 17–17; the seven black senators split their votes, four voting for Pinchback and three for Coupland. On the second ballot James B. Lewis switched his vote from Coupland to Pinchback, breaking the tie and placing Pinchback in the lieutenant governor's chair as president of the Senate. Feeling strengthened, Warmoth and his Senate allies immediately voted to adjourn to plot strategy for the regular session, which the governor had ordered to convene a month later on January 1, 1872.[78]

The alliance between Warmoth and Pinchback panicked the Custom House Ring into an ill-considered alliance with the Democratic opposition in New Orleans. With the machinery of state government firmly in Warmoth's hands and Pinchback ensconced as power broker in the Senate, only command of the House stood within their reach—and just out of Warmoth's grasp. In the House, Speaker George Washington Carter led a strange alliance of Custom House Republicans and Democrats against a nearly equal number of Warmoth Republicans. Carter, who had been a Confederate Texas cavalry colonel during the Civil War, was Warmoth's former political ally and business partner. In 1870 Warmoth used another of his favorite patronage tools when he signed a bill creating Cameron Parish in southwestern Louisiana as a political sinecure for his friend. Elected to the House in 1870, Carter quickly mastered the field and won election to Speaker before the 1871 session concluded. But the two men had a serious falling out after the 1871 legislative session when Warmoth vetoed a bill authorizing what he termed excessive per diem expenses for members of the legislature. Carter then joined forces with the Custom House Ring. While Warmoth sought to portray his veto as a good-government and economy measure, it is likely that he also intended to enforce party discipline on members and make them beholden to his political machine.[79]

In December 1871 the leadership of the Custom House Ring held a series of meetings with the leaders of the New Orleans Democratic Committee in which they agreed to join forces to bring down Warmoth's administration. Considering that the Demo-

77. War Department, *Official Army Register*, 4:1161; Jones, "Biographical Sketches," 85–86.

78. Warmoth, *War, Politics, and Reconstruction*, 119–20.

79. G. W. Carter to H. C. Warmoth, Nov. 30, 1868, Warmoth Papers, SHC.

crats represented included such "last ditch" ex-Confederates as E. L. Jewell and Albert Voorhies, a leader of the Rebel Legislature during the New Orleans street battle of 1866, it must have been difficult for many black politicians to participate. Nevertheless, this strange alliance hatched a scheme that called for Democratic and Custom House Republican senators to leave New Orleans together onboard the federal revenue cutter *Wilderness* before the January 1872 session began, preventing a quorum in Pinchback's Senate. Carter would then recognize a motion for the House to vote to impeach Warmoth, which would automatically remove him from office until tried by the Senate under the terms of the 1868 Constitution. Leaders of the Ring believed their ability to withhold a quorum in the Senate would generate enough pressure to oust Pinchback as president and then convict the governor in a trial. Theoretically, that would leave the Ring's man, Speaker Carter, next in line for the governor's office. What they did not count on was Warmoth's tenacity, his uncanny knack for staying one step ahead of his opponents, and his ability to deploy an armed force he could count on in a crisis.[80]

THE STREET BATTLE OF 1872

The Louisiana legislative session of 1872 convened on January 1 at the Mechanics' Institute. Without a quorum Pinchback could not conduct business in the Senate. The House opened its session but immediately adjourned until the following day as a memorial to the late Lieutenant Governor Dunn. When the House reconvened the next day, Carter survived a vote of confidence, 49–45, under a withering barrage of charges by Warmoth's faction that he had misappropriated more than $700,000 and had illegally signed state warrants. The next day Carter took the floor to defend himself against these charges. When Carter neared the end of his speech, Warmoth's supporters loudly moved to declare the Speaker's chair vacant. Carter refused to acknowledge the motion, and a brawl among the legislators ensued. Warmoth's allies rushed the dais, and the Speaker motioned for a dozen armed supporters to come to his aid. No one was badly hurt, but the tumult left Carter so shaken that he informed Warmoth's faction that he would consider stepping down the following day if they would agree to adjourn until then.[81]

This was clearly not the outcome anticipated by the anti-Warmoth alliance, which met to plot their next move in crisis atmosphere on the afternoon of January 3 at the Custom House. Besides Stephen B. Packard, representing the Ring were Postmaster

80. W. P. Kellogg to S. B. Packard, Dec. 7, 1871, ibid.
81. Pitre, "Collapse of the Warmoth Regime," 171.

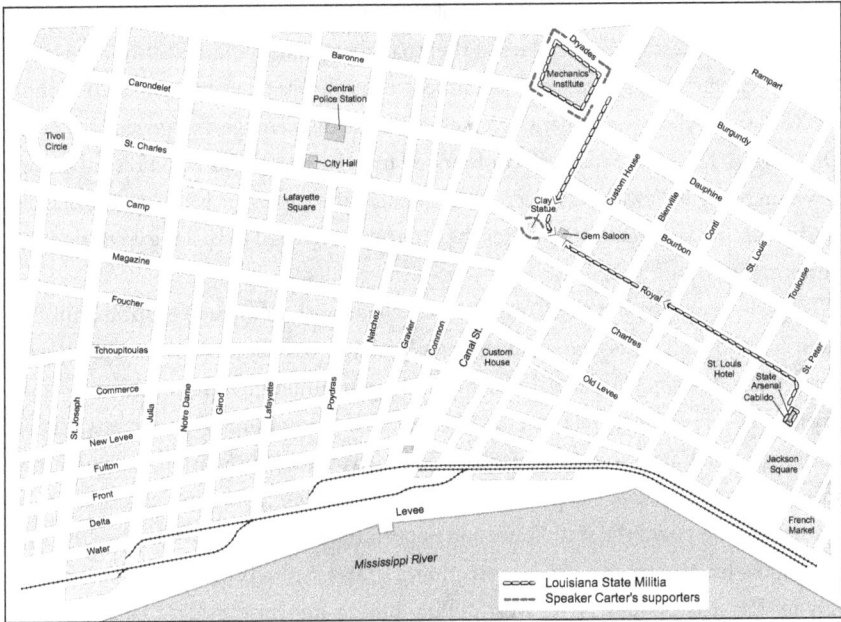

The Street Battle of 1872

Charles Lowell, Customs Collector Casey, and Speaker Carter. Democrats present included James B. Eustis, Frank B. Jonas, Albert Voorhies, Frank Zachary, J. B. Cotton, and E. L. Jewell. The group agreed to lend Carter some fortitude. Packard, in his capacity as U.S. marshal, would ask the local army commander, Maj. Gen. W. H. Emory, to bring troops into the city the following day to keep order and protect squads of Packard's deputies as they arrested the governor and his allies for conspiracy at the statehouse. Emory agreed to the request and moved four companies of troops from Jackson Barracks into the city, though only to prevent an armed clash between the factions and to protect federal property. He declined to help Marshal Packard arrest Warmoth without specific instructions from the War Department or the White House.[82]

The next day, January 4, Packard's deputies arrived at the statehouse to make the arrests at 11:30 A.M. They took Warmoth, Pinchback, Superintendent Badger, two captains from the Metropolitans, three state senators (Hugh J. Campbell, A. E. Barbour, and A. B. Harris), and thirteen House members into custody. After these arrests

82. Warmoth apparently had a spy inside the New Orleans Customs House at the time. His personal files contain Custom Ring members' private correspondence to one another during this crisis. See, for example, W. P. Kellogg to S. B. Packard [marked "Private," and written on U.S. Senate Chamber stationery], Feb. 2, 1872, Warmoth Papers, SHC.

Carter and his legislators expelled six of Warmoth's supporters on the grounds that they had spent less than sixty days in their parishes prior to their election. Considering that Carter's acquaintance with Cameron Parish was of a similar nature to those ejected, this hypocritical maneuver served to further enrage the governor's allies. Once again, however, Warmoth confounded his adversaries, for when his supporters saw him being led away under arrest, they exited the capitol as well, leaving Speaker Carter fuming and unable to muster the quorum he needed to seal the governor's impeachment.[83]

Upon posting bail at the Custom House, Warmoth immediately sprang into action. At 1:30 P.M. he issued a special proclamation warning Louisiana that "A conspiracy has developed to overthrow the State government by illegal and revolutionary means." He ordered the General Assembly into extraordinary session at 4:30 P.M., aiming to oust Carter from the Speaker's chair. To protect the legislature from further interference by Packard's deputies, he commanded General Longstreet to call out the state militia to guard the statehouse and Superintendent Badger to mobilize the Metropolitans for around-the-clock protection. He also sent a blistering telegram to his ally in Washington, Sen. J. R. West, telling him to inform President Grant that the Ring would cause "the *destruction* of the state government, unless the President takes immediate action and stops his officials." Rather meekly, and probably perplexed by the chaos now descending upon New Orleans, Grant replied that Packard's behavior as a "United States marshal is of such extraordinary character that I will have the matter investigated at once."[84]

Warmoth was in no mood to wait for a presidential investigation to solve the crisis. At 4:30 P.M. the House convened under heavy guard at the Mechanics' Institute, which Carter and his followers (having no further business after arresting their opponents) had vacated several hours earlier. Without delay Warmoth's supporters recognized a quorum (55 of 106 members reported present), voted to eject Carter from the House, declared the Speaker's chair vacant, and proceeded to elect a replacement. Warmoth's candidate and the winner of this unusual election was O. H. Brewster, a Republican representative from Madison Parish, near Vicksburg, Mississippi. Brewster had been a veteran of an Illinois regiment and had stayed on in Louisiana after the war to teach in the Freedmen's Bureau schools.[85] The House also passed a vote of

83. Warmoth, *War, Politics, and Reconstruction*, 130; Dawson, *Army Generals and Reconstruction*, 117.

84. Telegram, H. C. Warmoth to Sen. J. R. West, Jan. 4, 1872, in U.S. House, *Condition of Affairs in the Southern States*, 42nd Cong., 2nd sess., 1872, H. Exec. Doc. 268, 49–50; Telegram, Grant to Sen. J. R. West, Jan. 4, 1872, ibid., 50.

85. Pitre, "Collapse of the Warmoth Regime," 173; Warmoth, *War, Politics, and Reconstruction*, 134.

confidence in the governor and called upon him "to take all measures necessary to protect the General Assembly and the statehouse from violence and the members from intimidation."[86]

While the House met, General Longstreet organized the effort to turn the Mechanics' Institute into a fortress and prevent a coup d'état. The success of his mobilization must be partly inferred from incomplete state records, but most of the Metropolitans apparently answered the militia call up, probably because they were full-time state employees. The Louisiana State Militia, however, was another story. Several key militia commanders, including colonel and Republican state senator James Lewis, belonged to the Custom House Ring. Their units either did not answer Longstreet's order to muster or had to be reorganized on an ad hoc basis under the command of more politically reliable officers.[87] For the Third Regiment, Longstreet replaced Colonel Ingraham, a state senator and member of the Custom House Ring, with General Barbour, also a state senator but a political ally of Warmoth and Pinchback.[88] By the next day Longstreet had assembled a black regiment (under Barbour), a white regiment (under Colonel Owen), the artillery regiment (under Colonel Squires), and Captain Street's independent company to defend the statehouse and city armories. Estimates of the number of militia Longstreet actually managed to turn out vary considerably, from a high of three thousand (Warmoth's estimate) to a low of six hundred (General Emory's estimate). What remains beyond question is that Warmoth mobilized a military force with enough men, discipline, and firepower to deter Carter from ordering an assault on the capitol with his own outgunned sergeants-at-arms.[89]

On January 5, events began to turn decisively against Speaker Carter and the Ring, though it would be some time before they realized it. That morning Carter and his faction attempted to enter the capitol, but Metropolitan officers turned them away, citing their expulsion from the legislature the previous day. In frustration he attempted to form a new legislature at the Gem Saloon on Royal Street just off Canal Street in the French Quarter. Carter could hardly have made a more ill-advised site selection. The Gem Saloon was famed throughout Louisiana as a drinking and gaming establishment, notorious in the antebellum era as a place where planters entertained themselves while away from their wives and families when they came to the

86. The official journal of the extra session of the House, along with Warmoth's proclamation, is found in *New Orleans Republican*, Jan. 5, 1872, 1–6.

87. Special Orders No. 111, n.d., in Louisiana Adjutant General's Office, *Annual Report, 1872*, 56.

88. Special Orders No. 113, n.d., ibid.

89. Special Orders Nos. 54–55, n.d., ibid., 46.

city to sell their crops and confer with their factors.[90] As the crisis wore on over the next few days, the image of Carter's legislators heroically barricading themselves in this temple to sybaritic pursuits struck more and more Louisianians of every political stripe as ridiculous. Frustrated and still lacking a quorum, Carter turned to deputizing squads of newly minted sergeants-at-arms to prowl the city in search of Warmoth's representatives, whom he expected to detain and hold for a quorum in his rival House.

With tensions rising and General Emory pressed to keep the two sides apart, each faction appealed to Washington in an effort to break the deadlock. In the thinnest of veiled references to the fact that Grant's brother-in-law stood at the heart of the Ring's conspiracy, Warmoth craftily shifted the responsibility for any ensuing violence onto the president: "I respectfully request to be informed if, as claimed, you sustain the collector [James Casey, Grant's brother-in-law], the marshal [Stephen B. Packard, Grant's appointee], and other Federal officers in this revolutionary attempt to overthrow the State government—an attempt which, if not discontinued by your appointees and their democratic allies, must result in anarchy and bloodshed."[91] Grant did not rise to take the bait, however. He shot back a reply to Warmoth, insisting, "It occurs to me that you assume a false position in asking United States troops to suppress any insurrectionary or riotous movement until you have exhausted the power of the State; meanwhile the Federal troops should not molest you."[92]

Carter had no better luck in pressing Grant into action on his behalf. On January 6 he formally requested that the president "protect" his rival House.[93] In his endorsement to Carter's telegram, however, U.S. Attorney General Amos T. Akerman recommended to Grant that the "request should not be complied with; the House alone is not the legislature."[94] Like Louisiana during the Civil War, the state had two governments, neither of them complete, neither in unequivocal command of the capital or the state government, and neither fully recognized by Washington.

Three days later Carter's decision to hunt down Warmoth's legislators backfired, giving the governor the opening he needed to maneuver. On January 9 one of Carter's sergeants-at-arms killed Rep. Walter Wheyland, a Warmoth Republican from Sabine Parish, while trying to apprehend him; Wheyland had refused to be taken by force to

---

90. Pitre, "Collapse of the Warmoth Regime," 173; Taylor, *Louisiana Reconstructed*, 224; Dawson, *Army Generals and Reconstruction*, 118.

91. Telegram, H. C. Warmoth to U. S. Grant, Jan. 5, 1872, in House, *Condition of Affairs in the Southern States*, H. Exec. Doc. 268, 51.

92. Telegram, U. S. Grant to H. C. Warmoth, Jan. 6, 1872, ibid., 52.

93. Telegram, G. W. Carter to U. S. Grant, Jan. 6, 1872, ibid., 67.

94. Ibid.

Carter's legislature at the Gem Saloon.[95] Undeterred by a mass rally at Lafayette Square organized by the Democratic Committee of New Orleans the night before demanding his ouster, Warmoth responded by ordering his Metropolitans to break up the Gem Saloon House and arrest Carter and several others for murder. Commanding nearly three hundred police armed with Winchesters, Superintendent Badger occupied the Gem Saloon without a fight, but Speaker Carter eluded capture.[96] The next day the governor and his House attended Wheyland's funeral en masse, publicly demonstrating their solidarity and deploring Carter's resort to violence. After the funeral Warmoth issued another proclamation, declaring Carter's sergeants-at-arms (who now numbered in the thousands) "illegal, revolutionary, and in open insurrection" and commanding all legislators in the House and Senate to "return to the discharge of their duties at the State-house."[97]

Over the next ten days, the crisis subsided as absent legislators trickled back to the Mechanics' Institute to take their seats. On January 20 the Senate finally assembled a quorum and confirmed Pinchback's election as lieutenant governor, dashing whatever hopes the Ring still entertained of ejecting Warmoth by parliamentary maneuver. Twice more, however, on January 13 and 22, Carter whipped mass rallies of thousands into a frenzy and prepared to attack the capitol. Each time, though, General Emory averted violence and dispersed the crowds by informing Carter in no uncertain terms that the army would prevent an overthrow of Warmoth's government by use of force if necessary. After January 22 the city itself seemed worn out by the state of siege and glad to be done with political tensions for the time being. The young governor (still not thirty years old at the time of the 1872 crisis) had defeated his political opponents through a rare combination of tenacity, determination, and presence of mind under terrific pressure, but more than anything else, he owed his survival to the presence of a politically reliable militia and a tiny but well-led garrison of federal troops. It was a lesson his successors would grasp only too late.

UNDERSTANDING THE ROLES OF THE U.S. ARMY AND THE STATE MILITIAS DURING RECONSTRUCTION

One of the debates between historians revisiting Reconstruction during the 1960s involved the question of whether the U.S. Army could have done more to foster lasting

95. Lonn, *Reconstruction in Louisiana*, 125.

96. Dawson, *Army Generals and Reconstruction*, 121.

97. Warmoth's Proclamation, Jan. 10, 1872, in House, *Condition of Affairs in the Southern States*, H. Exec. Doc. 268, 65.

political change in the ex-Confederate states. John Hope Franklin in *Reconstruction: After the Civil War* argues that the U.S. Army's southern occupation force had been too small. He also states that military commanders refused to exert great enough pressure on defeated Confederates to achieve an enduring two-party political system that would permanently enfranchise the freed slaves. James Sefton, in *The United States Army and Reconstruction*, takes issue with Franklin, pointing out that the army had merely been the executor, not the maker, of federal policy. He stresses that, given the national struggle over Reconstruction policy, the army found itself constantly hampered in its peacekeeping duties by an atmosphere of uncertainty and frequent changes of policy. Under those circumstances the military did the best that could have been expected.[98] The New Orleans street battle of 1872 reveals that both sides of the argument fail to consider how the creation of new state militia forces complicated and divided security roles during Reconstruction.

After fulfilling the conditions of the Military Reconstruction Acts in each state, army generals shed their statutory responsibility for security and assumed a role remarkably similar to what scholars of contemporary international affairs would recognize as peacekeeping. The zenith of the army's ability to reshape the internal politics of the former Confederate states, as Sheridan's brief interregnum demonstrates, lasted only from the passage of the First Military Reconstruction Act in March 1867 until Congress readmitted each particular state. In Louisiana's case, that period was barely more than a year. In no southern state did it last longer than 1870, or little more than three years. Given the obstacles President Johnson deliberately threw in his way, Sheridan's efforts to remake Louisiana's political system from the ground up by conducting voter registrations open to the freedmen, organizing a constitutional convention, and ensuring free elections stand as remarkable achievements.

After readmission to full representation in Congress, the army's mission in the ex-Confederate states fundamentally changed. The Civil War altered the balance of power between the federal and state governments, but it did not entirely obliterate it. As an eyewitness to the massacre of 1866 and his own helplessness in 1868, Warmoth learned the bitter lesson that the first line of defense for his new government would have to be his own state police and militia. Paradoxically, the state forces he created proved far weaker than subsequently portrayed yet stronger and more resilient than some historians have concluded, especially given Reconstruction's ultimate demise. The impression left by one of William Dunning's own graduate students, Ella Lonn in

98. John Hope Franklin, *After the Civil War* (Chicago: University of Chicago Press, 1961); Sefton, *Army and Reconstruction*.

Reconstruction in Louisiana after 1868, is that the Metropolitan Police and Louisiana State Militia acted like jackbooted government thugs or criminal gangs of ignorant black savages who wantonly disregarded the rule of law and held the white population of New Orleans in the thrall of a new barbarism. Warmoth himself helped inflate that reputation in his later years. In his highly readable and often entertaining memoir published nearly sixty years after his tenure as governor, he boasts: "One thousand old Confederate soldiers under Colonel Squiers, and one thousand negro militia under General Barber, together with seven hundred Metropolitan Policemen under Superintendent Badger, with a battery all under the command of General James Longstreet, were quite able to protect the State House from the rabble of Carter, Packard, Casey, Eustis, Jonas, Voorhies, Zachary, and Jewell."[99] They were, of course, not "quite able" to protect the statehouse themselves, as Warmoth's desperate appeals to Grant in Washington and General Emory in New Orleans indicate. For while his state militia and police kept his government from falling at the beginning of the statehouse siege, the presence of federal troops helped break the siege and lend a visible legitimacy to Warmoth's authority. Had the army not been present, Carter's forces might well have been tempted to storm the capitol during the crisis. The consequences of such an assault remain incalculable, but the massacre of 1866 indicates the distinct possibility of another bloodbath. By 1872, however, Longstreet's impressively armed state militia suggests that such a street battle need not necessarily have been one in which Republicans would have been the losers, as they were in 1866.

Federal visibility did not demand a vast body of troops, as Franklin suggests. By the late 1860s the federal government found itself tempted by the pressures of fiscal economy to sharply reduce its detachments assigned for southern peacekeeping missions. Certainly the notion that the army occupied the South with massive force after 1868 is sheer legend, fabricated by the opponents of Radical Reconstruction. A cursory examination of the numbers of troops involved refutes that proposition. By 1871 there were fewer than seven hundred U.S. troops in all of Louisiana, a smaller garrison than the army routinely kept in the state before the Civil War. It was also only a small fraction of the twenty-five thousand troops in the state at the end of the Civil War or even the five thousand troops that hapless General Baird commanded at the time of the New Orleans street battle of 1866.

Nor was this brand of peacekeeping especially hazardous duty for the soldiers involved. Political opponents of Reconstruction shrank from the prospect of physically confronting federal intervention. Despite waves of apparently indiscriminate Recon-

99. Warmoth, *War, Politics, and Reconstruction,* 139–40.

struction violence, few if any U.S. soldiers were killed in action anywhere in the South under either the Reconstruction acts or the Enforcement acts that followed.[100] The experience of four years of large-scale conventional warfare had convinced Confederate veterans that fighting the federal army would have dared Washington to declare the Civil War not yet over.

Solving the internal-security dilemma of Warmoth's government, therefore, required a flexible military force that could accomplish, at a minimum, two principal tasks: defending the capital and the state's critical public buildings against a direct attack and keeping polling places throughout the state open and accessible during state elections, certainly for the newly enfranchised freedmen but more generally to all those who dared to vote for the Republican ticket. Sheridan's tight reign over both New Orleans, which served as his headquarters, and the military registrars he dispatched into the rural parishes provided a model that Warmoth studied with considerable profit. Given the persistent targeting of Louisiana Republicans of both races for violence, much more than that bare minimum was desperately desired, though beyond the immediate abilities of the new government. This proved to be the case both because of the feeble fiscal condition of the Reconstruction state governments as well as the pervasive anarchy attending the general collapse of the southern civil order by the end of the Civil War. It also goes far to explain Warmoth's single-minded quest to control not only the state's militia and capital police forces but the machinery of its voter registration and electoral count as well. Lacking a robust and reliable defense force to police every rural parish in the state, he tried to assure himself the power to nullify the security dilemmas created by the political dilemma he had to accept as a practical reality. It is within the context of these crosscutting challenges that Warmoth's achievements and compromises ought to be judged.

Like other newly created institutions during Reconstruction, such as churches and schools for the freedmen, the Louisiana State Militia remained a work in progress. Warmoth achieved little more than a preliminary start at extending the militia organization beyond New Orleans. It enraged some of his fellow Republicans that

100. The author has not found a record of a single U.S. Army combat fatality related to Reconstruction peacekeeping missions recorded in any of the secretary of war's annual reports to Congress, although some black soldiers may have been killed in vigilante violence before the passage of the Military Reconstruction Acts. For one example in South Carolina, see Richard Zuczek, *State of Rebellion: Reconstruction in South Carolina* (Columbia: University of South Carolina Press, 1996), 19–20. Another indication of how benign Reconstruction peacekeeping duty was considered within the army is suggested by the failure to award a campaign medal for the southern occupation, contrasting sharply with the numerous awards of the Medal of Honor made during campaigns against the Plains Indians during the same period.

he freely handed out commissions and weapons to ex-Confederates just as it enraged white Conservatives that he handed out commissions and weapons to ex-slaves. He certainly ran a considerable risk in trying to maintain such an unlikely and fragile political coalition. Still, that decision held at least a promise of obtaining white acquiescence toward the presence of the Republican Party in the Deep South. That prospect portended the possibility of an eventual acceptance of black political equality upon which his own political future, not to mention the political aspirations of the black community, ultimately rested. The biracial composition of Warmoth's militia was all the more remarkable because it included some of the same fraternity of Confederate veterans that had already inflicted a serious massacre upon black Union veterans in the street battle of 1866. Who could imagine General Longstreet and so many Louisiana Confederate veterans voluntarily taking the new militia oath to respect the civil rights of all men regardless of color or previous condition of servitude less than five years after Confederate defeat? And yet many of them did.

During the Civil War, Lincoln repeatedly courted prominent white slaveholders like the Blair family of Maryland through the deft application of political patronage, much to the consternation of abolitionist Republicans in Congress. Once won over, though, they eventually accepted his issuance of the Emancipation Proclamation, perhaps because Lincoln understood it is sometimes easier for most people to modify their ideology than their circumstances. Warmoth's government held out the promise of the acceptance of real gains in black political equality during Reconstruction, but this hope was dashed by the internal struggle for control over patronage. Within six months of the street battle of 1872, participation in the Louisiana State Militia had declined so far that the new adjutant general discharged the entire force and reconstituted it from scratch. Many of the ex-Confederate officers who had rallied to Warmoth's defense in early 1872 tired of Republican infighting. They resigned and did not return. Serious damage to the fragile militia institution had been done, and Republicans rather than Democrats or Conservatives did much of it.[101]

But the lion's share for the mismanagement of political patronage that brought on the street battle of 1872 must ultimately be laid at Grant's feet. As in other instances during his political career, Grant's loyalty to his friends and family during the Louisiana street battle of 1872 did not serve his presidency well. Allowing his politically inept brother-in-law, James Casey, to advise him was a serious political error that encouraged the Louisiana Republican Party's split into bitter factions, damaging its

101. General Orders No. 35, June 28, 1872, in House, *Condition of Affairs in the Southern States,* H. Exec. Doc. 268, 36.

future prospects at the moment it confronted serious threats to its very existence. Forced to choose between Warmoth's legally elected government and the Custom House Ring's assemblage at the Gem Saloon, the decisive victor of Vicksburg seemed paralyzed by indecision. By the time he made up his mind that he had no choice but to back Warmoth, Grant had permitted the army to play a far more prominent role in Louisiana politics than it should have. Nor was Louisiana the only example of this phenomenon. An eerily similar conflict over party patronage erupted two years later in Arkansas, with factions in the state Republican Party struggling for control of the statehouse in Little Rock during the "Brooks-Baxter War." As in New Orleans, the eventual intervention of federal troops in Little Rock helped resolve the dispute without large-scale bloodshed, though only after it became an embarrassing object of national scrutiny and fodder for a new round of partisan charges that Republicans had created puppet governments in the South sustained only at the point of a bayonet.[102]

Grant and the army both would eventually pay a price for their escalating involvement in disputes over local personalities and patronage. Strangely enough, the national Republican Party followed Louisiana's unhappy example and split into two factions in 1872: Grant and anti-Grant. The anti-Grants, calling themselves Liberal Republicans, attacked the president's supposed corruption and unsavory patronage appointments. Their nominee, Horace Greeley, pilloried Grant for inflicting "bayonet rule" on the prostrate South. The Democrats, finding the prospect of Republicans fighting with one another instead of themselves irresistible, also nominated Greeley as their candidate. As it had in 1866, Louisiana would foreshadow the rest of the nation in another turning point in Reconstruction.

---

102. An important essay on the problem of political patronage in Reconstruction state governments and its relationship to factional quarrels is Lawrence N. Powell, "The Politics of Livelihood: Carpetbaggers in the Deep South," in J. Morgan Kousser and James M. McPherson, eds., *Region, Race, and Reconstruction: Essays in Honor of C. Vann Woodward* (New York: Oxford University Press, 1982), 315–48. For an overview of the factional struggle in Arkansas, see Earl F. Woodward, "The Brooks and Baxter War in Arkansas, 1872–1874," *Arkansas Historical Quarterly* 30 (Winter 1971): 315–36. For a similar appreciation of political violence and factional turmoil in Texas, see Barry A. Crouch, Larry Peacock, and James M. Smallwood, *Murder and Mayhem: The War of Reconstruction in Texas* (College Station: Texas A&M University Press, 2003).

❧ 4 ❧

The Street Battle of 1873

The Battle of the Cabildo and the Spread of Paramilitary Insurrection

The bitter partisan infighting evident within the ranks of Republicans during the street battle of 1872 eventually shattered Louisiana's political parties into five factions. P. B. S. Pinchback found himself cast in the unexpected role of powerbroker in the state elections and then as the first African American to head a state government in U.S. history. Political factionalism led to the disputed state elections in November 1872, the establishment of rival state governments in New Orleans, and the mutiny of militia units. The battle of the Cabildo in March 1873 marked a new departure for the Republicans' enemies, who sponsored a desperate attempt to seize power in the capital with effects felt across the entire state—and eventually the entire South.

THE DISPUTED ELECTION OF 1872

Infuriated by Grant's support for his enemies in the Custom House Ring, Governor Warmoth sought a new political home with the Liberal Republican movement. Inside Louisiana, Liberal Republicans proved strongest in New Orleans, where the German immigrant community and business interests with northern connections sought to keep the party label but repudiate Grant and his opposition to patronage reform. Prominent Louisianians involved in the movement included Col. D. B. Penn, former commander of the Seventh Louisiana Infantry; Maj. E. A. Burke, a New Orleans businessman; Effingham Lawrence, state senator and co-owner of Warmoth's plantation in Plaquemines Parish; and F. J. Herron, the former Union general who advised Conservative leaders before the street battle of 1866. At least initially, however, it looked as though the Liberals might also be able to count on growing support in the rural parishes as well. One newspaper editor from upstate informed Warmoth: "The Democratic ticket has not a single supporter, or quasi-supporter, in the whole parish, as far as I have been able to learn. All look to the August Convention [of the Liberal Republicans] for the ticket to meet the emergency and if a good ticket is then made, as we confidently expect, you may put down the white vote as almost solid for it—and it is hoped that a considerable colored vote may also be secured."[1]

In May Warmoth led a delegation of one hundred Louisianians (including twenty blacks) to the Liberals' national convention, where Horace Greeley, the nationally influential editor of the *New York Tribune,* won the nomination for president. Warmoth had gone to the national convention backing Sen. Lyman Trumbull of Illinois but exhibited scant disappointment over the failure of his candidate. For his purposes, anyone but Grant would do.[2]

Others in Louisiana also wanted reform but disdained Warmoth as part of the problem rather than part of the solution. On June 5 a new Reform Party met in New Orleans, initially hoping to steer clear of affiliation with either major party. Many of the Reformers had been Whigs before the war and staunchly refused to back any legacy of the antebellum Democratic machine. They nominated George Williamson for governor but realized their support was too weak to carry the state alone. Their leaders immediately opened negotiations with Democratic leaders to merge the two tickets.

Just two days before the Reformers, the Democrats met in New Orleans with high hopes of recapturing state power for the first time since the war. At least some of their leaders understood that the Republican Party's turmoil gave Louisiana Democrats a unique opportunity to unite the opposition, but the convention nearly fumbled this away in a none too subtle appeal for the white vote.[3] The Democrats' nominee for governor, Col. John McEnery of Monroe, had been a lawyer before the war and commanded the Fourth Louisiana Battalion (CSA) at Vicksburg. After the war McEnery had been elected to the Rebel Legislature, acquiring a reputation as a fiery, race-baiting orator who backed the Black Codes and rejected the ratification of the Fourteenth Amendment. The *New Orleans Republican* warned, "We regard the McEnery ticket as representing the negro hating, schoolhouse burning, fire-eating Bourbonists." Warmoth, who was certainly in a position to know, claimed that McEnery's nomination cost the anti–Custom House alliance thirty thousand potential votes. The principal problem now for Louisiana Democrats was how to convince potential coali-

1. Charles J. C. Puckette, [editor of *The Weekly Natchitoches Times*], to Gov. H. C. Warmoth, June 19, 1872, Henry C. Warmoth Papers, LLMVC.

2. Taylor, *Louisiana Reconstructed,* 229.

3. The precise origin of the term "white line," possibly derived from the expression "to draw a line in the sand," is obscure. Southern Democrats frequently used it in the 1870s to denote the growing faction of their party that demanded white supremacy in local government.

tion partners that McEnery's election would not represent a wholesale repudiation of Reconstruction.[4]

Given the turmoil within Republican ranks, the Democrats' controversial choice for governor hardly seemed to matter. In addition to the Liberals, a second faction composed primarily of black Republicans split off to hold their own convention and declare their unhappiness with the Custom House Ring's domination. Led by P. B. S. Pinchback and state senator and militia general Hugh Campbell, this faction held the first of three state conventions in New Orleans on May 28. Pinchback clearly recognized the dangers in the coming election for black Louisianians. "As a race," he declared, "[we] are between the hawk of Republican demagogism and the buzzards of Democratic prejudice." Faced with the imperative to make a choice, however, he chose the demagogue by supporting Warmoth's renomination. The deal was not easy to consummate. Despite Pinchback's repeated pleas, the governor adamantly refused to appear on a state Republican ticket beneath Grant's name. Pinchback feared a Democratic attempt to use the Liberal movement as a Trojan horse to destroy Republican governments in the South from within. He might have joined with the Liberals if they had picked someone like Massachusetts senator Charles Sumner as their nominee, but not Horace Greeley, whom he considered impulsive and unreliable. When the Liberals finally settled on Greeley, Pinchback convened his faction's convention a second time in Baton Rouge during June, the same time the Custom House Ring would nominate regular Republican candidates for state office.[5]

On June 19 the leaders of the Custom House convened the Louisiana Republican Party Convention in Baton Rouge, the last of the five Louisiana factions to pick its ticket for the fall elections. Given the lingering bitterness engendered by the street battle of 1872, it is not likely Marshal Packard and Collector Casey ever considered allowing Warmoth to run for a second term. Pinchback and Campbell, however, believed that anyone else would prove too weak to master the chaos of Louisiana politics. They prepared to wage a floor fight to renominate Warmoth if he would only abandon Greeley in favor of Grant. Warmoth proved obstinate. He was determined to

---

4. William Pitt Kellogg, "Address of Governor Kellogg to the People of the United States on the Condition of Affairs in Louisiana, with Official Facts and Figures," in U.S. House, *Condition of Affairs in the Southern States*, 43rd Cong., 2nd sess., 1875, H. Rpt. 261, 1035; *New Orleans Republican*, July 26, 1872; Warmoth, *War, Politics, and Reconstruction*, 199–200. The term "Bourbon," like the term "Radical," was originally a pejorative that acquired such common currency during Reconstruction that even Bourbon Democrats used it to describe themselves. While the term's American evolution remains obscure, it came from the name for the defenders of the old regime in France, who had "learned nothing and forgotten nothing."

5. Taylor, *Louisiana Reconstructed*, 231; Haskins, *Pinchback*, 135.

either master or wreck the power of the Custom House Ring. With Grant set to return to the White House and his brother-in-law still ensconced at the Custom House, the former seemed out of the question. Pinchback tried to stall for time again, calling yet a third convention for his faction in New Orleans for August 5. There he at last admitted failure and resigned himself to fusing his faction with the Custom House Ring. William Pitt Kellogg, a white carpetbagger born in Vermont, accepted the nomination for governor, which he gained by just one vote on the third ballot. Pinchback's gens de couleur libre friend, business partner, and frequent political rival, César C. Antoine, received the nomination for lieutenant governor. For his troubles and the votes he commanded, Ring leaders offered Pinchback the party's nomination for U.S. representative-at-large from Louisiana and also named two other prominent black politicians, P. G. Deslondes and William G. Brown, to the ticket as candidates for secretary of state and superintendent of public education respectively.[6]

Once the Republican ticket took shape, attention shifted to whether or not Liberals, Democrats, and Reformers could reconcile their differences and settle on a fused ticket in time for the fall campaign. On July 18 the Reform Party combined its ticket with the Democrats in return for the promise of a few minor state positions. On August 5 the Liberals met in New Orleans for their state convention. Warmoth set the tone by announcing he would refuse the nomination for a second term as governor to clear away all concerns about his ambitions. The convention responded by nominating D. B. Penn for governor; John Young, a planter from Claiborne Parish, for lieutenant governor; and Maj. F. E. Dumas for secretary of state. Dumas's nomination underlined the Liberals' attempt to avoid a complete alienation of black voters and stood in sharp contrast to the all-white Democratic-Reform ticket.

Throughout August, Liberals and Democrat-Reformers argued over how to broker a fused ticket. Later congressional questioning of one of the deal's brokers, Major Burke, hinted that the Democrats bought Warmoth's support in exchange for a promise to elect him U.S. senator.[7] Considering the formidable power Warmoth would hold as the incumbent governor over voter registration and the Returning Board that fall, a Senate seat was certainly not too high a price to pay in return for recapturing the state government. Whatever the case may have been, it is certain that Democrats paid no heed to Warmoth's advice to craft a more racially moderate appeal. On August 28 the Fusion ticket (as it became known) announced its nomination of McEnery for governor and Penn for lieutenant governor. Fusionists did endorse one black can-

---

6. *New Orleans Republican*, Aug. 13, 1872.

7. Testimony, E. A. Burke, in House, *Condition of Affairs in the Southern States*, H. Rpt. 261, 656–57, 665.

didate for state office, Samuel Armistead of Caddo Parish as secretary of state, but that hardly balanced the nomination of such notorious "white liners" as R. M. Lusher, the candidate for superintendent of public education, who had fought T. W. Conway's integration of the New Orleans's public schools, or H. N. Ogden, candidate for attorney general and brother of white paramilitary leader Col. Frederick N. Ogden.[8]

After the uncertainty of all the factional jockeying, the election itself seemed almost anticlimactic. Reports of violence were rare, particularly compared with the presidential election of 1868. More important than violence, as Louisiana historian Joe Gray Taylor has observed, the voting was "so shot through with fraud that no one ever had any idea who had actually won. . . . The election was dishonest, the count was dishonest, and there was no honest way in which the result could be decided."[9] The election was dishonest primarily because Warmoth's power over local registrars gave Fusionists every opportunity to manipulate the votes cast at the parish level. The count was dishonest since Warmoth also commanded the statewide Returning Board. And the result was dishonest because both sides had already dedicated themselves to winning no matter what the vote or the count.

It has never been precisely certain what happened when the Louisiana Returning Board met on November 14 to certify the official ballot count. The only certainty is that the board split in two after the meeting, with each side declaring itself the legal Returning Board and the other a fraudulent rival. According to Warmoth, Custom House Ring leaders approached him after the election and also offered him a U.S. Senate seat, just as the Fusionists had, in exchange for returning the election in favor of the Republicans. He claimed he refused their bribe. Instead, on the morning the Returning Board met, he removed Secretary of State Herron from the panel, arguing that Herron's accounts as tax collector for New Orleans had not been settled as required by law. He then used his appointive powers as governor to install one of his friends, Col. Jack Wharton, as the new secretary of state. This automatically made Wharton Herron's replacement on the board. Warmoth and Wharton came to the meeting confident they would control its outcome since two of the five members (Lieutenant Governor Pinchback and state senator T. C. Anderson) became ineligible to take part in the proceedings by running for office in November. That left only the Ring's man, state senator John Lynch, to oppose them in the selection of two new members to fill Pinchback's and Anderson's places. When he arrived, the governor notified Herron of his replacement and produced Wharton's commission. Warmoth

8. Pitre, "Collapse of the Warmoth Regime," 161–87; Taylor, *Louisiana Reconstructed*, 235–36.

9. Taylor, *Louisiana Reconstructed*, 241.

and Wharton then passed a motion to elect their own candidates, Durant DaPonte and Frank Hatch, to the board, which would give them a four-to-one voting advantage over Lynch.[10]

Senator Lynch denied Governor Warmoth's version of the story to General Emory, President Grant, a federal circuit-court judge, and the congressional committees that eventually investigated the proceedings. He insisted that when the board met, Herron immediately made a motion to fill the two empty seats with General Longstreet and Jacob Hawkins, whom Lynch seconded and then voted for. According to Lynch, the legal Returning Board consisted of himself, Warmoth, Herron, Longstreet, and Hawkins; Warmoth's recognition of DaPonte and Hatch was illegal. Eventually Lynch obtained a court order from a state judge voiding Warmoth's removal of Herron and declaring his own Returning Board the legal one.[11]

After Lynch obtained the court order, Warmoth responded with a novel maneuver, creating yet a *third* Returning Board. In 1872 the legislature had passed a new election law that revised the board's membership. When Lynch got his court order voiding Herron's removal, Warmoth took the 1872 election bill from his office safe and signed it, effectively nullifying the two previous boards, or so he maintained. On December 3 he appointed new members and named a Fusionist, Gabriel DeFeriet, chairman. The following day the DeFeriet Board canvassed Louisiana's election returns and declared the McEnery-Penn ticket elected. To confirm his command over the statehouse, Warmoth ordered the new legislature, with Fusionists in the majority in both houses, into extraordinary session on December 9, 1872, well in advance of the inauguration date for the new governor on January 13, 1873.[12]

THE STRUGGLE OVER THE STATE HOUSE AND THE STATE MILITIA

Pinchback and the Custom House Ring leaders had anticipated that Warmoth might make some sort of move and procured the Grant administration's prior support. After the November election Colonel Casey went to Washington to consult with his brother-in-law about Louisiana politics. When he returned, the attorney general telegraphed Marshal Packard on December 3 with orders to "enforce the decrees and mandate of the U.S. courts, no matter by whom resisted, and General Emory will fur-

10. Executive Order, H. C. Warmoth, Nov. 13, 1872, in U.S. House, *Condition of Affairs in Louisiana*, 42nd Cong., 3rd sess., 1873, H. Exec. Doc. 91, 259. See also "Affidavits of Jack Wharton and H. C. Warmoth," Nov. 25, 1872, ibid., 259–60.

11. "Affidavit of John Lynch," Nov. 19, 1872, ibid., 258–59.

12. Taylor, *Louisiana Reconstructed*, 243–44.

nish you with all necessary troops for that purpose."[13] When the DeFeriet Board declared the Fusionist ticket elected the next day, Packard acted to prevent Warmoth from taking control of the statehouse, as the young governor had done in the street battle of 1872. At midnight on December 5, Packard obtained a court order from federal judge Edward H. Durrell authorizing him to take possession of the capitol using federal troops. At 2:00 A.M. on December 6, Packard and his deputy marshals along with two batteries of Emory's troops, acting as a posse comitatus, occupied the state offices at the Mechanics' Institute.[14]

Possession of the statehouse and the active support of federal troops gave Republicans a decisive advantage. On December 9 the Lynch Board met and confirmed Kellogg as governor and Antoine as lieutenant governor. They also confirmed the election of seventy-seven Republicans and thirty-two Fusionists in the House and twenty-eight Republicans and eight Fusionists in the Senate. Using Warmoth's own call for the new legislature to meet in special session, they convened at the Mechanics' Institute and repeated the 1872 strategy, this time with more success. With federal troops guarding the statehouse for them, Ring leaders admitted only those legislators certified by the Lynch Board. The House elected Postmaster Lowell, Ring leader, as the new Speaker. In the Senate, Lieutenant Governor Pinchback opened the session by accusing Governor Warmoth of offering him a bribe of $50,000 to exercise control over the Senate. Pinchback immediately sent his charges to the House, which obligingly voted to impeach the governor by a vote of 57–6. Impeachment automatically suspended Warmoth from office and elevated Pinchback in his stead. The new acting governor then notified President Grant and General Emory of the day's startling developments and requested federal troops to defend the statehouse against any attack.[15]

Perhaps forgetting that they had been an active party to a similar scheme in the street battle of 1872, enraged Fusionists screamed foul and protested the intrusion of federal troops into the internal affairs of the sovereign state of Louisiana. On December 10 Governor-elect McEnery and his supporters held a mass rally at Lafayette Square to denounce the Republicans' "usurpation" of the state government. The following day Warmoth delivered another gubernatorial proclamation commanding the Fusionist legislature to meet in the New Orleans City Hall, now guarded by the

13. Telegram, Atty. Gen. George H. Williams to U.S. Marshal Stephen Packard, Dec. 3, 1872, in House, *Condition of Affairs in Louisiana*, H. Exec. Doc. 91, 13.

14. Dawson, *Army Generals and Reconstruction*, 136.

15. Pitre, "Collapse of the Warmoth Regime," 182–83; Lonn, *Reconstruction in Louisiana*, 208.

Orleans Parish sheriff, William P. Harper, a Hays's Brigade veteran and Warmoth militia general turned Fusionist politician. Warmoth also declared the Republican-
organized legislature illegal and demanded that they withdraw from the statehouse.[16]

Turmoil in the state government produced turmoil in the state militia. On November 13 Warmoth named Colonel Street adjutant general of Louisiana and ordered
the state militia in New Orleans to active duty.[17] Much to Warmoth's consternation,
however, Street proved loyal to the Pinchback–Custom House coalition. After the legislature impeached Governor Warmoth, Street began taking his orders from Acting
Governor Pinchback. With his grip over the state government still precarious, Pinchback bolstered his authority by purging the officer ranks of the militia of the disloyal.
On December 11 he ousted his own former political ally, Hugh Campbell, from the
position of major general commanding the militia division in New Orleans. Campbell
had supported Pinchback in his factional wrangling with the Custom House Ring, but
he went over to the Fusionists in the fall; they rewarded him with the presidency of
the Fusionist Senate.[18] In Campbell's place Pinchback named General Longstreet,
who had continued to support Grant for president through the fall campaign.[19] Within
two days Street named ten additional officers to critical positions in the New Orleans
militia. In addition to ensuring party loyalty, their commissions reflected the tight-
ening grip of interlocking patronage appointments at the federal, state, and local levels within the capital. Longstreet's new chief of staff, Col. Theodore DeKlyne, was also
Packard's deputy U.S. marshal at the Custom House. Two of Superintendent Badger's
captains in the Metropolitan Police, Thomas Flanagan and P. H. Boyle, also became
high-ranking staff officers in the state militia.[20]

Paper appointments alone did not ensure Republicans' undisputed command over
the militia. Warmoth's mobilization order had aimed in part to take possession of armories located at Carondolet Street and Davidson Court as well as the state arsenal

16. Pitre, "Collapse of the Warmoth Regime," 184; Forman, "William P. Harper," 58. Harper was adjutant general of the state militia from June to November 1872. See also General Orders Nos. 33–35, 45, Nov.
13, 1872, in Louisiana Adjutant General's Office, *Annual Report, 1872,* 42.

17. General Orders Nos. 45–47, Nov. 13, 1872, in Louisiana Adjutant General's Office, *Annual Report,*
1872, 42–43.

18. Campbell later explained and recanted his defection to the Fusionists in a speech to a black church
in 1875. See Hugh J. Campbell, *The White League Conspiracy against Free Government* (New Orleans: New
Orleans Republican, 1875), 10 (copy in Western Americana Collection, Firestone Library, Princeton University).

19. General Orders No. 48, Dec. 11, 1872, in Louisiana Adjutant General's Office, *Annual Report, 1872,*
43.

20. General Orders No. 51, Dec. 13, 1872, ibid., 45.

at St. Peter Street. The state arsenal was a massive Greek Revival edifice built in 1839 just off Jackson Square and adjacent to the building known as the Cabildo, which had been constructed as the seat of colonial government during Spanish rule and housed the Louisiana Supreme Court in 1872. Struggling to keep control over the militia, Warmoth relied on a few handpicked commanders, all white, all ex-Confederate officers, and all recently commissioned by him. They included Brig. Gen. J. B. Walton, original commander of the Washington Artillery in 1861; Brig. Gen. William M. Owen; and Col. Eugene Waggaman, former commander of the French-speaking Tenth Louisiana Infantry. Together, Warmoth's new commanders assembled a force of almost five hundred troops, including the militia's artillery regiment and at least two companies of infantry, to defend the Carondolet Street armory against the Republicans.[21]

His purge completed, Pinchback ordered General Badger to seize the disputed arsenals after Warmoth's militia refused to surrender their weapons and vacate the premises. Badger assembled three hundred Metropolitans to overwhelm the Carondolet Street armory on December 13, reminiscent of his decisive seizure of the Gem Saloon in the street battle of 1872. But by the time they arrived, Warmoth's force was too well armed and the arsenal too well defended to take the building without casualties.[22] The two forces, "face to face with arms in their hands," stood opposed to one another. General Emory surveyed the situation and tersely informed the War Department that there was "imminent danger of immediate conflict between two bodies of armed men." He appealed for a definitive decision by Washington on which side the army should support.[23]

The following day Pinchback sent Grant a telegram with his version of events and requested that the president authorize the use of federal troops "for the purpose of suppressing this mutiny."[24] While Grant had informed Pinchback through the attorney general that the acting governor had his full support, he had neglected to convey this critical information to the War Department, hence General Emory's confusion about whom the army was supposed to aid. A cable from Adj. Gen. E. D. Townsend

21. Telegram, Acting Gov. P. B. S. Pinchback to Atty. Gen. George H. Williams, Dec. 14, 1872, in House, *Condition of Affairs in Louisiana*, H. Exec. Doc. 91, 24–25; Special Orders Nos. 94, 96, n.d., in Louisiana Adjutant General's Office, *Annual Report, 1872*, 52.

22. Special Orders No. 101, n.d., ibid., 53.

23. Telegram, Maj. Gen. W. H. Emory to Adj. Gen. E. D. Townsend, Dec. 13, 1872, in House, *Condition of Affairs in Louisiana*, H. Exec. Doc. 91, 25.

24. Telegram, Acting Gov. P. B. S. Pinchback to Atty. Gen. George H. Williams, Dec. 14, 1872, ibid., 24–25.

followed, clarifying Grant's support for Pinchback. Emory then dispatched an officer to inform Warmoth's rival militia of the president's decision.[25] Not wanting a collision with a force supported by President Grant, but not wanting to appear to recognize Pinchback's legitimacy either, Colonel Waggaman agreed to surrender to the U.S. Army, which Emory was only too happy to arrange. After more negotiations and further threats by Pinchback, Warmoth's militia marched out of the armories, and the Metropolitans took possession. Emory had once again defused a tense confrontation in New Orleans, but perhaps more significantly, Pinchback had inflicted a telling blow on Warmoth's claim to be both the de facto and de jure chief executive of Louisiana. Over the next several weeks, those members of the Fusionist legislature who also held credentials in Pinchback's legislature drifted back to the Mechanics' Institute. Declining membership forced the Fusionist legislature to adjourn for lack of a quorum. Compounding his woes, Warmoth ran out of parliamentary maneuvers to prevent the start of his impeachment trial in the House. He found himself forced to instruct his lawyer to request a delay until January to prepare a defense, an embarrassing recognition of the authority of Pinchback's administration.[26]

THE RIVAL GOVERNMENTS OF 1873

Despite the setback they had suffered, McEnery and his supporters resolved to go forward with plans to convene a Fusionist legislature and hold his inauguration in January 1873. Missteps by Governor-elect Kellogg and their own hopes that Congress would intervene to reverse Grant's de facto recognition of the Republican government encouraged them. Some lower-ranking Fusion officials (including Louis Wiltz, mayor of New Orleans, and William P. Harper, sheriff of Orleans Parish) had already taken office thanks to commissions from both Kellogg and McEnery. They began working to pave the way for a Fusionist revival. Pinchback, though scheduled to depart office upon Kellogg's inauguration on the thirteenth, was not sanguine about Fusionist intentions and wanted to prevent them from maintaining even the appearance of a shadow government. On January 3, after the Fusionists held another mass rally on Lafayette Square to show their support for McEnery, Pinchback delivered an address justifying his actions and warning his opponents that "no pretended governor shall be inaugurated . . . no pretended General Assembly shall convene and disturb the pub-

25. Telegram, Adj. Gen. Edward D. Townsend to Maj. Gen. William H. Emory, Dec. 14, 1872, ibid., 25; Telegram, W. H. Emory to E. D. Townsend, Dec. 14, 1872, ibid., 26.

26. Special Orders No. 102, n.d., in Louisiana Adjutant General's Office, *Annual Report, 1872*, 54. For details of the negotiations, see *New Orleans National Republican*, Dec. 14, 1872.

lic peace. Parties participating . . . are public wrongdoers, and shall be promptly dealt with as such. The whole force of the State shall be used for this purpose."[27]

To underline his determination to prevent the formation of a rival government, he telegrammed Grant the same day, telling him that to "prevent a subversion on the present State government and to suppress riot, it may be necessary for me, as executive, to use police or other forces to prevent this revolution." Pinchback also requested that the president ensure that General Emory received the necessary orders to "furnish troops to sustain the State government."[28]

Pinchback's blunt declaration of his intent to use force against McEnery stunned Grant and provoked a flurry of meetings between the White House, the War Department, and the Justice Department in Washington. Grant and his cabinet believed McEnery's government would fade away after a few days of excitement if Louisiana Republicans simply ignored it rather than trying to force it out of existence. The next day Grant, through his attorney general, curtly warned Pinchback not to use force: "I think there ought to be no forcible interference with any proceedings to inaugurate McEnery, if they are not accompanied by violence, and there is no attempt to take control of the State government."[29] He also instructed General Sherman to cable Emory and inform him that he was authorized to deploy his forces to "preserve the peace." He refused to authorize the army to prevent either McEnery's inauguration or the convening of a rival legislature.[30]

Grant's decision not to support Pinchback's effort to suppress McEnery's regime removed the last obstacle to the peculiar establishment of rival state governments in 1873, the third time since 1862 Louisiana had been so divided. On January 6 Kellogg's legislature convened at the Mechanics' Institute accompanied by two thousand supporters. Vigilant against the possibility of any trouble, General Badger ordered patrols at the statehouse and held a large contingent of Metropolitans, with four harnessed cannon teams, in reserve at the nearby Carondolet Street arsenal. At Lafayette Square four thousand looked on while the Fusionists inaugurated their legislature, which promptly adjourned for lack of a quorum in either chamber. Over the entire city General Emory maintained a steady watch, backed by a small yet balanced force of infantry, cavalry, and artillery. A week later the same tensions returned when Kellogg and McEnery both took the governor's oath and delivered inaugural addresses to their

27. Pinchback quoted in Lonn, *Reconstruction in Louisiana*, 219.

28. Telegram, P .B. S. Pinchback to U. S. Grant, Jan. 3, 1873, in House, *Condition of Affairs in Louisiana,* H. Exec. Doc. 91, 30.

29. Telegram, Atty. Gen. G. H. Williams to S. B. Packard, Jan. 4, 1873, ibid., 30.

30. Telegram, Asst. Adj. Gen. William D. Whipple to W. H. Emory, Jan. 4, 1873, ibid., 30.

respective legislatures. After Kellogg's inauguration, Pinchback gave a brief farewell address, defending his tenure against both the "bitter antagonism of race" displayed by McEnery's followers and some Republicans' "hypercriticism upon which they have been pleased to call my indiscreet exercise of power." Despite the defensive tone of his remarks, Pinchback evinced some pride for having saved the state government for the Republicans in a moment of crisis. He received scant thanks from those who benefited most from his actions—the carpetbaggers of the Custom House. When he departed the governor's chair, he left office as the first, last, and only black governor of a southern state for more than a century.[31]

The spectacle of rival state governments fixed a spotlight of national attention on Louisiana's internal politics once again. Grant had hoped that recognizing Pinchback and refusing to see McEnery's representatives in Washington would encourage the controversy to die down. It did not. When the president refused to see their envoys, the Fusionists made a public appeal by distributing "An Address to the People of the United States" to newspapers across the nation. It called on Congress to either investigate the election of 1872 or dissolve the present government and return the state to military rule.[32] Public opinion in the North, piqued by Greeley's campaign charges of "bayonet rule" during the presidential election, had already cast the problems of Louisiana Republicans in an unsympathetic light. By late December northern newspapers carried editorials attacking the unseemly details of the rival Returning Boards as well as the manner in which Emory's troops had seized the statehouse under Packard's orders and assisted Pinchback during the militia mutiny. Objecting to the militarization of the Grant administration's southern policy, the *New York Herald* posed the timely question, "IS THIS A REPUBLIC, AND IS LOUISIANA ONE OF THE UNITED STATES?"[33]

Congress had little choice except to take up the issue of the disputed election. Democrats and Liberal Republicans felt no reticence at all about scrutinizing the Grant administration's dealings with what they viewed as an increasingly unsavory regime in New Orleans. Other concerns also sparked interest in Louisiana. Both sides there claimed to have gained their ticket's electoral votes for president and vice president, which had to be approved by the vote of Congress. In the end neither house of Congress decided to count Louisiana's electoral votes. Grant would have won reelection in either case, but the decision not to count a readmitted state's electoral votes

---

31. Pinchback's farewell address, *New Orleans Republican*, Jan. 14, 1873, 1.

32. Lonn, *Reconstruction in Louisiana*, 217–18.

33. *New York Herald*, Dec. 26, 1872, 1.

only heightened pressures for a full-scale inquiry into Louisiana's elections. On January 16, 1873, the U.S. Senate instructed a special committee chaired by Sen. O. H. P. Morton of Indiana to investigate the November election and to establish if there indeed was a "legal state government in Louisiana."[34]

Beginning on January 26, Morton's committee spent the better part of a month examining documents and witnesses. By the end of the proceedings, it was clear that congressional Republicans were as divided and paralyzed as Grant had been over what to do about Louisiana. The president, smarting from white southern criticism, urged Congress to decide upon a policy and start sharing responsibility for federal military intervention in the southern states.[35] The majority report, defended by Sen. M. H. Carpenter of Wisconsin, recommended Warmoth's retention as governor until March 1873, at which time a new election under federal supervision would be held. Democrats supported a minority report calling for the outright recognition of McEnery and the Fusionist ticket. Senator Morton denounced the Fusionists, defended Kellogg's government, and argued against Carpenter's bill for a new election on the floor of the Senate: "I recommend masterly inactivity. . . . If McEnery attempts to make any trouble, Governor Kellogg is able to take care of him without any assistance from the Government of the United States; but if he requires it he will get it. The President has said he would give it."[36] For two full days, February 27 and 28, 1873, the debate raged in the Senate, with personal feelings between Republicans running higher in some cases than those between Republicans and Democrats. Test amendments by both sides failed. In the end Morton's nonpolicy of "masterly inactivity" prevailed by default rather than design. Congress adjourned on March 4, 1873, without supporting either government in New Orleans.[37]

THE BATTLE OF THE CABILDO

Back in New Orleans, "masterly inactivity" made a bad situation worse. Throughout the congressional inquiry and debate, Kellogg and McEnery kept their respective legislatures in session and producing laws to demonstrate their legitimacy to Washington. Kellogg's Republicans distanced themselves from Warmoth by passing bills supporting financial retrenchment and debating a new civil rights measure. McEnery's legislature tried to cripple Kellogg's by voting to prohibit the payment of taxes to their

34. Lonn, *Reconstruction in Louisiana*, 231–32.

35. Ulysses S. Grant, "Fourth Annual Message," Feb. 25, 1873, in Richardson, *Messages and Papers of the Presidents*, 7:212–13.

36. *Congressional Globe*, 42nd Cong., 3rd sess., 1872.

37. Lonn, *Reconstruction in Louisiana*, 232–40.

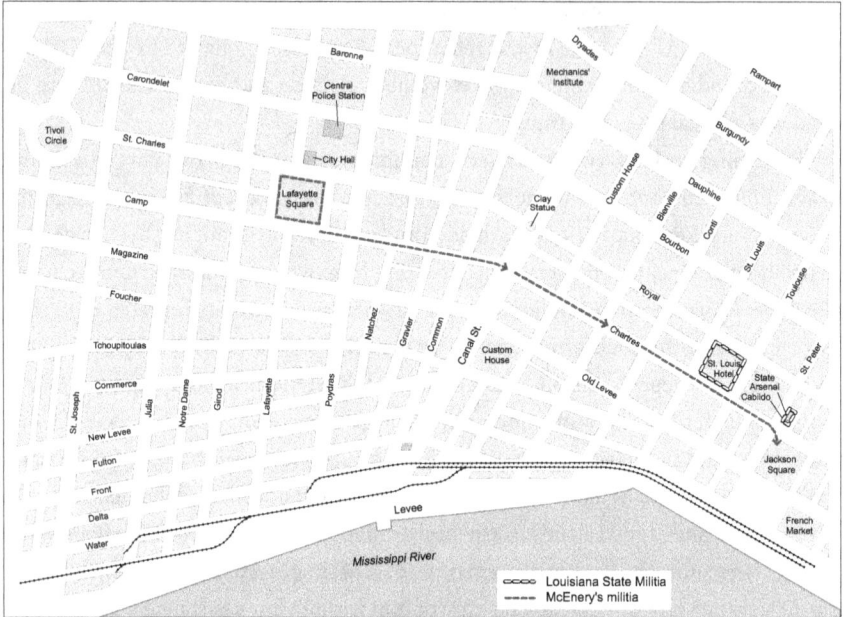

The Street Battle of 1873

rivals' parish tax collectors. Republicans retaliated with bills mustering the Metropolitans into the state militia and authorizing them to collect taxes from defaulting
parishes. By the end of February, strains began to show in McEnery's actions, betray-
ing his faltering hope of finding aid from Congress. In frustration he issued a proclamation on February 26 calling on all able-bodied men to assemble on March 1 for state
militia service. The following day he appointed an ex-Confederate officer, Frederick N.
Ogden from New Orleans, brigadier general and provisional commander of his militia. In interviews with New Orleans newspapers over the next few days, Ogden indicated that he would occupy the police stations and militia arsenals that Warmoth had
so recently lost to Pinchback.[38]

The clash was not long in coming. On March 1, 1873, McEnery held another mass
rally for his supporters, including the militia, at Lafayette Square. Informed daily of
Congress's drift toward inaction, he demanded an immediate end to Kellogg's "usurpation." McEnery later disavowed ordering any military action, but after the rally Ogden interpreted McEnery as having given him an open-ended order to attack the Kellogg government's police stations and militia arsenals.

38. Ibid., 226–28; Taylor, *Louisiana Reconstructed,* 260–62; Dawson, *Army Generals and Reconstruction,* 143.

On March 5 Ogden and about two hundred militia, the nucleus of whom were drawn from veterans of Warmoth's militia mutiny in December, assembled at Lafayette Square for an attack on the St. Peter Street state arsenal at the Cabildo. Things went badly from the start. Ogden's bellicose interviews with the city newspapers had tipped off General Longstreet and the state militia well in advance. When he finally struck, the arsenal building was heavily defended, and General Badger's Metropolitans stood waiting in reserve.[39]

At about 9:30 P.M. Ogden and his men marched from Lafayette Square through the streets of the French Quarter, throwing up barricades at street intersections as they went. By the time they reached Jackson Square, however, the Louisiana State Militia had been fully alerted. Metropolitan Police in the Cabildo and the arsenal refused Ogden's personal demand for surrender and pinned down his force in Jackson Square. By 10:00 P.M. Badger and 125 well-armed Metropolitans arrived at Jackson Square, firing booming shots over the heads of the McEnery militia with a twelve-pound cannon charged with grapeshot. At about the same time, officers from Emory's Nineteenth U.S. Infantry arrived on the scene. Under a flag of truce, they informed Ogden that Emory had ordered them to disperse. Wounded and demoralized by his lack of success, Ogden gave the order and his men departed. In the ensuing confusion Longstreet's force arrested fifty-three of Ogden's militiamen and held them on state and federal charges. By midnight McEnery's putsch against the Kellogg government had ignominiously collapsed.[40]

Republicans wasted no time in capitalizing on their military success. The next day, March 6, Governor Kellogg ordered Longstreet to disperse the McEnery legislature, located in Odd Fellows Hall just off Lafayette Square. At noon Badger and the Metropolitans surrounded the building and ordered the occupants out. Because the Fusionist legislators had assumed President Grant would not allow Acting Governor Pinchback to use force against them, they appeared surprised and angered that Governor Kellogg chose to breech this convenient arrangement without advising them.

39. See Special Orders Nos. 14–18, n.d., in Louisiana Adjutant General's Office, *Annual Report, 1873,* 79–80. These orders mobilized black militia companies, the Metropolitans, and Longstreet's staff. No dates are given in the first three, but the text of the last makes it clear that Longstreet completed the mobilization by February 24 and stood ready after that date to repel Ogden's attack.

40. *New Orleans Daily Picayune,* Mar. 6, 1873 (morning ed.), 1. A list of all those arrested is found in *New Orleans Daily Picayune,* Mar. 6, 1873 (afternoon ed.), 1. The New Orleans U.S. district attorney eventually dropped all charges against those arrested. Kellogg's attorney general filed state charges of inciting a riot but later dropped those as well. See *New Orleans Daily Picayune,* Mar. 7, 1873 (afternoon ed.), 1; and Mar. 13, 1873 (afternoon ed.), 1.

(Actually, Kellogg had decided not to inform General Emory in advance of his plans.) Lacking available forces of their own, Fusionist legislators had no alternative but to abandon the building and depart between the triumphant parading files of Badger's troops. After months of political stalemate running from New Orleans to Washington and back again, it appeared that Louisiana finally had one government again, and this time it owed more to the Republicans' own initiative than to the ultimate sanction of federal bayonets.[41]

INSURRECTION SPREADS THROUGH LOUISIANA

Because the battle of the Cabildo ended in a complete rout of the Fusionists, it seemed to presage a new ascendancy for Louisiana Republicans. Longstreet had scattered Ogden's insurgent white militia, crushing the putsch. Badger and the Metropolitans had forced a humiliating public disbandment of the Fusionist Legislature, destroying McEnery's claim to head a functioning and legitimate government. For the moment it appeared Republicans had overcome their internal differences and defeated their opponents with only minimal aid from federal forces. That appearance proved illusory. For while the Republican leadership had preoccupied itself with legitimacy and succession struggles in the capital, unrest had fanned out from the city into the rural parishes, eventually pitting Republicans against Fusionists in dozens of local reenactments of the battle of the Cabildo.

The battle for the Louisiana countryside erupted first at Colfax, the parish seat for Grant Parish along the Red River between Alexandria and Shreveport. Fittingly enough, Grant Parish was itself an offspring of Reconstruction, created in 1869 by the first Republican legislature under orders from Governor Warmoth. In his ceaseless quest to create more patronage opportunities in parts of the state that had been especially hostile to Republicans, Warmoth signed bills carving out new parishes containing carefully tailored black electoral majorities from adjoining majority-white parishes. Beside new seats in the state legislature, this offered opportunities for local patronage since the governor's expansive appointive powers granted him the authority to appoint new slates of parish officials.[42]

The land chosen to form Grant Parish was an uneasy amalgam of two starkly contrasting geographic and demographic regions.[43] Its western edge bordered the Red

41. Dawson, *Army Generals and Reconstruction*, 144; Taylor, *Louisiana Reconstructed*, 255; Lonn, *Reconstruction in Louisiana*, 228–29.

42. Tunnell, *Crucible of Reconstruction*, 157–59.

43. Robert Ransom and Richard Sutch use Grant Parish as one of their "typical" counties for the economic study of the southern transition from slave labor to sharecropping. See *One Kind of Freedom*, 292.

River, whose alluvial plain antebellum cotton planters had prized for its fertile soil, long growing season, and easy access to New Orleans by steamboat. It also stood at the northernmost edge of Louisiana's sugar-producing region. This fact alone kept a number of the area's planters, who would probably otherwise have become Democrats, clinging to the last remnants of the Whig Party.[44] In 1860 the wealthiest of the dozen large planters in what would become Grant Parish was Meredith Smith Calhoun of Calhoun's Landing (later Colfax), who owned four plantations totaling more than fourteen thousand acres and more than seven hundred slaves. On the eve of the Civil War, the census valued his estates at more than $1,000,000; they were profitable enough to allow him to invest $100,000 in a new sugar mill. With few exceptions, the Grant Parish freedmen present after the Civil War had grown up on Calhoun's plantations, and in 1873 most still lived in small communities, like Smithfield Quarters just north of Colfax, that had been slave quarters just a few years earlier.[45]

Not unlike the alluvial plain of the Red River, the white planter elite of Grant Parish represented only a narrow demographic band. Beyond the three-mile-wide river bottoms, the land rose into low hills covered by poorly irrigated soil and long-needle pines, most of which later became part of the Kisatchie National Forest. On this land cotton growing was not so profitable, and the greater number of antebellum whites who lived there had few if any slaves. The general poverty of this area is suggested by noting that before 1869 the northern part of the parish belonged to Winn Parish, the hotbed of white Populism in Louisiana in the 1890s and birthplace of Huey Long. The 1870 Census, while notoriously inaccurate, nevertheless conveys a revealing portrait of population of the area at the time: residing there were twenty-four hundred blacks and twenty-two hundred whites, a rough racial balance with a narrow black majority deliberately crafted to keep Grant Parish in Republican hands.[46]

In the struggle to gain the upper hand, both Louisiana state governments sought

44. An example of this phenomenon was James Madison Wells, the Whig planter from Rapides Parish, just south of Grant Parish, who became governor during presidential Reconstruction. See Lowrey, "Political Career of James Madison Wells," 995–1123.

45. On the extent of Calhoun's holdings, see Menn, *Large Slaveholders*, 104–5. On the antebellum history of the parish area, see Mabel Fletcher Harrison and Lavinia McGuire McNeely, *Grant Parish, Louisiana: A History* (Baton Rouge: Claitor's, 1969). Grant Parish was not the site of any significant fighting during the Civil War, though Maj. Gen. Nathaniel P. Banks moved up the Red River past Calhoun's Landing in his 1864 campaign against Maj. Gen. Richard Taylor's forces in the vicinity of Shreveport. See Ludwell H. Johnson, *Red River Campaign: Politics and Cotton in the Civil War* (Baltimore, Md.: Johns Hopkins University Press, 1958).

46. Department of Commerce, *Negro Population, 1790–1915* (Washington, D.C.: Government Printing Office, 1918; reprinted with introduction by James McPherson, New York: Arno, 1968).

to demonstrate their authority by recognizing different slates of officials in Grant Parish.[47] McEnery recognized Alphonze Cazabat as judge and C. C. Nash as sheriff of the parish in December 1872, before his own inauguration. Early in March 1873 Kellogg certified the Republican candidates, R. C. Register and Daniel Shaw, as parish judge and sheriff respectively. On March 25 Register and Shaw broke into the courthouse to take possession of their offices. After rumors reached the town that hostile whites had organized ten miles away in Montgomery to retake the courthouse by force, the two deputized a posse comitatus of twenty to thirty men. Attempts to negotiate a compromise failed, then on April 5 the situation sharply worsened when a band of unidentified white men murdered a black man, Jesse McKinney, in front of his own house near Colfax. William Ward, a Union veteran, black Republican state representative, and militia captain, immediately mustered his company and may have distributed some Enfield rifles from the state militia arsenal in New Orleans. An influx of three hundred black men and their families seeking safety at Colfax ensued over the following days. Once summoned to the town, black militiamen divided into watches and began drilling under arms. Pickets posted at the major roads leading into town forbade some whites from entering. Some whites in town, including Judge Rutland (the previous parish judge) and his family, either fled or left under duress. Fearing an imminent attack by whites from the surrounding area, Captain Ward and Judge Register left Colfax on April 8 for New Orleans, hoping to persuade Governor Kellogg to send reinforcements. They left Levin Allen, another black army veteran, in command.[48]

47. As is more often than not the case concerning battle narratives, contemporary reports of what happened at Colfax are contradictory, often confused, and always colored by the allegiances of the eyewitnesses. For a view sympathetic to the white supremacists involved, see Johnson, "Colfax Riot." The author has attempted to reconstruct a plausible—if by no means definitive—narrative of the confusing events of the battle from the lengthy congressional testimony on Colfax. Particularly useful is the testimony of J. R. Beckwith, the U.S. prosecuting attorney at both of the Colfax trials held in 1874. Beckwith interviewed more witnesses to the fighting than anyone else and tried to vigorously prosecute the case in federal court. See Testimony, J. R. Beckwith, in House, *Condition of Affairs in the Southern States*, H. Rpt. 261, 409–21. His testimony before the congressional committee that investigated Louisiana's election violence substantially agrees on all major points with the text of the charge of the judge in the original trial (reprinted in ibid., 856–65).

48. William Ward received a commission as a captain in the state militia on December 1, 1871, but almost immediately caused General Longstreet and the state militia staff difficulties by his provocative parading and drilling of the Colfax militia company, which upset a number of local whites. Longstreet eventually ordered an investigation of Ward and subsequently forbade him from drilling his company without permission—a rather mild disciplinary measure. The adjutant general's reports for 1872 and 1873 are silent on whether his company returned their weapons to the state arsenal, a charge made by the defenders of

Fears of an attack were well justified. James West Hadnot, a Confederate veteran and reputed head of the local Ku Klux Klan in 1868, led a mounted force of twenty men to the outskirts of Colfax on April 1, where Cazabat and Register met to discuss their political quarrel. When Register refused to yield, Cazabat broke off negotiations but promised he would defend his claim to office by force if necessary. Over the next five days an armed camp of several hundred armed white men coalesced at Bayou Darrow, about five miles north of Colfax, consisting of paramilitary companies from Grant and a number of surrounding parishes. On April 5 another armed reconnaissance party under Capt. C. C. Nash approached Colfax, but Levin Allen, Alexander Tillman (another black Union veteran), and a force of armed black militia drove them off after word reached them of Jesse McKinney's murder.[49]

While tensions rose in Colfax, Governor Kellogg prevaricated in New Orleans. On April 9 Judge Rutland, who had made his way downriver by steamboat, pleaded with Kellogg, General Longstreet, and General Emory to send troops. Longstreet wanted to send a detachment of the Metropolitan Police right away, but Kellogg refused Rutland's request, preferring to pass the action to the U.S. Army. Emory, who had yet to receive word from Washington on whether Kellogg or McEnery was the de jure governor of the state, declared the standoff at Colfax a local matter and declined to intervene without explicit orders from Washington. After fresh pleas from Ward and Register, who arrived in New Orleans on April 10, Kellogg reversed himself and sent two militia officers to investigate. It was too little and too late. The stage had already been set for battle.[50]

THE BATTLE AND MASSACRE AT COLFAX

Captain Nash gathered his paramilitary force just north of Colfax for an assault to take the town on Easter Sunday, April 13. Precise numbers have never been clear for either side, but the white supremacist forces probably amounted to nearly three hundred armed men. Beside more than one hundred from Grant Parish, Nash had three companies from Rapides Parish, commanded by Capt. George W. Stafford, Capt. David C. Paul, and Capt. Joseph W. Texada; a company from Winn Parish commanded by Capt. James Bird; and a company from Catahoula Parish commanded by Capt. J. W. Wig-

---

the Colfax paramilitaries in court and before the congressional investigating committees but unsupported by evidence after the battle. See Louisiana Adjutant General's Office, *Annual Report, 1871*, 22; and Special Orders No. 52, Dec. 11, 1871, ibid., 39. On William Ward's political career, see Vincent, *Black Legislators*, 268–70.

49. Testimony, J. R. Beckwith, in House, *of Affairs in the Southern States*, H. Rpt. 261, 410.

50. Dawson, *Army Generals and Reconstruction*, 144–45.

gins.[51] As paramilitaries without formal commissions or support, they came with their own weapons, but many of these men carried Winchester repeating rifles and revolvers firing cased ammunition, easily outmatching the black militia's Enfields and shotguns. Nash also procured a small cannon from the Red River steamboat *John T. Moore*, and a blacksmith from Montgomery forged ammunition for it. Besides being well armed, Nash's men were mobile. While no source explicitly mentions it, most allude to the fact that every man under his command had his own horse and most had probably grown up in the saddle. Against this force Levin Allen had mustered somewhere near 150 black militiamen, armed mostly with shotguns and several crudely fashioned cannons. Most were natives of Grant Parish, and while some had their own mules, they could not hope to match Nash's mobility. On Saturday, after rumors reached Colfax of the impending assault, militiamen started digging a ring of breastworks encircling the courthouse, but by Sunday morning their trench line was only two feet deep and had encompassed just three sides of the building.[52]

At noon Nash formed a battle line several miles north of town and prepared to assault this black Alamo on the Red River. Riding up to the militia picket line under a flag of truce, he offered Allen one last opportunity to surrender the courthouse and his men's weapons. Allen curtly refused, insisting that he and his men would not share Jesse McKinney's fate. Nash then offered thirty minutes in which to remove all the women and children who had taken refuge in the town before his assault commenced. Allen dared Nash to come get the men he wanted and rode back to Colfax to prepare his defenses.[53]

The attack began thirty minutes later. Nash's force advanced in line southward, unhindered by fire from the defenders' homemade cannons, and occupied Smithfield Quarters. Moving on the center of town, the paramilitaries encountered heavy fire from blacks entrenched in the earthworks around the courthouse, and their advance stalled. For more than an hour this stalemate continued, with the whites unable to dislodge the black militia. Stymied, Nash sent a detachment led by James Daniels, an-

51. All six of the commanders of paramilitary companies at Colfax (James Bird, David C. Paul, C. C. Nash, Joseph W. Texada, G. W. Stafford, and J. W. Wiggins) were Confederate veterans, and of these six at least four (Paul, Nash, Texada, and Stafford) were ex-Confederate officers. Janet B. Hewett, *The Roster of Confederate Soldiers, 1861–1865*, 16 vols. (Wilmington, N.C.: Broadfoot, 1995). Captain Wiggins and the Catahoula Parish paramilitaries later shielded men implicated in the battle of Colfax from detection and prosecution. Testimony, James Forsythe in House, *Condition of Affairs in the Southern States*, H. Rpt. 261, 377–84.

52. Testimony, J. R. Beckwith, in House, *Condition of Affairs in the Southern States*, H. Rpt. 261, 411.

53. Ibid.; Johnson, "Colfax Riot," 411.

other Confederate veteran, to move west of the courthouse with the paramilitaries' cannon, positioning them to flank the militia position from the levee on the river, while the rest of Nash's line kept up a masking fire. Shortly after 2:00 P.M. Daniels's force moved out and achieved complete surprise. Cannon fire suddenly enfiladed the defenders' trenches, and the militia's resistance crumbled. Half of the militiamen retreated into the safety of the courthouse building itself. The remainder ran for concealment in the fields of Calhoun's Plantation south of town, pursued by Nash's men on horseback.[54]

Determined to finish the fighting quickly, the paramilitaries forced one of their black prisoners, Benjamin Brimm, to torch the roof of the courthouse. As the building burned, Nash sent James West Hadnot forward with another flag of truce to demand an immediate surrender. In the smoke and confusion that followed, shots rang out, and both Hadnot and Sidney Harris fell mortally wounded, probably shot by their comrades. Some black militiamen, including Alex Tillman, refused to surrender and probably perished in the flames. Those attempting to flee the burning courthouse were reportedly "ridden down in the open fields and shot without mercy," and the wounded lying about the courthouse grounds were leisurely "pinned to the ground with bayonets" by their attackers. At least thirty-seven black defenders had been taken prisoner by the time the fighting ceased around 3:00 P.M. That night most of the paramilitaries left town for their homes. A smaller number remained in Colfax to guard their prisoners, however, and some time after 9:00 P.M., following desultory discussions about how to dispose of their captives, they assembled the survivors and summarily executed each one with a pistol shot to the back of the head. Astonishingly, and probably only because some of the paramilitaries had celebrated their victory by getting drunk, several of the prisoners survived these executions and later testified about the details of the massacre to federal investigators.[55]

Considerable dispute remains about the number of killed and wounded in the battle and massacre. Three whites died from their wounds, though a subsequent medical examination by a U.S. Army surgeon supported the claim that paramilitaries had mortally wounded Harris and Hadnot. The number of blacks estimated killed in the battle and massacre varies from as low as sixty-four to as high as four hundred. Some of the accounts were either fanciful or based on sheer guesswork. Republican newspapers, particularly in the North, probably reported the higher numbers in an attempt

---

54. Testimony, J. R Beckwith, in House, *Condition of Affairs in the Southern States,* H. Rpt. 261, 412–13.

55. Johnson, "Colfax Riot," 412–13; Testimony, J. R Beckwith, in House, *Condition of Affairs in the Southern States,* H. Rpt. 261, 413, 415–16.

to reap the maximum partisan benefits of this sensational event. Those sympathetic to the attackers at first denied any massacre; others blamed the extent of the slaughter on a justifiable retaliation against "negro treachery" in the reputed shootings of Hadnot and Harris under a flag of truce. The actual number killed is probably closer to the lower end of the range of estimates since the tiny courthouse building could not have held more than a hundred people. T. W. DeKlyne, the U.S. deputy marshal who investigated the scene and supervised the burial party, counted fifty-nine bodies buried at the site. He also noted that family members had already claimed at least four other bodies before he arrived, and others were probably killed or mortally wounded but never officially reported. At least another twenty-five had been wounded but escaped from the battlefield before the massacre. No one ever found the body of Levin Allen, the black militia commander, and it remains unknown whether he perished in the fire or escaped.[56]

In the following weeks and months, Louisiana Republicans discovered Colfax was no isolated incident. Across the state local Fusionist leaders abandoned any earlier pretense of legality and tried to oust Republicans from office by force or intimidation. Just three days after the battle of Colfax, disturbances in Livingston Parish forced Governor Kellogg to dispatch General Longstreet with a "sufficient force" of Metropolitans to put down unrest.[57] On April 19 General Street ordered a company of fifty-five Metropolitans under Colonel Flanagan to Amite in Tangipahoa Parish (also a creation of Governor Warmoth in 1869) to quell disputes between Fusionists and Republicans.[58] While Livingston and Tangipahoa were both "Florida parishes" (that is, east of the Mississippi River), no area of the state seemed unaffected. Not long after this, General Street sent "fifty or sixty" Metropolitans, complete with cavalry and a small cannon, under General Badger and Longstreet's son, Maj. John Garland Longstreet, to patrol against white reprisals at New Iberia and St. Martinsville in the French-speaking southern parishes of Iberia and St. Martin.[59]

56. Manie Johnson discusses the various estimates of the contemporary sources in "Colfax Riot," 418 n. 115. See also Testimony, J. R Beckwith, in House, *Condition of Affairs in the Southern States*, H. Rpt. 261, 413. Like much else about the battle of Colfax, the perspective of those telling the story influenced the numbers reported killed. A precise number probably cannot be fixed at this late date.

57. General Orders No. 13, Apr. 16, 1873, in Louisiana Adjutant General's Office, *Annual Report, 1873*, 43.

58. General Orders No. 14, Apr. 19, 1873, ibid., 43.

59. Special Orders Nos. 26–28, n.d., ibid., 81. A brief account of the successful action dispersing Colonel De Blanc's force was discovered in the Adjutant General's Office papers and later reprinted in the Conservative press after Republicans fell from power. See *New Orleans Daily Picayune*, May 15, 1877, 1.

BATTLES AND STRATEGIES IN AN UNCIVIL WAR

At first glance the connection between the relatively bloodless battle of the Cabildo and the frenzied butchery of the battle of Colfax may not seem readily apparent. Taken together, however, they defined a new departure in white supremacist efforts to oust Republicans from power. Perhaps because they drew so little blood, one recent historian of Reconstruction has described the struggles in Louisiana state government motivating the street battles of 1872 and 1873 as "a series of tragicomic episodes."[60] Even historians of Reconstruction Louisiana have usually reduced their descriptions of the battle of the Cabildo to a series of bizarre events unreflective of its significance to the evolving struggle for power between Republicans and their opponents.[61]

The Reconstruction street battles in Louisiana hardly compare with the high drama of Civil War battles if they are measured by the numbers of their participants or casualties. In the street battle of 1872, there was only a single fatality, the unfortunate Warmoth representative Walter Wheyland. In the street battle at the Cabildo in 1873, there were fewer than a thousand participants, including three companies of federal troops. Unconfirmed reports in local newspapers recorded only two deaths and perhaps twenty men wounded, including General Ogden himself.[62]

It is essential, however, to recall that numbers of participants and death tolls have always been imperfect measures of the political implications of any battle in military history. When measured by their effect on public opinion or on the outcome of the war, the list of Civil War battles that one may properly describe as "decisive" begins to narrow significantly—arguably to a list no longer than First Bull Run, Antietam, Gettysburg and Vicksburg, Atlanta, and the long siege of Richmond and Petersburg. Of the many others (including, for example, the famous two-day bloodbath at Shiloh in 1862 that featured more than 100,000 soldiers and 20,000 casualties), however important they were in terms of ground gained or raw numbers of casualties inflicted, their influence on the political course of the struggle was, at best, indirect. By contrast, when they are measured by their political influence instead of by sheer military scale, the street battles of 1872 and 1873 grow in historical significance. By 1872 all the Republican state governments across the South showed dangerous signs of strain, though none could claim to be as chronically endangered as Louisiana's. The success of Warmoth and Kellogg in mobilizing the state militia to defend the statehouse not only turned back their opponents' attempts to destroy the Republican government but

60. Foner, *Reconstruction*, 349.

61. Lonn, *Reconstruction in Louisiana*, 228; Taylor, *Louisiana Reconstructed*, 254–55.

62. *New Orleans Daily Picayune*, Mar. 6, 1873, 1.

also considerably raised the threshold of violence their enemies felt they had to match.

Republicans' success in keeping their new southern state governments in power was not unqualified. The finality of Union victory in the Civil War had been secured not only by the direct means of death and destruction deliberately inflicted by Union armies in battle but also by the indirect means of the appropriation of property in the form of slaves and sometimes land, the suspension of civil liberties and local governments, and eventually the disfranchising and proscriptive policies of the Military Reconstruction Acts. These indirect means, while not a part of warfare per se, had all been implemented by military occupation authorities to punish the enemies of the federal government and prevent them from rising again in rebellion. The security dilemma of Warmoth's and Kellogg's governments is underlined by their failure to capitalize upon their martial victories in the street battles of 1872 and 1873 with measures that punished their adversaries and deterred others from joining future uprisings. Warmoth faced special difficulties, given that one of his antagonists was the president's own brother-in-law and others lay beyond his reach as governor, protected by their status as federal officials. Kellogg's opponents in the battle of the Cabildo held no such immunity, however, and yet he still proved unwilling to punish them for trying to bring down his government. In the end participants in the militia mutiny of December 1872 suffered no criminal prosecution despite their illegal occupation of state property, illegal possession of state militia weaponry, and refusal to obey orders from state authorities. It was no wonder they had no compunction about joining in the putsch at Jackson Square a few months later. Refusal to vigorously prosecute those arrested after the battle of the Cabildo similarly underscores the inability of Kellogg's government to make its opponents fear, if not obey, its demands for public order. It is therefore not surprising that Kellogg incited in his opponents an increasingly virulent measure of contempt mixed with rage.

The deadliest documented incident in America during Reconstruction, the battle of Colfax, emerged as a grim milestone in the search for a blended strategy of grassroots violence coupled with white-line voter mobilization. Before Colfax, politically oriented violence in Louisiana had aimed at either capturing or solidifying control over the statehouse—as had been the case in each of the street battles of 1866, 1872, and 1873—or delivering the state's electoral votes in a national election—as in the Knights of the White Camellia's brief but bloody campaign in 1868. Neither of those options proved fruitful. By trial and error Colfax and the unrest that followed demonstrated that neither federal nor state officials possessed the ability to maintain public order far beyond the capital city.

Colfax also demonstrated the dramatic new appeal of the racially oriented mas-sacre as a favored paramilitary tactic, especially if applied with a certain discretion. Unlike the street battle of 1866, the 1873 battle and massacre in Colfax occurred far away from the closely policed streets of urban New Orleans and the scrutiny of the national press. Because a racial massacre could rarely be prevented by forces outside the local community before the fact and usually went unobserved by large numbers of people, it proved to be a peculiarly potent instrument of terror. Republicans car-ried Grant Parish in the 1870 and 1872 elections. For nearly a century after the battle of Colfax, Grant Parish remained an unshakable bastion of single-party, white-line Democratic politics. Most of the black men in the parish willing to stand up to white pressure perished in the fighting, and those who did not either went into exile or got a never-to-be-forgotten message to stay away from politics altogether. From Missis-sippi in 1874 to South Carolina in 1876, racial massacres would ignite similarly vio-lent campaigns to oust Republicans from local office and fashion white supremacist legislative majorities in Deep South states where black voters outnumbered whites.

Like the battle of the Cabildo, paramilitary action at Colfax ultimately went un-punished. The day after, a contingent of Metropolitan Police arrived by steamer from New Orleans. They were too late to do anything except hunt for the white attackers, who by then had scattered. Two days later federal troops under the command of one of General Emory's officers arrived and began to arrest suspects. They eventually found and detained ninety men, but only nine actually faced trial for crimes under the 1871 Enforcement Act (also known as the Ku Klux Klan Act), created to enforce the provisions of the Fourteenth Amendment. The first trial, held in February 1874, ended in a mistrial. The second, held in May 1874, acquitted four but found the other five guilty of conspiracy against a peaceful assembly. After a lengthy appeal the U.S. Supreme Court ruled in *United States v. Cruikshank* (1876) that the Enforcement Act of 1871 and the Fourteenth Amendment applied only to actions committed by state governments, not private individuals. The high court's decision returned the case to the jurisdiction of the state of Louisiana. None of the paramilitaries participating in the attack on Colfax ever stood trial again. Long before the Supreme Court ruled, how-ever, Conservatives had reached the appropriate conclusions. White supremacists had at last discovered the mix of paramilitary action and racialized politics that just might jettison Reconstruction in their state and perhaps across the entire South.[63]

63. Robert M. Goldman, *Reconstruction and Voting: Losing the Vote in Reese and Cruikshank* (Lawrence: University Press of Kansas, 2001).

❧ 5 ❧

The Street Battle of 1874

The White Leagues Seize Power

Enraged by the battle of the Cabildo and inspired by the massacre at Colfax, more than ten thousand white men from Louisiana joined paramilitary companies, which came to be known as the White Leagues in 1874, fired with a new determination to oust Republicans from power. Unlike the vigilantes of the Knights of the White Camellia or the Ku Klux Klan, the White Leagues were not secret organizations. In dozens of rural parishes across the state, hundreds of white men armed themselves, held daylight rallies, and forced or intimidated scores of black and white Republicans out of political office. In New Orleans, well-organized White League companies abandoned any pretense of subterfuge and openly conducted military drills in the streets under the command of Confederate-veteran officers. On September 14 General Ogden, now at the head of a larger and more disciplined body of men than he had led at the Cabildo in 1873, moved to overthrow the Kellogg government in a carefully orchestrated coup d'état.

GOVERNOR KELLOGG REORGANIZES THE LOUISIANA STATE MILITIA

Compared to Henry Clay Warmoth, William Pitt Kellogg, Louisiana's second Republican governor, cut a feeble figure. Born in Vermont, he grew up in Illinois and moved to Nebraska Territory as a young man. After serving as a colonel in the Union army, President Lincoln named him to the position of surveyor at the U.S. Custom House on Canal Street in the spring of 1865. Like Warmoth, Kellogg's army service and connections to the Republican's national party organization made him a prominent candidate for high office in Louisiana. In 1868 the new legislature elected him U.S. senator, and he spent the next four years in Washington. Nothing about Kellogg's tenure in the Senate was particularly distinguished. Indeed he probably owed his nomination for governor in 1872 to his absence from New Orleans during the internecine struggle between Warmoth and the Custom House Ring as much as anything. Had he been better acquainted with the fratricidal nature of Louisiana politics, he might have decided to stay in Washington rather than run for governor.[1]

Kellogg has appeared to at least some historians as a more sincere advocate of political racial equality than his predecessor. A closer examination reveals that his actions rarely matched his rhetoric. In 1873 the Louisiana legislature passed, and Kellogg signed, a new state civil rights bill. This law mandated equal access to accommodations and public transportation without regard to race—it was to some extent a forerunner of the federal Civil Rights Bill of 1875, Congress's last successful enactment of civil rights legislation during Reconstruction. In practice, however, the Louisiana measure was, as one historian has pointedly observed, "ignored outside of New Orleans." Kellogg's administration made practically no effort to enforce the provisions of the law, either through the extensive police powers Warmoth ramrodded through the legislature or through the state courts, which remained mostly in the hands of Republican judges throughout Kellogg's tenure.

The governor also signed a number of measures intended to reform state government in order to clear the cloud of corruption charges that had gathered over the capital. Stung by the Fusionists' accusations of election rigging in 1872, Kellogg decided to support a new election law designed to overhaul the Warmoth administration's intricate registration and voting procedures. The new bill passed, but it retained the state Returning Board as the ultimate authority over elections.[2]

Kellogg devoted most of his energy as governor trying to revive economic growth by reducing government spending, which he thought would be popular across racial and party lines. In addition to reining in expenditures, he reduced the bonded indebtedness accumulated by both the Rebel Legislature and the Warmoth administration. Kellogg disposed of much of the contingent bonding of new railroads underwritten since 1865 by liquidating bankrupt railroad corporations, a number of which had collapsed in the wake of the Wall Street panic of 1873. In other cases he repudiated some of the more dubious bond issues through court challenges to their legality. These financial write-offs improved the state's balance sheet but came at the price of depriving Louisiana of the transportation infrastructure that Warmoth and his allies had hoped would make New Orleans a dynamic commercial hub for expanding markets in Texas, California, and Mexico. Kellogg personally devoted several long trips to

---

1. John Edmond Gonzalez, "William Pitt Kellogg: Reconstruction Governor of Louisiana, 1873–1877," *LHQ* 29 (1946): 394–495.

2. Taylor, *Louisiana Reconstructed*, 258–62.

New York to discuss the state's finances with investors. These attempts to argue against the depressed prices and high interest rates of state bond issues proved unsuccessful. Louisiana warrants typically sold at fifty to sixty cents on the dollar during Kellogg's administration, a steep discount to their face value, but an accurate indicator of northern capital's lack of faith in his government.[3]

The new governor's positions on civil rights and financial reform did not strengthen black political support for his administration. In one of the first actions of the new legislative session of 1873, all the black state senators banded together to elect P. B. S. Pinchback to the U.S. Senate, denying the white officials of the Custom House Ring that particular prize. Kellogg did not actively oppose Pinchback's election, and he may secretly have been glad to have a popular and potentially dangerous rival out of the capital. But he offered him no active support through his former Senate colleagues in Washington when Pinchback came under serious fire for supposedly accepting a bribe back in New Orleans. Pinchback blamed the Custom House Ring in general, if not Kellogg in particular, for failing to support him on Capitol Hill, and he eventually would exact revenge when he returned to New Orleans after a long but futile struggle to take Kellogg's old Senate seat.[4]

By midsummer of 1873 black political support for Kellogg had slumped further. After President Grant issued a proclamation in May recognizing Kellogg as the de facto governor, the white business community of New Orleans hatched a new scheme to undermine the carpetbaggers that became known as the Unification Movement.[5] Using P. G. T. Beauregard as a figurehead, the group offered to negotiate a comprehensive political deal with the richest and most influential leaders of the gens de couleur libre, with whom they frequently shared discrete financial and sometimes familial relations. If black leaders would quit the Republican party, Unification leaders promised to accept all the post–Civil War amendments, acknowledge black civil rights, open public schools to black children, condemn election violence, and divide state and local offices between the races. Beauregard's impeccable Confederate military credentials served as a kind of insurance policy against the possibility of white

---

3. Kellogg persuasively defended his management of the fiscal affairs of the state before the Hoar Committee sent to investigate Louisiana in 1875. See Testimony, W. P. Kellogg, in House, *Condition of Affairs in the Southern States*, H. Rpt. 261, 242–68.

4. Ex-Governor Warmoth, relishing his own revenge for Pinchback's role in his impeachment in 1872, insisted that he played the key role in the Senate's decision not to seat his sometime friend and frequent rival. See Warmoth, *War, Politics, and Reconstruction*, 234–38.

5. "Proclamation of Pres. Ulysses S. Grant," May 22, 1873, in Richardson, *Messages and Papers of the Presidents*, 7:223–24.

backlash against this proposal, which called for explicitly acknowledging black political power. But it is difficult to gauge just how genuinely Unification leaders wanted such a sweeping compromise. The fact that some of them later joined the White Leagues suggests that they were not altogether sincere. There can be no question, however, that the public extension of such a comprehensive offer of reconciliation by the upper crust of New Orleans's white elite indicates that the public façade of solid Conservative opposition to black political power concealed some serious tensions. White business leaders realized that Grant's public declaration of support for Kellogg meant the continued presence of federal troops in the city. While many remained attached to support for McEnery's legitimacy in principle, in practice it offered them little prospect of turning the Republicans out of office. That being the case, a continuing political impasse seemed dangerous for business at a time when economic conditions had collapsed following the bank crash of 1873.

Some of the most important and influential black merchants of the city seriously considered the idea of a compromise. Among them were Aristide Mary, Dr. J. B. Roudanez (former publisher of the *New Orleans Tribune*), and even C. C. Antoine, Kellogg's lieutenant governor. Had a deal been struck, it would have shattered the Louisiana Republican Party, which could not survive without black votes. Fortunately for the party, most of the freedmen and their leaders had images of the battle of Colfax and similar incidents fresh in their minds. They remained suspicious that Conservatives could change their stripes overnight and suddenly embrace a comprehensive political platform they had spent years bitterly opposing at every turn. For many black Republicans, abandoning the party that had won emancipation, civil rights, and the franchise in exchange for mere promises made no sense. At a political rally in New Orleans on July 15, 1873, J. Henri Burch, a black state representative from Baton Rouge who had married Lt. Gov. Oscar Dunn's widow, spoke for many when he denounced the Unification Movement as a plot to wreck Reconstruction. He argued that those who had most bitterly opposed black freedom and black votes had engineered it. Within weeks of the rally, the movement stalled and then vanished as rapidly as it had appeared, leaving behind no trace of one of the few efforts to effect a political compromise between native black and white southerners in nineteenth-century America.[6]

Despite the dangers revealed in the white militia mutiny and the failed putsch at the Cabildo, Governor Kellogg devoted scant attention to the problem of rebuilding the militia in the first two years of his administration. Nevertheless, his adjutant gen-

6. T. Harry Williams, "The Louisiana Unification Movement of 1873," *JSH* 11 (Aug. 1945): 349–69.

eral, Brig. Gen. Henry Street, acknowledged the need for a vigorous recruitment effort to replace the exodus of white militia companies recruited during Warmoth's reign. The table of organization in the adjutant general's report for 1874 reveals that the outline of a plan for revitalizing the state militia existed on paper, though it did not get much further than that (see appendix 1, table 1.2). As had been the case under Warmoth, the best trained, best armed, and most reliable state forces were the Metropolitan Police, which Street formally enrolled as a militia brigade under the command of Brig. Gen. A. S. Badger. One of Badger's police captains, Thomas Flanagan, a Union army veteran and Irish immigrant from Boston, became regimental colonel for the infantry. Beside the infantry companies organized by police precinct, the Metropolitans also had a battery of artillery composed of both cannons and Gatling guns garrisoned at the state arsenal on St. Peter Street and a mounted troop of cavalry. In 1873, after many delays, General Street obtained new uniforms, Winchester repeating rifles, and other equipment from federal stores and New York contractors to upgrade the Metropolitan Brigade. With the exception of their erratic pay, the Metropolitans were probably as well-organized and equipped as postwar National Guard regiments of the northeastern states. After the battle of the Cabildo, the Metropolitans (who, it will be recalled, contained both black and white companies) also contained most of the white militia still loyal to the Republicans.[7]

In 1874 Brig. Gen. A. E. Barbour, the black state senator from Orleans Parish who had staunchly supported Warmoth in the street battle of 1872, commanded two regiments of black troops. The Third Regiment remained the stronghold of the gens du couleur libre, as it had been under Governor Warmoth, with the most military and political experience among its officers. Col. A. J. Dumont, the regiment's commander, was a distiller from New Orleans. He had been educated in Mexico City and served as an officer in Maximilian's army during the French occupation, returning to New Orleans when the French withdrew. He held a variety of appointed and elected offices during Reconstruction, including deputy U.S. marshal, state representative, and state senator.[8] His second in command was Lt. Col. Emile Detiege, a quadroon who belonged to a family of wealthy New Orleans jewelers. He had been a lieutenant in the Seventy-Third USCT and had fought at the battle of Port Hudson but resigned during General Banks's purge of black officers. Like Dumont, he had held office under the Republicans. He was an inspector in the Custom House after 1871 and won

7. See Street's narrative sections in Louisiana Adjutant General's Office, *Annual Report, 1873*, 1–10; and idem., *Annual Report, 1874*, 1–13.

8. Foner, *Freedom's Lawmakers*, 66–67.

election as state senator (1874–76) and then state representative (1877–80) from Saint Martin Parish. Detiege reorganized and mustered all five companies of the Third Regiment in 1873 after the battle of the Cabildo, but Dumont took command of the regiment during the street battle of 1874.[9]

About the Second Regiment, which was newly organized in 1874, little information is available concerning it or its commander, Col. Rudolph B. Baquie. Baquie's name does not appear in surveys of appointed or elected black Reconstruction officials. Given the English surnames of most of the company-grade officers in this regiment and their commission dates in July and August 1873, it seems reasonable to infer that the regiment probably included more working-class black migrants from rural parishes who lacked the social standing and wealth of the gens de couleur libre.[10]

The table of militia organization suggests that Republicans wanted to expand the state militia after the fallout of the 1872 election became clear, but they never mustered the political will or resources to carry out the plan. Kellogg did award a brigadier general's commission to Thomas Morris Chester, a talented black Civil War journalist for the *Philadelphia Press* and lawyer from Harrisburg, Pennsylvania. After the war Chester moved to New Orleans and became a popular state education superintendent. He had no formal military training or experience, but he had helped recruit black regiments in the North during the Civil War. More importantly, he lacked the local social connections in New Orleans that successful militia recruitment demanded. Chester and his staff officers never managed to muster a single new company of militia volunteers in 1873 or 1874.[11]

After the alarming slaughter at Colfax, state militia leaders did recruit some new black companies in rural parishes. Under Col. O. H. Brewster, the Union army veteran and white carpetbagger who became Warmoth's Speaker of the House during the street battle of 1872, a regiment of eight black companies mustered for state service in 1873 and 1874 in the northeastern parishes bordering the Mississippi River. Brewster's second in command was Lt. Col. William Murrell Jr., a black Union veteran who served as state representative from 1872 to 1876, 1879 to 1880, and in 1884. He was also editor of the *Madison Vindicator* during Reconstruction, and his father was a politician in Lafourche Parish.[12] Ouachita Parish, where Brewster lived, had a repu-

9. Ibid., 62–63.

10. Louisiana Adjutant General's Office, *Annual Report, 1874*, 20–21.

11. R. J. M. Blackett, *Thomas Morris Chester: Black Civil War Correspondent* (Baton Rouge: Louisiana State University Press, 1989); Foner, *Freedom's Lawmakers;* Louisiana Adjutant General's Office, *Annual Report, 1874*, 18.

12. Vincent, *Black Legislators,* 147–48; Foner, *Freedom's Lawmakers,* 156–57.

tation as a bastion of white supremacist sentiment. Monroe, the Ouachita Parish seat and largest town in northeastern Louisiana, was the home of John McEnery, the Democratic candidate for governor in 1872, and his brother Samuel McEnery, who became governor in the 1880s. The mustering dates of Brewster's companies and their location in small towns in Madison Parish suggest that these militia units probably organized as a defensive reaction to the burgeoning white supremacist movement just across the river in Vicksburg, Mississippi.[13]

Maj. Robert R. Ray of Clinton mustered in another incomplete regiment of five companies. Ray was a black Union veteran who had served in the Eighty-Second USCT and was a native of East Feliciana Parish, northeast of Baton Rouge. He had a long career in Reconstruction politics, beginning as a delegate to the 1867 constitutional convention. From 1870 to 1872 he served as the East Feliciana Parish sheriff (one of the very few blacks to do so in any southern state during Reconstruction), and he was also elected to the Louisiana House for one term (1874–76). In addition to a company in East Feliciana, he also mustered companies in Saint Tammany, Lafourche, Terrebonne, and Assumption parishes in 1873 and 1874. The geographical range of these companies (two in the Florida parishes and the other three in the Cajun parishes southwest of New Orleans) suggests that they were not organized to act in concert with one another. What they had in common was their rural location and the problem of hostile white paramilitary mobilization after Colfax.[14]

The single troop of independent cavalry mustered in Catahoula Parish in northeastern Louisiana was something of an anomaly for Louisiana, though the presence of cavalry was common enough in several other southern state militias during Reconstruction. B Troop Cavalry, commanded by Capt. James Forsythe, was a white militia unit composed of upcountry Confederate-veteran farmers who joined the Republican Party after the war. Forsythe was an Irish immigrant and served in the Rebel army from 1861 until furloughed because of illness in 1863. During Reconstruction he served as parish tax collector, president of the Republican Party's Parish Executive Committee, and organized black voters during election campaigns. This earned him the enmity of local White Leaguers and an assassination attempt by Capt. J. W. Wiggins, one of the paramilitary leaders indicted for taking part in the Colfax massacre. Forsythe's testimony before the 1875 congressional commission sent to investigate Louisiana is a fascinating record of the terrific pressure faced by those few whites who

13. On the incident at Vicksburg, inspired by the White League organizing in Louisiana, which became the catalyst for Mississippi's "shotgun campaign" in 1875, see William C. Harris, *The Day of the Carpetbagger: Republican Reconstruction in Mississippi* (Baton Rouge: Louisiana State University Press, 1979), 645–48.

14. Foner, *Freedom's Lawmakers*, 178; Vincent, *Black Legislators*, 221.

dared to resist the white supremacist onslaught that ended Reconstruction in the Deep South.[15]

Compared with Warmoth's militia, Kellogg's was a different force in both size and racial demographics. James Longstreet remained field commander, but almost all of the rest of the Confederate veterans in the Louisiana State Militia bolted to the Conservatives. Even Longstreet's closest friends and former comrades, including Col. William Owen, Col. Charles Squires, and Col. W. J. Behan, eventually joined the White Leagues. While Longstreet mustered thirty-nine companies in New Orleans in 1870 under Warmoth, by 1874 only twenty-six companies swore allegiance to the Kellogg government, a one-third drop in strength. Of those twenty-six companies, eleven came from the Metropolitan Police, who had not been formally counted as part of the militia in 1870. Even the gens de couleur libre regiment raised fewer companies (five in 1874 versus nine in 1870), an ominous indicator of their waning support. Kellogg managed to muster a few more companies in the rural parishes than Warmoth (fourteen versus eleven), and at least on paper the rural militia had better-qualified leaders than had earlier been the case. But beneath a tidal wave of white supremacist reaction that arose from the countryside after the battle of Colfax, this small step toward strengthening the state militia quickly vanished.

FROM VIGILANTES TO PARAMILITARIES:
THE RISE OF THE WHITE LEAGUES

On April 14, 1873, the day after the battle of Colfax, the U.S. Supreme Court handed down its most important decision interpreting the Fourteenth Amendment and the constitutionality of the Grant administration's attempts to enforce the post–Civil War amendments in the South. Its outcome profoundly shaped the violent campaigns against state Reconstruction governments that followed. The *Slaughterhouse Cases* arose out of Louisiana Republicans' effort to create a modern and sanitary meatpacking facility that would make New Orleans the destination of choice for Texas cattle ranchers over Kansas City or Chicago. In 1869 the legislature passed, and Governor Warmoth signed, a bill confining all butchering in the Metropolitan District to a state-chartered facility located downriver from the city water supply. White butchers sued in state court to overturn the law, claiming the state had infringed upon their right under the Fourteenth Amendment to make a living. Complicating the case itself were the usual accusations of bribery, corruption, and conflicts of interest endemic to Warmoth's reign, not to mention nearly interminable rounds of injunctions and counter-

---

15. Testimony, James Forsythe, in House, *Condition of Affairs in the Southern States*, H. Rpt. 261, 377–83.

injunctions by both parties to the lawsuit. After the Louisiana Supreme Court upheld the state's corporation law in 1870, the butchers appealed to the federal courts. The high court heard oral arguments in 1872. Their 5–4 decision, written by Justice Samuel F. Miller, upheld the state-court decision, but his *obiter dicta* dealt a major blow to federal enforcement of civil rights by construing the Fourteenth Amendment's protection of "privileges and immunities" extremely narrowly. In effect the court held that states retained the principal responsibility for protecting civil rights, particularly those that had traditionally been guaranteed by state constitutions.[16]

The announcement of the decision excited attention in New Orleans over the next few months. R. H. Marr and E. John Ellis, the New Orleans defense attorneys for the nine white paramilitaries charged in the federal case growing out of the battle at Colfax, immediately seized upon the legal reasoning in *Slaughterhouse*. They argued against their clients' indictment by denying the constitutionality of the 1871 Enforcement Act under which they had been charged. In the first Colfax trial, begun in February 1874 and held in New Orleans, the jury acquitted one of the defendants and declared a mistrial for the other eight. The federal prosecutor, J. R. Beckwith, immediately retried the other eight and won conviction of three defendants on conspiracy charges. Marr then appealed in the federal courts to quash the indictments, citing the *Slaughterhouse* verdict as precedent. On June 27 Justice Joseph Bradley agreed with Marr's argument, voided the indictments, and set in motion the legal journey to the landmark decision in *United States v. Cruikshank*, handed down by the Supreme Court in 1876.[17]

In the meantime the gathering forces of white supremacy did not need to wait two years to get the clear message that federal prosecutions for terrorism had ground to a halt. Governor Kellogg noticed the sudden shift in white sentiment: "The opinion of Judge Bradley was hailed with the wildest demonstrations of approval; it was regarded as establishing the principle that hereafter no white man could be punished for killing a negro, and as virtually wiping the Ku-Klux laws off the statute books."[18]

Bradley's decision fanned the flames ignited by the spark at Colfax into a wildfire blaze of paramilitary mobilizations across Louisiana (see appendix 2, table 2.1). Hunger for the latest news of the Colfax trials and the growth of the White Leagues, as the paramilitary companies came to be known, underwrote a boom in Louisiana-style tabloid journalism specializing in stories of black depravity, carpetbagger corruption,

16. Ronald M. Labbé and Jonathan Lurie, *The Slaughterhouse Cases: Regulation, Reconstruction, and the Fourteenth Amendment* (Lawrence: University Press of Kansas, 2003).

17. Robert J. Kaczorowski, *The Politics of Judicial Interpretation: The Federal Courts, Department of Justice, and Civil Rights, 1866–1876* (New York: New York University Press, 1985), 141–51, 176–83.

18. Testimony, W. P. Kellogg, in House, *Condition of Affairs in the Southern States*, H. Rpt. 261, 242–68.

and white supremacist valor in battle against the inferior race. The *Alexandria Caucasian*, the first newspaper dedicated to the White League cause, published its inaugural issue on March 28, 1874, while lawyers prepared to argue the first Colfax case in New Orleans. Alexandria was the parish seat of Rapides Parish, which bordered on Grant Parish. It was also the home of Capt. George W. Stafford, the commander of the Rapides Parish paramilitary company at the battle of Colfax, who had been among those originally indicted in the Colfax case. Stafford and two other ex-Confederate officers published the newspaper. All three had served with Brig. Gen. Leroy A. Stafford (George's father), who had commanded the Ninth Louisiana Infantry and then the Second Louisiana Brigade of the Army of Northern Virginia until he was killed during the battle of the Wilderness in 1864.[19] Inspired by the battle of Colfax and emboldened by the failure of federal prosecutors to make headway in the trials and appeals of those indicted for what were, in effect, war crimes, the *Caucasian* issued a call to arms. It demanded an end to all party factionalism in order to make the election campaign in 1874 an all-out contest of race against race: "There will be no security, no peace, and no prosperity for Louisiana until the government of the state is restored to the hands of the honest, intelligent, and tax-paying masses; until the superiority of the Caucasian over the African in all affairs pertaining to government, is acknowledged and established."[20] To accomplish this end, the editors appealed to white men in every parish of the state to create their own armed companies and oust every Radical, black or white, from office in the state.

Historians who have studied Reconstruction Louisiana have sometimes stressed that the White Leagues had no central organization or chain of command. That judgment is correct, but it is also somewhat misleading if the lack of a centralized command structure is taken to mean that this made the White Leagues weak or ineffective. Much of their power to terrorize opponents stemmed precisely from this decentralized and ubiquitous nature. In rural parishes across the state, the White Leagues created a highly successful campaign of intimidation, terror, and assassination that placed a premium on the ability to assemble, strike quickly, and then disperse before either the state militia or federal troops could respond. Had the White Leagues retained a permanent high command, it would have proven an irresistible target for the Republican state government and federal prosecutors. Making a virtue out of a necessity, local league leaders decided to ruin the Radical government in Louisiana from the bottom up.

19. Freeman, *Lee's Lieutenants*, 3:237, 351; Seymour, *Civil War Memoirs*, 46–47 n. 10.
20. *Alexandria (La.) Caucasian*, Mar. 28, 1874, 1.

Across the state paramilitary companies followed a stereotypical pattern of mobilization. In the spring and summer of 1874, sensational new partisan newspapers initiated the mobilization with a steady drumbeat of propaganda. Those with a strong regional base of readers, such as the *Alexandria Caucasian*, the *Shreveport Times*, the *New Iberia Sugar Bowl*, and the *New Orleans Bulletin*, denounced local and state government by Radicals, denied their legitimacy, and called on all white men to arm themselves and assemble in mass meetings. Declared the *Natchitoches Vindicator*, "Your only succor lies in your own right arms, and you must immediately be prepared to meet any and every emergency."[21]

At these mass meetings an organizing committee drew up a simple constitution and platform for action and then nominated a slate of Confederate veterans, sometimes by vote and sometimes by acclamation, for officers. The White Leagues almost always disavowed any connection to any political party, preferring to stress the need for white racial unity above all else. Their leaders insisted that the time for political debate had passed and that the crisis of "carpetbagger misrule" demanded direct action. This had the not entirely unintended effect of intimidating the southern white community into a conspiracy of silence about the campaigns of terror that followed. Despite their disavowals of political intent, there is no question that White Leaguers understood exactly who their political friends and political enemies in the coming struggle would be. There is no record of their ever having intimidated or assassinated a single Conservative official in Louisiana or that they endorsed a single Republican, black or white, for any office. In effect, if not in name, the White Leagues became the unofficial paramilitary wing of the Conservative/Democratic Party at a time of intense political crisis.

In some parishes White League leaders kept their civilian status, but former Confederate officers took command and gave military-style orders to members when the leadership decided on direct action. In most cases the local leadership of the White Leagues was the same as the Conservative or Democratic Party leadership, though this was not necessarily always the case. In the Red River parishes J. C. Moncure of Shreveport, a local Democratic politician, assumed overall direction and advised leaders in charge of individual parish companies, such as Capt. T. W. Abney of Red River Parish, who would later played a leading role in the Coushatta massacre. In southern Louisiana parishes Col. Alcibiades De Blanc, the former commander of the Eighth Louisiana Infantry and head of the Knights of the White Camellia, became the undisputed head of White Leaguers among the white French-speaking population. Describing De Blanc's

---

21. *Natchitoches Vindicator*, July 25, 1874, 1.

charismatic sway over his men, a U.S. Army officer sent to monitor elections in Saint Martin Parish insisted, "He is an acknowledged leader of the White League, and I believe they would follow him anywhere; they would obey his orders as soldiers obey the command of their officers."[22] In New Orleans Frederick Ogden, head of the Orleans Parish Democratic Club and McEnery's militia commander at the battle of the Cabildo, acted both as a member of the Orleans Parish White League Committee and as its field commander. By August 1874, active White Leagues had organized in almost half of the state's parishes, with as many as fourteen thousand men enrolled.[23] Perhaps the most striking feature about this paramilitary mobilization during the summer of 1874 was how closely it resembled the Confederate army's mobilization in 1861. Almost overnight a popular volunteer army sprang up without benefit of either a state or the bureaucracy usually associated with the mobilization of modern armies.

The emerging paramilitary movement borrowed freely from the battle and massacre at Colfax for tactics and goals. A favorite and frequently successful opening gambit was to organize a mass rally of armed white men and issue a public ultimatum to local Republican officeholders to resign their offices, just as Captain Nash had done before the final assault on Colfax. In June 1874, armed whites began assembling at Natchitoches (just above Grant Parish on the Red River) and issued a public demand for the resignation of four Republican parish police jurors no later than July 4.[24] By that date nearly eight hundred armed paramilitaries had encamped outside of town to await word of the officials' decision. After conferring with Raeford Blunt, the black Republican state senator for Natchitoches, the police jurors decided resistance would be futile and surrendered their offices. Nash himself was reported to have been at Natchitoches during the encampment, but it is not recorded whether he offered them advice or mere moral support.[25] In Saint Martin Parish Colonel De Blanc paraded the White League company he had raised through the streets of the parish seat and then summarily demanded the resignations of the parish judge and his son for the crime of "drilling Negroes." After they resigned, Colonel De Blanc ordered them to leave the parish and never return.[26]

White Leaguers showed no compunction about spilling blood when they felt it

22. Testimony, Capt. J. H. Gageby, in House, *Condition of Affairs in the Southern States*, H. Rpt. 261, 704–5.

23. Lonn, *Reconstruction in Louisiana*, 256–58.

24. Parish police jurors in the Louisiana system of parish government are roughly equivalent to county commissioners.

25. Testimony, Raeford Blunt, in House, *Condition of Affairs in the Southern States*, H. Rpt. 261, 214–30.

26. *New Orleans Republican*, Aug. 29, 1874, 1.

necessary and the mood seized them. In August 1874 the Red River Parish White
League commanded by Captain Abney demanded that state representative Marshall
Harvey Twitchell's six family members and friends resign from their parish offices at
Coushatta after an intimidating armed mass rally in the town. Despite their resignations, members of the De Soto Parish White League assassinated all six men a few days
later after they left Coushatta on horseback. Resort to murder, however, brought un-
desired attention to the White Leagues' seizure of power, and they eventually staged
a mopping-up operation. After the federal attorney in New Orleans dispatched investigators to Red River Parish, unidentified whites lynched two black men in Coushatta, apparently to ensure there would be no hostile witnesses to their seizure of
power. Similar mopping-up assassinations also occurred in Grant Parish for several
years after the battle of Colfax, both as reprisals for testifying against the Colfax defendants in federal court and as part of the continuing drive to snuff out the last ves-
tiges of the local Republican Party.[27]

THE MAKING OF A WHITE SUPREMACIST MILITIA

In New Orleans the White League assumed its most organized form, a white militia
bent on overthrowing the Republican government in a well-planned coup d'état. Considerable information is available about the membership of the Crescent City White
League, as it was formally known, because its veterans took great pride in its accomplishments, which they celebrated in public ceremonies for decades. From their own
records a clearer composite portrait can be drawn than on probably any white supremacist group during Reconstruction.[28]

The commander of the Crescent City White League was Maj. Gen. Frederick N.
Ogden. Ogden came from a long line of citizen-soldiers. His great-grandfather, Robert
Ogden II, was a graduate of the College of New Jersey (later Princeton University) and
served as George Washington's quartermaster general during the American Revolution. Frederick Ogden's own colorful military service probably began even before secession. A document in his personal papers suggests that, under an assumed name,

27. Tunnell, *Crucible of Reconstruction*, 173–209; Testimony, Capt. Arthur W. Allyn, in House, *Condition of Affairs in the Southern States*, H. Rpt. 261, 155–56.

28. For the complete roster of the White League militia in the street battle of 1877 (which also anno-
tates members participating in the street battle of 1874), see J. Curtis Waldo, "The Roll of Honor: Roster of
the Citizen Soldiery Who Saved Louisiana," 1877 (unpublished manuscript, rev. ed. by Works Progress Administration, 1938), White League Papers, Special Collections Division, Howard-Tilton Memorial Library,
Tulane University, New Orleans. See also "List of Those Who Took Part in the Battle of 14th September,
1874," in Landry, *Battle of Liberty Place*, 234–40.

he had joined one of William Walker's filibustering expeditions in the 1850s, a failed attempt to create a new slave state in Nicaragua.[29] Volunteering for one of New Orleans's first units raised for the Confederacy (Dreux's Battalion), he fought in Virginia in 1861 and then as a major in another Louisiana battalion at the siege of Vicksburg in 1863. After Vicksburg fell he accepted a parole and exchange from the Union army, then broke his parole and raised a new Confederate cavalry regiment, which served under Nathan Bedford Forrest. After the war Ogden returned to New Orleans, where he became a merchant specializing in the cotton-bagging and tie trade. No record exists of a correspondence between Ogden and his former commander, but like Forrest he bitterly opposed black enfranchisement, serving on the Orleans Parish Democratic Committee during the wave of violence in the national elections of 1868. As a Democratic Party activist, an unusually dedicated Confederate officer, and a member of the New Orleans business class, Ogden was a natural candidate for command of McEnery's forces at the battle of the Cabildo in 1873. Creating the Crescent City White League on July 2, 1874, required him to do little more than change the name of the Crescent City Democratic Club and publish a white supremacist manifesto in the local newspapers.[30]

Historians of the South have endlessly debated the class origins of the Ku Klux Klan and other white supremacist vigilantes during Reconstruction. Dunning-era historians usually insisted, based mostly on anecdotal evidence, that lower-class whites caused the worst of the violence, a view to which even the revisionist historian Kenneth Stampp ascribed. More recently, social historians have challenged this assertion by documenting the direction and participation of upper- and middle-class whites in Reconstruction violence. The difficulty in establishing an accurate profile stems from the Klan's ritualistic secrecy and the veil of silence in the white community that concealed their identities. Hard evidence about membership in the Ku Klux Klan and similar organizations remains fragmentary at best. In contrast the White League of New Orleans kept a meticulous roster of its original membership that it published and revised in the late 1870s, which can be compared to other known records of the era, such as census records and Confederate veteran records (see Appendix 2, table 2.2).[31]

29. Letter, signed by William Walker, Dec. 28, 1856, accepting resignation of 2nd Lt. C. L. Jackson [pseudonym for F. N. Ogden?] from Walker's army in Nicaragua effective Jan. 15, 1857, Frederick Nash Ogden Papers, 1856–1910, Special Collections Division, Howard-Tilton Memorial Library, Tulane University, New Orleans.

30. Landry, *Battle of Liberty Place*, 201–4.

31. Kenneth Stampp, *The Era of Reconstruction, 1865–1877* (New York: Vintage, 1965), 199; Foner, *Reconstruction*, 431–33; Hewett, *Roster of Confederate Soldiers*; "List of Those Who Took Part in the Battle of 14th September, 1874," in Landry, *Battle of Liberty Place*, 234–40.

Confederate-veteran status is a central factor in understanding the growth and de-velopment of the violent white supremacist campaigns against Reconstruction. Ap-pendix 2 contains the names of all 111 White League officers participating in the street battle of 1874. Of those, 90 out of a possible 102, or 88 percent, can be positively identified as Confederate veterans who served in Louisiana units during the Civil War.[32] This side-by-side comparison of White League leadership and Confederate-veteran status reveals much about how white supremacists saw themselves. While not every former Rebel became an enemy of Reconstruction in the 1870s, this study strongly supports the conclusion that, in practice, the violent movement against Re-construction was led by a solid vanguard of Confederate veterans.

Among Confederate units, however, not all were equally represented, and here it would appear that overtones of class origin emerge. White League officers in the street battle of 1874 came from a total of thirty-eight different Confederate units, few of which produced more than one or two White League officers. The most promi-nently represented unit, however, was the Washington Artillery, one of the most so-cially exclusive units in the entire Confederate army. It recruited primarily from the Anglophone business community in New Orleans. All of its members volunteered for Confederate service; none were conscripts. Most joined before the Confederacy adopted a draft in the spring of 1862, and its leadership joined even before Louisiana seceded from the Union in January 1861. From this unit alone came eighteen White League officers, including Colonel Behan, commander of the Crescent City White League Regiment and a future mayor of New Orleans; E. I. Kurscheedt, a merchant who offered the use of his store for General Ogden's command post during the battle; and Colonel Walton, a staff officer for Ogden and the Washington Artillery's antebel-lum leader. No other unit provided more than five officers.

In addition to eighteen officers, a cross-comparison of the entire Civil War roster of the Washington Artillery and the roster of the White League of 1874 reveals that thirty other White Leaguers of enlisted rank served in the unit during the Civil War. This made the Washington Artillery the most prominently represented Confederate unit in the Crescent City White League, with forty-eight veterans participating (see Appendix 2, table 2.3). An aggregate total of 550 men served in the Washington Ar-

---

32. Five officers who were not Confederate veterans themselves, and probably not old enough to have fought in 1865, can be positively identified as sons of known Louisiana Confederate veterans. Four other White League officers were listed without their first names and therefore could not be positively matched with veterans records. Among the remaining nineteen names, some may have served in Confederate units in other states, but multiple entries with identical names make it practically impossible to positively iden-tify their veteran status.

tillery during the Civil War, of whom 69 died from sickness, wounds, or combat by 1865. Therefore, even without accounting for those who probably died, moved away from New Orleans, or emerged from the Civil War too incapacitated to ever fight again over the subsequent decade, more than 10 percent of those who served with the Washington Artillery joined the White Leagues in 1874. It seems that those most likely to have volunteered for a civil war to establish an independent southern nation in the 1860s were those most likely to volunteer for a civil war to overthrow Reconstruction in the 1870s. The high number of enlisted men of the Washington Artillery joining the White Leagues also supports the unsurprising but nevertheless telling conclusion that Confederate soldiers tended to follow the lead of their officers in joining the violent campaign against Reconstruction.[33]

THE STREET BATTLE OF SEPTEMBER 14, 1874

If the White Leagues had an Achilles' heel in late summer of 1874, it was a lack of the modern military weaponry they needed to win a firefight against the Louisiana State Militia. Their determination to acquire such arms led directly to the street battle of 1874. By the beginning of September, General Ogden and his staff had enrolled twenty-six companies of infantry and two improvised batteries of artillery in New Orleans, with new companies mustering every week. This force, comprising more than fifteen hundred men with impressive combat experience in both its leadership and ranks, represented a dangerous threat to the Republican militia. By late August, White League companies had begun openly drilling in the evenings in the residential streets of the capital. These men drilled without arms, not only to avoid an unplanned confrontation with the Metropolitan Police but also because most of them possessed only personal weapons, such as revolvers and shotguns, which might have been acceptable for guerrilla ambushes in the countryside but would not be effective against the state militia's modern rifles and artillery in a pitched street battle.

Alarmed by reports of White League organizing, General Badger ordered the Metropolitan Police to scour the city for weapons during the last weeks of August. His detectives searched cotton-press halls, railroad terminals, and ships docked along the levees of the Mississippi. On September 8, Metropolitan Police seized a wagonload of weapons at Camp and Canal streets. Three days later they boarded the recently ar-

33. "Roster of the Washington Artillery," in Owen, *Washington Artillery*, 437–64. Owen served as adjutant of the Washington Artillery during the Civil War and meticulously compiled battery rosters in the 1880s. A total of 550 men served in the unit from 1861 to 1865. Sixty-nine died of wounds, sickness, or were killed outright. No figures are available on subsequent deaths or debilitating illness, so the 10 percent participation rate for the street battle of 1874 is a conservative estimate.

rived ship *City of Dallas* and confiscated six crates of Springfield muskets. On the night of September 12, the *Mississippi* docked at New Orleans, and rumors raced through the city that the vessel held weapons bound for the White Leagues. The following day, September 13, Badger dispatched a force of fifty or sixty Metropolitans to seal off the levee and prevent access to the ship's cargo.[34]

Badger's campaign to deny them arms provoked the White Leagues' leadership to launch an impromptu coup d'état. The timing was not ideal, for their goal had been to topple the Radical government on the eve of the November elections and present Washington authorities with a fait accompli. But several factors pushed them to act now. First, they had predicated their hopes of ejecting the Republicans on the continued absence of General Emory's federal troops, who were still in summer camp at Holly Springs, Mississippi, but might return any day with the arrival of fall weather. Second, they feared losing the momentum generated by the paramilitary mobilization across the state if they lost a major cache of weapons and had to postpone the planned coup to await a new shipment. On Friday night, September 11, D. B. Penn (McEnery's running mate for lieutenant governor) and General Ogden secretly met. They decided to demand abdications from Governor Kellogg and all state officials at the beginning of the following week. If Kellogg refused to resign, they would immediately order the overthrow his government by force. The operational plan for the coup called for the White Leagues to construct barricades along the length of Julia Street. This would effectively cut the city in two, with the Republican state government and its forces isolated inside the French Quarter. Within those narrow streets, the old St. Louis Hotel served as statehouse, the Cabildo on Jackson Square as supreme court chambers, and just around the corner on St. Peter Street was the site of the state militia's principal arsenal. The unexpected arrival of the *Mississippi* and the discovery of its cargo by Badger's Metropolitans forced the coup plotters to advance their timetable again. Later that night (September 12) the White League leaders decided to stage a mass rally the following Monday, seize their weapons from the Metropolitans aboard the *Mississippi*, and forcibly occupy all the state government buildings in the French Quarter. At midnight White League companies distributed their existing stocks of weapons at Leeds Foundry on Joseph Street in the American Quarter.[35]

The plan, while conceived in haste, represented a significant advance over Og-

34. Testimony, James Buckner, in House, *Condition of Affairs in the Southern States*, H. Rpt. 261, 670.

35. Davidson B. Penn, interview, *New Orleans Times*, Sept. 23, 1874, 1; Testimony, A. S. Badger, in House, *Condition of Affairs in the Southern States*, H. Rpt. 261, 400.

den's abortive putsch the previous year. This time the conspirators left fewer details to chance. Among Governor Penn's staff officers was Maj. E. A. Burke, the local agent for the New Orleans, Chicago, and St. Louis Railroad. Burke hatched an ingenious scheme to control the return of Emory's federal troops by arranging for their train to move slowly and spend hours stopped on sidings awaiting fuel and water. If all went as he planned, the soldiers might not be able to return to the city in force until several days after a new government had been fully installed.[36] Ogden assigned a White League company, commanded by Capt. Frank McGloin, the mission of capturing City Hall on Lafayette Square intact just before the main attack began and cutting the telegraph lines to all the Metropolitan Police precinct stations. This would make it harder for Louisiana State Militia leaders to sound a general alarm or track the movements of the White Leagues within the city. On Sunday broadsheets printed by the conspirators' favorite newspaper, the *New Orleans Bulletin,* saturated white neighborhoods in New Orleans in preparation for Monday's mass meeting. It advised merchants to close their stores that day to support the mass meeting and clear the streets, helping limit the possibility of property damage and friendly casualties.[37]

The atmosphere on Canal Street on the morning of September 14 was electric. By 11:00 A.M. a crowd started to gather along the storefronts near a statue of Henry Clay for the afternoon rally. At noon Penn emerged from the Boston Club (the most exclusive social club in the city) and made his way through a throng of well-wishers to his headquarters at 58 Camp Street. Once in his office he signed three proclamations as "acting governor" of Louisiana, which justified the coup and set it in motion.[38] The first, addressed to "the People of Louisiana," denounced Governor Kellogg for "usurping" the legal state government and demanded his immediate abdication. The second appointed General Ogden as the provisional commander in chief of the state militia and called upon all Louisianians to arm themselves and come to the defense of Penn's

36. Maj. E. A. Burke, one of the most enigmatic figures of Reconstruction and Redemption Louisiana, claimed before the congressional committee sent to investigate Louisiana in 1875 that he was not a member of the White League. He did not deny his role in the events of September 14, but he stopped testifying and invoked his Fifth Amendment privileges when directly asked by committee attorneys whether he had ever provided military arms to the White Leagues. See Testimony, E. A. Burke, in House, *Condition of Affairs in the Southern States,* H. Rpt. 261, 653–60.

37. *New Orleans Bulletin,* Sept. 13, 1874,1; Testimony, A. S. Badger, in House, *Condition of Affairs in the Southern States,* H. Rpt. 261, 404.

38. D. B. Penn claimed to be acting governor of Louisiana based upon his presumption of the de jure election of John O. McEnery in 1872 and McEnery's absence from the state on September 14, 1874. Penn did not testify before the congressional committee investigating Louisiana in 1875, probably because he feared prosecution under the Enforcement Act of 1871.

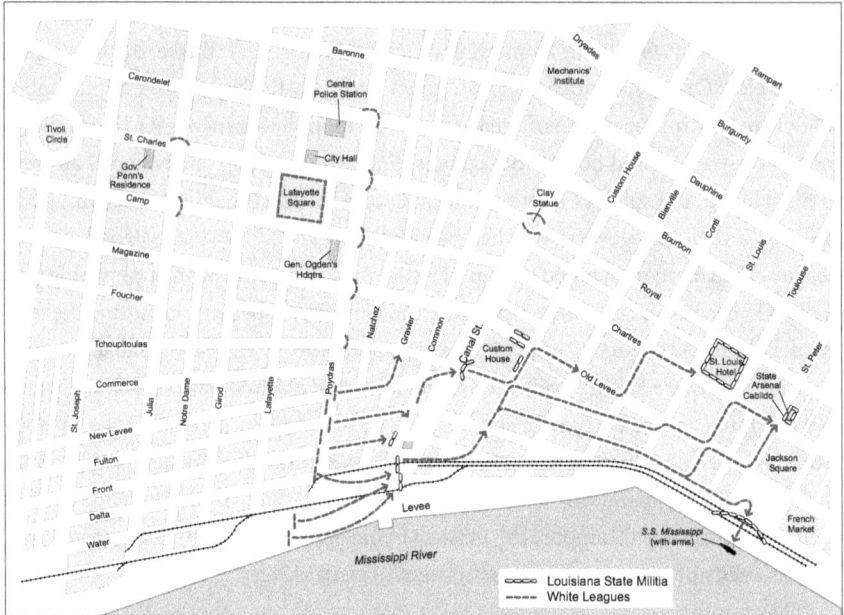

The Street Battle of 1874

government. The third was a carefully worded appeal "to the colored people of Louisiana" denying any intention of harming them or their rights.[39]

By the time Penn signed his proclamations, General Ogden had already taken up residence at his own headquarters in Kurscheedt and Bienvenue's store, also on Camp Street. White League companies across the city had been sequestered in their meeting rooms all morning, tensely awaiting orders. While they waited for the mass rally to begin, Ogden's staff decided at the last moment to move their defensive line forward from Julia to Poydras Street, bringing them to within a block of Canal Street and the U.S. Custom House. By 2:00 P.M., even before the rally began, companies of White Leaguers began barricading Poydras from the Mississippi levee to St. Charles Avenue with overturned street cars, excavated iron street crossings, and a colorful mélange of furniture, mattresses, and bales of cotton. To some observers New Orleans had assumed the appearance of Paris under siege during the Franco-Prussian War.[40]

At 11:30 A.M. R. H. Marr, the lead attorney for the Colfax defendants, and a com-

39. D. B. Penn, "Proclamation to the People of Louisiana," Sept. 14, 1874; Penn, General Orders No. 1, Sept. 14, 1874; and Penn, "To the Colored People of the State of Louisiana," Sept. 14, 1874, White League Papers.

40. "Fourteenth September—Official Report of General Fred. N. Ogden," Sept. 17, 1874, White League Papers; Testimony, A. S. Badger, in House, *Condition of Affairs in the Southern States,* H. Rpt. 261, 400.

mittee of dignitaries mounted the steps of the Clay statue in the center of Canal Street. Before an estimated crowd of between two thousand and five thousand mostly angry white men, Marr repeated "Acting Governor" Penn's objections to Kellogg's "usurpation" and demanded his resignation to prolonged cheers. By popular acclamation the crowd endorsed his proposal to send a committee to the statehouse to demand Kellogg's "immediate abdication." Marr and his committee left immediately, advising the crowd to wait for their return. After an hour they returned with the news that the governor had snubbed them with only the most perfunctory notification sent through a subordinate that he would not communicate with them. Kellogg warned them that he regarded the presence of large numbers of armed men in the streets as a "menace." To a chorus of shouts and applause, Marr exhorted the crowd to overthrow the Radical government, urging them to go to their homes, get their weapons, and reassemble back at Clay's statue by 2:00 P.M. to express the popular will of white Louisiana.[41]

As Marr spoke, General Longstreet and his lieutenants met in the statehouse to decide on a plan of action. Since Captain McGloin's White Leaguers had already seized City Hall and cut the telegraph lines to police precinct stations, Longstreet did not know that only a block beyond the tumultuous crowd on Canal Street, well-armed and disciplined White League companies had assembled behind a line of barricades. In what must have seemed at the moment to be a simple and reasonable plan, the general decided to split his forces into two. Suspecting the White Leaguers would attempt to mob the statehouse and Jackson Square, he left a defensive force consisting of all the black militia he could muster (around 475) in the vicinity of the capitol under the command of Major General Campbell and Brigadier General Barbour. The remaining force of 500 men, consisting of the best-armed companies from the Metropolitan Brigade along with its artillery and cavalry under General Badger's command, would march from Jackson Square to Canal Street on either side of the Custom House. From there they planned to disperse Marr's rally, fan out to prevent any reassembly, and then methodically reoccupy the city above Canal Street.[42] At that moment Governor Kellogg, in a show of exceptionally bad political judgment, decided to remove himself from the statehouse. Rather than stay in the governor's office, he took up residence inside the U.S. Custom House on Canal Street, which offered the sanctuary of federal sovereignty and the protection of a small detachment of U.S. troops.[43]

41. *New Orleans Bulletin*, Sept. 14, 1874, reprinted in House, *Condition of Affairs in the Southern States*, H. Rpt. 261, 800–801.

42. "Longstreet's Statement," reprinted in *New Orleans Daily Picayune*, Oct. 20, 1874, 4; Testimony, A. S. Badger, in House, *Condition of Affairs in the Southern States*, H. Rpt. 261, 400.

43. Testimony, W. P. Kellogg, ibid., 242–68.

The firefight on Canal Street between the Louisiana State Militia and the White League lasted less than sixty minutes. After marching to Canal Street, General Badger ordered his cavalry to read the riot act to the taunting crowd of whites lining the thoroughfare and then clear the street north of the Custom House toward the Clay statue, where Marr had delivered his address. The mounted police deployed in line and advanced until one of Badger's sergeants fell, apparently shot by an unseen sniper from one of the buildings along the street. This temporarily halted the Metropolitans' advance. At that moment of confusion, a messenger arrived warning Badger and Longstreet that White Leaguers had been spotted moving down the levee toward the foot of Canal Street. Longstreet ordered Badger to wheel his troops about and deploy in a blocking position to the south to prevent being outflanked. Ordering two Napoleon field guns and a Gatling gun into action, the Metropolitans established a dangerously exposed position in the middle of Canal Street close to the levee. No sooner had this battery set up than it opened fire on White Leaguers furtively advancing from behind the thousands of cotton bales scattered along the levee. Two White League companies returned heavy fire on the Metropolitans, killing or wounding all but four of the men in the exposed battery. Seeing the carnage and watching his troops begin to retire toward the Custom House, Badger tried to rally his Metropolitans, but at that moment his horse was shot from under him and he pitched to the ground, riddled by gunshots and nearly bleeding to death.[44]

Sensing that the Republican militia had begun to waver, Colonel Behan, commanding five companies of White Leaguers at the foot of Poydras, ordered a charge down the levee and then wheeling up Canal Street. For what was perhaps the last time in American history, the troops let out a rebel yell and attacked at a run. In panic the Metropolitans' ordered ranks broke down, and men scattered in all directions. Some made their way into the safety of the Custom House. Others ran back to the statehouse on Royal Street. Still others fled deeper into the French Quarter until they reached the relative safety of the state arsenal off Jackson Square. In the crossfire Longstreet had been thrown from his horse, badly reinjuring his right arm, which had been wounded during the battle of the Wilderness in 1864; he had to be carried into the safety of the Custom House. Curiously, and at about the same time, General Ogden also fell from his horse as he tried to make his way down Canal Street after leaving his headquarters to see what was happening.[45]

The loss of both Generals Badger and Longstreet, not to mention the untimely dis-

---

44. Testimony, A. S. Badger, ibid., 400.

45. *New Orleans Bulletin-Supplement*, Sept. 22, 1874, 1.

appearance of Governor Kellogg, utterly demoralized the militia. A large White League detachment raided the huge cache of weapons aboard the *Mississippi,* and smaller groups ransacked the militia arsenals and police stations across city.[46] By the end of the day, the White Leaguers were much better armed than they had been that morning, and their numbers had swelled with new volunteers excited by Marr's call to arms. They were in firm command of most of the city, advancing patrols across Canal Street into the French Quarter and occupying all state buildings and police stations except for the statehouse and the arsenal. Republican officeholders, Metropolitans, and militia crammed into the statehouse, a formidable defensive position, but they were uncertain of what to do next. Several of the toughest young Metropolitan officers barricaded themselves and some two hundred militia inside the arsenal, secure in the knowledge that its massive walls would be costly for the White Leaguers to assault. Unfortunately, they too had a leadership problem, for their ranking officer, Capt. Joseph Lawler, had been shot in the stomach and was sinking in and out of consciousness under the influence of opiates administered to relieve his pain.[47]

Late into the night White League leaders took stock of their incomplete victory and debated their next move in an atmosphere of uncertainty. One of their major objectives for launching the coup, securing the weapons onboard the *Mississippi,* had been achieved. Governor Kellogg, however, had eluded their grasp and remained ensconced within the inviolable confines of the Custom House. They had a number of men killed and wounded, but they suspected that the Radicals' losses might be even higher than theirs. They feared more loss of life if they had to launch an all-out assault on the statehouse or the arsenal. Above all they feared Washington's reaction when authorities learned of the battle to overthrow a de facto government recognized by President Grant. They did not know, but they suspected, that Custom House officials might have already somehow contacted Washington or General Emory in Holly Springs. Even if they had not, federal authorities were sure to become suspicious when they realized that the telegraph lines to New Orleans had gone dead in the middle of another acute Louisiana political crisis.

Instead of fire, Penn and Ogden decided to call upon propaganda to win the holdouts' surrender. Once again White League printing presses turned out handbills, blanketing the area around the remaining Radical strongholds. The White Leagues now offered pardon, safe passage, and amnesty to all Republican militiamen who laid

46. Col. John Angell, letter, Sep 15, 1874, Battle of Liberty Place Papers, 1874, Special Collections Division, Howard-Tilton Memorial Library, Tulane University, New Orleans; Louisiana Adjutant General's Office, *Annual Report, 1874,* 7.

47. *New Orleans Bulletin,* Sept. 17, 1874,1.

down their weapons and went home.[48] At 3:00 A.M. patrols under a flag of truce approached the arsenal, requesting to speak with the officer in charge. They transmitted the amnesty offer and then threatened to shell the building with cannon unless the holdouts surrendered. A Metropolitan captain stalled for time by asking for permission to consult with Governor Kellogg and General Longstreet in the Custom House. White League officers granted his request, but the courier returned after an hour with word from the governor to hold the arsenal at all costs. By that time, however, Kellogg had lost the moral authority of his office as well as the obedience of his troops. His soldiers refused his order to fight on to the bitter end. Instead, following his personal example, they deserted individually and en masse, despite the protests of a few of their officers. By sunrise on September 15, the Louisiana State Militia had ceased to exist.[49]

THE MAKING AND UNMAKING OF RECONSTRUCTION MILITIAS

The street battle of 1874 and its aftermath bring the processes underlying the making and unmaking of Reconstruction militias into sharper focus. Defeat disintegrated the fledgling institution of the Louisiana State Militia. After the ignominious mass desertion at the arsenal on the day following the battle, moral disintegration accelerated. Governor Kellogg, aided by the presence of federal troops, eventually managed to reconstitute the Metropolitan Police, but not the volunteer state militia. Adding to the humiliation of defeat in the battle itself, General Street court-martialed several black militia officers for dereliction of duty. While their punishments amounted to mere administrative slaps on the wrist—each was admonished and then ordered to "resume his sword," in the pompous language of the court—these trials were especially insulting, considering the self-evident cowardice of Governor Kellogg, who fled from the statehouse before the shooting started.[50] After 1874 there is no record that any volunteer black militia company ever mustered to defend the Reconstruction government in New Orleans again. Dissatisfaction within the capital's black militia regiments reinforced growing black political dissatisfaction with the Republican state government and party. Black challenges to domination by the white leadership of the Custom House Ring afterward grew more vocal, acrimonious, and divisive.

As if the demoralization of the militia's regimental officers was not enough, the

48. "Proclamation" [signed by E. John Ellis, acting assistant adjutant general], Sept. 14, 1874, White League Papers.

49. *New Orleans Bulletin-Supplement*, Sept. 22, 1874, 1.

50. General Orders Nos. 26 [court-martial of Lt. Col. Emilie Detiege] and 27 [court-martial of Lt. A. R. Demange], n.d., in Louisiana Adjutant General's Office, *Annual Report, 1874*, 51–53.

leadership suffered key losses that proved all but impossible to replace. General Badger barely survived the battle. His wounds forced physicians to amputate his leg, and his recuperation took months. General Longstreet, also injured in the battle, was probably more hurt by the defection of nearly all of his old Confederate comrades to the other side. After the street battle he fell into a running dispute in New Orleans newspapers over whether he or Governor Kellogg had ordered the Metropolitans' advance on Canal Street, which he felt undermined his credibility as a commander. Longstreet distanced himself from Louisiana politics and in early 1875 resigned his commission.[51]

The Louisiana State Militia, born of Governor Warmoth's harrowing memories of the massacre at the Mechanics' Institute in 1866, was always a precarious organization, embodying the contested legitimacy and weaknesses of the Reconstruction state government itself. Militias had existed in America for more than two centuries by this time, but they flourished only where they had been predicated upon broad political consensus within local communities. A divided state government in New Orleans produced a divided state militia, as the 1873 struggle painfully demonstrated. Southern Republicans' attempt to create a functional interracial democracy was a radical and deeply divisive project that placed terrific stresses on the cohesion of their volunteer military forces. The state militia survived and remained a force for stabilization in the hands of flexible and wily political masters like Warmoth and Pinchback. When commanded by an incompetent leader like Kellogg, it failed and then collapsed into a ruin from which there was little chance of rebuilding.

The year 1874 also witnessed a rapid transition in the search for homegrown institutions to overthrow Republican rule. In the countryside, paramilitary action scored a series of smaller incremental gains that created a massive problem for the state government in New Orleans. It was a new brand of Reconstruction violence, which produced a kind of visceral excitement lacking in previous anti-Republican political campaigns. During the national election of 1868, indiscriminate vigilante action killed and wounded eighteen hundred black Louisianians—far more than the totals in 1873 and 1874 combined. But because earlier vigilante action had been oriented toward influencing the state's electoral votes in a presidential election rather than focused on actually seizing local power, it produced no tangible political effect and triggered forceful reactions from Republican administrations in Washington and New Orleans.

The battle of Colfax became a blueprint for the future of white supremacy across

51. *New Orleans Daily Picayune,* Oct. 20, 1874 (morning ed.), 4; and Dec. 21, 1874 (morning ed.), 1.

Louisiana because it pointed the way toward a successful strategy of paramilitary action narrowly aimed at seizing local political power and destroying the Louisiana Republican Party from the bottom up. Rather than trying to directly attack federal or even state forces, paramilitary companies seized power in a number of parishes of Louisiana's racial middle ground that had been lost to local Republicans since the implementation of the Military Reconstruction Acts. In parishes where blacks made up 80 percent or more of the population, like Concordia and Tensas, white supremacists did not even bother to try to organize White Leagues in 1874. In parishes with large white majorities, like Cameron and Ouachita, no White League proved necessary because Republicans had little prospect of winning elections there anyway. For parishes where whites and blacks stood more evenly matched in numbers, paramilitary terror became an irresistible choice to tip the local balance of power against Republicans.

Paramilitary action alone, though, could not overthrow the state government in New Orleans, as General Ogden's forces discovered at the battle of the Cabildo. Defeating a well-armed and well-led state militia while avoiding the danger of collision with federal troops required a superior force, not only in terms of size but also in lethality and discipline. The street battle of 1874 demonstrated how far Louisiana white supremacists had progressed toward the creation of such a force. Despite Marr's earnest rhetoric depicting the 1874 engagement as a spontaneous popular uprising, General Ogden's White League militia behaved more like a Civil War field army than the vigilantes of the Mechanics' Institute massacre in 1866 or even the paramilitary companies that descended on Colfax in 1873.

In several respects a case could be made that Ogden's militia was superior, soldier for soldier, to many Civil War armies, which, it should be recalled, also began their existence as state volunteer militias in 1861 before being mobilized for national service on both sides. Civil War armies retained militia-like qualities throughout the conflict, stubbornly resisting their officers' despairing attempts to transform them into standing armies like those of Europe, which nearly all professionally trained American soldiers believed to be the superior model of the nineteenth century. In 1874 the White League in New Orleans possessed an organization with the fully articulated command and staff of a Civil War field army, including a formal headquarters complete with telegraphers, staff officers, and aides shuttling messages between the various levels of command and its civil authority. Numerous sources testify to the emphasis placed by White League officers on close-order drill in the weeks leading up to the street battle. Every drill conducted by White League company officers, nearly all of whom were Confederate veterans, represented a tribute to the fundamental importance of drill that Civil War soldiers who survived the shock of first combat grew to appreciate, however grudgingly. Drill made nineteenth-century American militias more disciplined. Discipline made them more formidable in battle, more cohesive and much less likely to break under fire, as the scattering of Longstreet's force on Canal Street unhappily demonstrated. The White Leagues possessed more firepower and better weapons than most Civil War armies. Indeed the decision to attack on September 14 had been precipitated precisely by their leaders' fears that they would lose their secret cache of up-to-date breechloaders, superior to the state militia's muzzleloading rifled muskets left over from the Civil War. When the U.S. Army returned to New Orleans a few days later, the White Leaguers obeyed every command given them by General Emory except one: they refused to return the fifteen hundred modern rifles and two cannons they had seized in the surrender of the St. Peter Street arsenal.[52]

A militia the White League remained, however, and for reasons that were both political and instrumental in nature. Acting Governor Penn carefully asserted their legal status as his state militia by signing a written order appointing Ogden as field commander and empowering him to muster new companies into state service. Other orders issued by Ogden's command during the White League's brief occupation appeared on official stationery seized from the state Adjutant General's Office. The reasons for these formalities are clear enough. The architects of the 1874 street battle hoped not simply to win a firefight but to assert their legitimacy by persuading Washington and public opinion across the United States that they represented the popularly elected authority, one that could exercise all the functions of a state government in the nineteenth century, which included raising a state militia and using it to establish civil order.

Unlike other nineteenth-century American militias, though, the White Leagues possessed a special kind of zeal. They intended not only to defeat their opponents in a street battle but also to secure a coup d'état. Little scholarly literature has appeared on the coup d'état as a political technique, despite the assertion by historian Edward Luttwak that more governments have been changed by them than any other method in the twentieth century.[53] There is, somewhat surprisingly, no general military history of the coup d'état, but several general features are apparent. As British historian E. J. Hobsbawm has pointed out, coups were comparatively rare before the twentieth century and appeared, with the notable exception of Latin America, only in the most

---

52. W. H. Emory to E. D. Townsend, Oct. 1, 1874, RG 94, Records of the Adjutant General's Office, NA.

53. Luttwak, *Coup d'Etat*, 1–6. See also ibid., App. C, which gives an impressive list of successful coups during 1945–67.

modern countries with republican forms of government, such as France. Only the centralization and growth of military power characteristic of modern bureaucratic/ technocratic states in the nineteenth century, combined with the organizational skills of a trained officer corps, has even made the sudden overthrow of governments possible. This confluence of trends helps explain why a wave of coups in the First World in the first half of the twentieth century preceded a similar wave in the Third World after 1945.[54] Much of the ineptness of white supremacist attempts to overthrow the Louisiana government before 1874 can be explained by the absence of domestic examples upon which the plotters might have drawn. What they knew about undertaking a successful coup was essentially the halting product of their own failed efforts.

While the coup d'état of 1874 ultimately proved unsuccessful because federal troops intervened and reversed it, the White Leagues learned many technical lessons that would prove valuable in the near future. First, their careful preparations, including the early seizure of the Metropolitans' telegraph lines and Major Burke's sabotage of the railroads, confirmed the importance of a well-organized plan to paralyze the communications and transportation network in the city. This crippled the capacity of both the state militia and the federal army to prevent the coup, even after they saw it coming. The day before the fighting, General Emory had actually received reliable intelligence from within New Orleans claiming that an armed clash was "inevitable," but he could not move his troops fast enough to prevent it.[55] Success in isolating New Orleans gave the White Leagues time to finish off the remnants of the state militia early on the day after the coup and then formally install Penn as acting governor at the statehouse before federal troops arrived.

Second, the street battle of 1874 taught a bitter lesson for future plotters about the relationship between using violence and gaining power. Historically, the most successful coups have been those in which comparatively little bloodshed occurs. Ideally, instigators do not act until their potential opposition has been neutralized, intimidated, or subverted. A badly organized coup attempt is likely to either collapse altogether or lead to undesirable consequences. When Spanish army generals abruptly moved to overthrow the Loyalist government in 1936 without first gaining a full consensus of the military leadership, they ignited the very social revolution that they

54. Eric J. Hobsbawm, *Age of Extremes: The Short Twentieth Century, 1914–1991* (London: Michael Joseph, 1994), 348. See also Malaparte, *Technique du Coup d'Etat*. Malaparte emphasizes the fragility of the modern state and its susceptibility to overthrow by extreme political factions in times of general crisis or instability.

55. Telegram, Maj. Gen. Irvin McDowell to Lt. Gen. William T. Sherman, Sept. 13, 1874, RG 94.

feared and brought on a much wider and larger conflict that became the Spanish Civil War.[56]

The spectacular and deadly violence of the street battle of 1874 drew national attention to political affairs in Louisiana yet again. After reports of pitched gun battles in the streets leaving dozens dead or wounded, President Grant could hardly acquiesce in the overthrow of a state government he had publicly recognized, whatever private reservations he may have held about its leaders. In the future, Louisiana's white supremacists would have to seek ways to organize an overwhelming display of force that made overt violence unnecessary in New Orleans by perfecting a matching set of political skills that would also make federal military intervention in the state impossible to continue.

56. Luttwak, *Coup d'Etat,* 11–12. On the complicated relationship between Spanish army generals' attempted coup d'état, the social revolution in Spain, and the onset of the Spanish Civil War, see Paul Preston, "The Making of a Generalíssimo, July–August 1936," in *Franco: A Biography* (New York: Basic Books, 1994), 144–70.

❧ 6 ❧

The Statehouse Incident of 1875

The U.S. Army Returns to New Orleans

For the White Leagues, the street battle of 1874 was a victory that felt like a defeat. Routing General Longstreet's state militia dismantled the Republican government's first line of defense against the paramilitary campaign in the countryside and destroyed its ability to put down future uprisings in the capital. Without a state militia, Louisiana Republicans could be exposed as utterly dependent on the U.S. Army for defense against future attacks. As events would soon demonstrate, the 1874 battle felt like a defeat because it provoked another large-scale federal military intervention that easily swept aside the government the White Leagues had installed.

THE ARMY RESTORES THE KELLOGG GOVERNMENT

The perspective of time has permitted some historians to see the overturning of Reconstruction as a kind of long retreat in which the federal government gradually distanced itself from the lofty ideals of the Fourteenth and Fifteenth Amendments. It certainly did not seem that way in New Orleans in the late fall of 1874. Refusing to concede anything, the Grant administration responded vigorously to the White League overthrow of the Kellogg government by sending in a powerful new cohort of federal troops. This new effort became, in effect, a full-scale attempt to reconstruct Louisiana all over again, including a surprise reappearance by the master of the state's first Reconstruction military government, Lt. Gen. Philip Sheridan.[1]

On September 15, 1874, as the White Leagues celebrated the inauguration of D. B. Penn as acting governor at the statehouse in the French Quarter with mass rallies, Grant issued a presidential proclamation commanding "turbulent and disorderly persons" in New Orleans to disperse. Late on September 17 a train bearing General Emory and federal troops finally arrived in New Orleans after ingenious delays concocted by General Ogden's imaginative aide, Major Burke. Emory enforced Grant's

---

1. William Gillette, *Retreat from Reconstruction, 1869–1879* (Baton Rouge: Louisiana State University Press, 1979).

proclamation with orders of his own. He appointed an interim military governor and commanded the White Leagues to return all state property, including the weapons they commandeered in the surrender of the state arsenal. On September 19 Emory oversaw the return of a hapless Governor Kellogg to his offices in the statehouse.[2]

Over the next few weeks the War Department ordered an impressive array of units to New Orleans to underline Grant's determination to do everything possible to shore up Kellogg's government and prevent another coup d'état. The army sent three regiments of infantry and a battery of artillery to the new occupation. The navy deployed a flotilla of gunboats anchored in the Mississippi River, complete with detachments of marines. Washington also sent mobile forces in the form of the Seventh Cavalry, anticipating more violence across the state before the November 1874 elections. New Orleans became host to the largest garrison of federal troops in the United States and assumed the appearance of an occupied city, much as it had during the Civil War.[3]

The White Leagues' leadership protested the restoration of Kellogg's government step by step, but they knew any real resistance was futile. On September 15 Penn answered Grant's proclamation with a telegram of his own, defending the overthrow of Kellogg's government but offering his "sincere loyalty" to the federal government. John O. McEnery arrived back in New Orleans on the same train as General Emory to lay claim to the governorship. He too protested the return of state offices to the Kellogg administration in interviews with local newspapers but declined to threaten resistance. Some of his White League supporters may have debated something more than verbal resistance. Just before federal troops reappeared in New Orleans, Ogden felt compelled to publish a proclamation resolving "That as a body we will not come in conflict with United States troops." Two days later his militia demobilized itself after surrendering all occupied state offices, police stations, and militia arsenals to federal officers. Trying to put the best possible face on this reversal of fortune, the *New Orleans Daily Picayune* issued its own defiant démarche: "The idea of frightening New Orleans, an old war-worn, battered and bombarded city, full of scarred soldiers and

2. Ulysses S. Grant, "By the President of the United States of America, a Proclamation," Sept. 15, 1874, in Richardson, *Messages and Papers of the Presidents,* 7:276–77; Telegram, W. H. Emory to E. D. Townsend, Sept. 17, 1874, RG 94, Records of the Adjutant General's Office, NA.; Circular, W. H. Emory, Sept. 17, 1874, ibid.; Telegram, W. H. Emory to E. D. Townsend, Sept. 19, 1874, ibid.

3. U.S. Army, *Outline Descriptions of the Posts and Stations of Troops in the Geographical Divisions and Departments of the United States* (Washington, D.C.: Government Printing Office, 1872), 233–50 [with handwritten 1875 annotations], William Worth Belknap Papers, Special Collections, Firestone Library, Princeton University, Princeton, N.J.

tried veterans, with a couple of regiments of United States troops, is a little too pre-posterous."[4]

Given the powerful new concentration of armed force and the focused attention of the Grant administration, it is not surprising that the November 1874 election passed without a major incident. But it produced ominous signs of how badly the White Leagues' paramilitary campaign had hurt the Louisiana Republican Party. The most telling indicator was the loss of Republican seats in the Louisiana House. In their first election in 1868, Republicans had won a 56–45 majority, an eleven-vote margin eventually expanded by Warmoth's creative gerrymandering and zealous pursuit of party patronage. In the January 1875 legislative session, even by the Returning Board's own partisan count, Republicans would be evenly deadlocked with Conservatives (as the opposition now preferred to call themselves) 53–53, with five elections still in dispute. Those representatives certified by the board would choose which of the disputed contenders would be seated and, by doing so, determine which party would take control over the House.[5]

The complicated electoral deadlock in the legislature was not the only sign that Louisiana politics had taken a violent turn. Emboldened by the White Leagues' open show of force in the streets, gangs of "boy regulators" began to resegregate New Orleans public schools. The usual pattern was for a group of older white boys (some of whom appeared to contemporary observers to be well beyond school age) to disrupt a mixed classroom of black and white students and demand the ejection of all children who appeared to be other than white. They accepted no refusal to comply with their demands. Even P. B. S. Pinchback's two sons, who attended one of the best public schools in the city, were subjected to this humiliation. Commented one of their tormentors, "They're good enough niggers, but they're niggers."[6]

Inflammatory editorials in the *New Orleans Bulletin,* the quasi-official newspaper of the Crescent City White League edited by two of its members, E. L. Jewell, and D. C. Byerly, egged on the school resegregation campaign. Undaunted by the removal

4. Telegram, D. B. Penn to U. S. Grant, Sept. 14, 1874, in House, *Condition of Affairs in the Southern States,* H. Rpt. 261, 1027; Gen. Frederick Nash Ogden, "Proclamation," Sep 17, 1874, Folder 2, Frederick Nash Ogden Papers, 1856–1910, Special Collections Division, Howard-Tilton Memorial Library, Tulane University, New Orleans; *New Orleans Daily Picayune,* Oct. 24, 1874 (morning ed.), 4.

5. Lonn, *Reconstruction in Louisiana,* 287–91; Taylor, *Louisiana Reconstructed,* 302–4.

6. Louis R. Harlan, "Desegregation in New Orleans Public Schools during Reconstruction," in Kenneth Stampp and Leon Litwack, eds., *Reconstruction: An Anthology of Revisionist Writing* (Baton Rouge: Louisiana State University Press, 1969), 332–33; boy regulator quoted in Lonn, *Reconstruction in Louisiana,* 357.

of Penn's government, the *Bulletin* maintained a steady drumbeat of propaganda demanding a return to segregated schools and segregated "star cars" on the city's streetcar lines. Debate over the issue turned ugly after former governor Warmoth attacked the *Bulletin's* editors in print for their rank hypocrisy. The former governor noted that Jewell and Byerly had endorsed the Fusionist platform in 1872, which pledged equal rights for blacks and whites in public accommodations. Jewell responded with a furious editorial that likened Warmoth's defense of black rights to a "dog returning to its vomit" for his quitting the Fusionists and rejoining the Republicans after the battle of the Cabildo in 1873. Warmoth had silently ignored a raft of challenges to duel while governor, but he refused to disregard another deliberate slander since he was no longer constrained by the dignity of high office. Following another exchange of mutually recriminating notes, he accepted Jewell's challenge. While preparing for the duel, Warmoth and Byerly, who had agreed to serve as Jewell's second in the duel, met by chance on Canal Street and exchanged harsh words, the editor striking the ex-governor repeatedly over the head with a cane. The two then brawled in the street until Warmoth stabbed Byerly to death with a knife.[7]

The gathering cloud over Louisiana politics further darkened due to storms on the national political horizon in the fall of 1874. For the first time since before the Civil War, the Republican Party lost control of the U.S. House of Representatives. Following the Jay Cooke and Company bank collapse in 1873, the New York Stock Market crashed, sending the American economy spiraling downward into depression. Republicans reeled under the ensuing weight of revelations about corruption in Grant's cabinet and among several of his most trusted aides. These scandals were certain to be the subject of investigations in the new session of the House, which would now be controlled by Democrats. One New Orleans Custom House official wrote to Benjamin Butler, a leader of the Radicals in the House who was fighting to keep his own seat, that "Every time a Republican standard falls north, a new impulse for mischief quickens here." Just when the Louisiana Republican Party most needed help from the national party, Republicans everywhere seemed vulnerable. When the electoral smoke cleared, Butler had lost his seat, and Louisiana Republicans an important ally in Washington.[8]

7. *New Orleans Daily Picayune*, Dec. 27, 1874 (morning ed.), 1. Prosecuting attorneys charged Warmoth with murder, but a jury trial later exonerated him. See Current, *Those Terrible Carpetbaggers*, 295–96; and Warmoth, *War, Politics, and Reconstruction*, 240–43.

8. [Col.] J. R. G. Pitkin to Benjamin F. Butler, Oct. 24, 1874, Benjamin Butler Papers, LC. On the political effect of the depression of the late 1870s on southern Republican state governments, see J. Mills Thornton III, "Fiscal Policy and the Failure of Radical Reconstruction," in Kousser and McPherson, *Region, Race, and Reconstruction*, 349–94.

Despite the shift in the political winds, Grant tried to fight back. In his annual message to Congress in December 1874, he pointedly noted the "unsettled condition of affairs in some of the Southern States," paying particular attention to Louisiana's problems. After summarizing events in the state since the disputed election of 1872, he reminded Congress that it still had taken no action to solve the continuing crisis there. He exhorted senators and representatives to adopt some plan to back a legitimate government in Louisiana, insisting that "in the event of no action by Congress I must continue to recognize the government heretofore recognized by me." In secret, though, Grant decided to send his old favorite lieutenant, General Sheridan, back to New Orleans, armed with explicit orders to investigate the situation and implicit authority to exercise whatever military powers he deemed necessary.[9]

THE INCIDENT AT THE LOUISIANA STATE HOUSE, JANUARY 4, 1875

Against this troubled backdrop, the new Louisiana legislature met in January 1875. On January 3, Republicans caucused in the statehouse, ringed by a heavily armed guard of Metropolitan Police, wrapped within a phalanx of U.S. Army infantry on full alert. Conservatives maintained their silence about their own strategy for the new session, but rumors raced through New Orleans that another attempt would be made to seize control of the state government.

The following day, January 4, capacity crowds thronged the streets surrounding the capitol building (the St. Louis Hotel) in anticipation of the new session of the legislature and the prospect of a spectacle. The spectators was not disappointed. Precisely at noon the clerk of the House began to read the roll of members certified by the Returning Board. Fifty-two Republicans and fifty Conservatives answered the roll call. In the instant the clerk finished—or perhaps just an instant sooner—Louis A. Wiltz, a White Leaguer and state representative from New Orleans, unleashed a prearranged blitz of resolutions. In swift succession Conservatives nominated, seconded, and elected Wiltz as temporary Speaker by acclamation—or so he later claimed. Even as Republican legislators shouted out objections and hurled points of order from the floor, Wiltz forcefully mounted the rostrum and took the oath from a justice of the peace who magically appeared. Without a moment's hesitation, Speaker Wiltz recognized motions for a new clerk and sergeant-at-arms, who instantly materialized from the doorways of the hall. Conservatives then moved, seconded, and voted on the five disputed seats, each miraculously resolved to the advantage of their party. Fistfights

---

9. Ulysses S. Grant, "Sixth Annual Message," Dec. 7, 1874, in Richardson, *Messages and Papers of the Presidents,* 7:296.

and a general brawl broke out as Republican legislators, who had considerable experience with such disorderly parliamentary scenarios, fought Wiltz's deputy sergeants-at-arms to exit the House chamber and force a quorum call. Metropolitan Police from outside heard the commotion and joined in the fray by attempting to physically pull Republican legislators out of the jammed doorways of the chamber.

At that point a Conservative representative had the presence of mind to move for the House to call upon the nearby troops of the federal army to restore order. Col. Phillipe Régis Dénis de Keredern de Trobriand, a dashing Civil War hero and the colorful French-born commander of the Thirteenth U.S. Infantry charged with the immediate security of the statehouse, appeared in civilian clothes to the applause of the assembled Conservatives.[10] With Wiltz's urging, a reluctant Trobriand personally ordered all unauthorized persons to leave the House chamber and, assisted by several aides, cleared the lobby outside the hall as well. Within a few minutes, to another round of applause from the Conservatives and the effusive thanks of Speaker Wiltz, the colonel departed the House, order apparently restored.[11]

This was not the show of federal force that Kellogg and the Republicans had in mind. Within an hour, fifty-two House Republicans signed a letter of protest and deposited it on the governor's desk. Kellogg in turn dashed off notes to both Colonel Trobriand and General Emory protesting the illegality of Wiltz's proceedings and requesting the intervention of federal troops to "clear the hall and State-house of all persons not returned as legal members of the house of representatives by the returning-board of the State."[12]

By two o'clock in the afternoon, bayonet rule was once again on public display in New Orleans. Trobriand, now in uniform and accompanied by squads of armed soldiers, marched back into the House chamber. Notwithstanding a torrent of protest by Speaker Wiltz, Trobriand commanded his soldiers to remove all five of the recently

10. De Trobriand was the son of a French general but became a naturalized American citizen and colonel of the 55th New York Volunteers in 1861. He rose to the rank of brevet major general of volunteers during the war, distinguishing himself in the heavy fighting at the Peach Orchard on the second day of the battle of Gettysburg. In 1866 he accepted an appointment as colonel in the regular army. See Ezra J. Warner, *Generals in Blue: Lives of the Union Commanders* (Baton Rouge: Louisiana State University Press, 1964), 121–22.

11. Colonel de Trobriand's original handwritten fourteen-page account of the incident at the Louisiana State House on January 4, 1875, along with many of the original copies of his correspondence with General Emory and Governor Kellogg (only some of which appear in the congressional investigation of the incident), are located in the Phillipe Régis de Trobriand Papers, U.S. Military Academy Library Special Collections, West Point, N.Y.

12. W. P. Kellogg to W. H. Emory, in U.S. House, *Condition of Affairs in Louisiana*, 43rd Cong., 2nd sess., 1875, H. Rpt. 101, pt. 2, 306.

seated Conservatives, helpfully pointed out to him by Hugh J. Campbell, the former state militia general. Aware that the Republicans would now reorganize the House to their advantage, the Conservative legislators solemnly followed their disgraced brethren out of the House chamber as a protest against this use of federal troops. After they left, the overwhelmingly Republican House voted to remove Wiltz and elected Michael Hahn, the former governor and a wounded survivor of the Mechanics' Institute massacre of 1866, as the new Speaker of the House by unanimous acclamation.[13]

Recognizing the gravity of the day's events, General Sheridan took personal charge of the military in New Orleans that evening. At about 9:00 P.M., using the president's prior grant of discretionary authority, he annexed the entire Department of the Gulf to his own command, effectively making General Emory and all forces in New Orleans subject directly to him rather than the War Department in Washington. He then informed Grant of developments in New Orleans and advised the commander in chief to take a more vigorous course of action in what became a famous (or infamous) message. Declared Sheridan:

> I think that the terrorism now existing in Louisiana, Mississippi, and Arkansas could be entirely removed and confidence and fair dealing established by the arrest and trial of the ringleaders of the armed White Leagues. If Congress would pass a bill declaring them banditti they could be tried by a military commission. The ringleaders of this banditti, who murdered men near here on the fourteenth of last September, and also more recently at Vicksburg, Mississippi, should in justice to law and order and the peace and prosperity of this southern part of the country be punished. It is possible that if the President would issue a proclamation declaring them banditti, no further action need be taken, except that which would devolve upon me.[14]

In reply Grant sent word to Sheridan through the secretary of war advising him that "the President and Cabinet confide in your wisdom and rest in the belief that all acts of yours have been and will be judicious."[15]

Sheridan's "banditti message," with its blunt discussion of the merits of a return to martial law, and Grant's reply, which did nothing to deny Washington's interest in such a proposal, ignited a furious national debate. Was the Grant administration

---

13. Differing partisan accounts of what actually transpired in the Louisiana House of Representatives are found in *New Orleans Republican,* Jan. 5, 1875, 1; and *New Orleans Daily Picayune,* Jan. 5, 1875, 2.

14. Telegram, P. H. Sheridan to W. W. Belknap, Jan. 5, 1875, RG 94.

15. Telegram, W. W. Belknap to P. H. Sheridan, Jan. 6, 1875, in ibid.

justified in its willingness to use force to defend Republican governments in the ex-Confederate states? Much of the reaction was predictably partisan. In Louisiana, Republicans of both races sensed that events had reached a climax, and they cheered Sheridan's uncompromising stand against White League terrorism. Hugh Campbell told a mass rally of black Republicans at Bethel Chapel in New Orleans several days later: "We are now standing at the critical point in the fortunes of Republicanism in the Southern States. The destinies of the Republican party, and with them those of the colored people . . . who have been the supporters of the Republican party, are now in the scale, and the scale is literally trembling on its balance."[16] Just as predictably, the White League's *Bulletin* attacked Sheridan and the president in blistering language, accusing Grant of aspiring to the role of an American "Caesar" and ominously predicting that "if the army and navy are prepared to support him in his treasonable designs, then is the doom of the Republic sealed and liberty is dead."[17]

In Washington, debate over the army's actions at the Louisiana Statehouse also tended to follow party lines, but the defenders and opponents of the president's Reconstruction policies did not always fall into such predictably partisan camps. In the U.S. Senate on January 11, 1875, Carl Schurz of Missouri gave his final address as senator. Schurz, who was a German refugee from Prussian repression in the revolution of 1848, a major general in the Union army, a persistent supporter of black emancipation, and an equally persistent critic of Johnson's restoration policy, could not be simply dismissed as another partisan enemy of Reconstruction. He used his final speech to the Senate as an opportunity to pillory Grant and the army in terms that proved both eloquent and merciless.

Challenging the president to justify the legality of military intervention in Louisiana's state government, he demanded to know, "where is the law authorizing United State soldiers, with muskets in their hands, to determine who is a legally-elected member of a State legislature and who is not?" He took Sheridan the war hero to task for employing roughshod tactics more suitable to battlefields than legislative halls: "Nobody respects General Sheridan more than I do for the brilliancy of his deeds on the field of battle; the nation has delighted to honor his name. But the same nation would sincerely deplore to see the hero of the ride to Winchester and of the charge at the Five Forks stain that name by an attempt to ride over the laws and the Constitution of the country, and to charge upon the liberties of his fellow-citizens." He warned the Senate of the dangers to the future of liberty if they upheld the inter-

16. Campbell, *White League Conspiracy*, 6 (Western Americana Collection copy).
17. *New Orleans Bulletin*, Jan. 7, 1875, 1.

vention of federal troops in the Louisiana House. He demanded to know, "if such things be sustained by Congress, how long will it be before it can be done in Massachusetts and in Ohio? . . . How long before a soldier may stalk into the National House of Representatives, and, pointing to the Speaker's mace, say, "Take away that bauble!'?" Finally, he connected America's growing military power and the growing corruption of the Gilded Age, a connection that came uncomfortably close to merging the two with the Grant administration's already soiled reputation: "It is not, indeed, the success of any Napoleonic ambition in this country that I fear. . . . But what I do see reason to fear if we continue on our course is this: that our time-honored Constitutional principles will be gradually obliterated by repeated abuses of power establishing themselves as precedents; that the machinery of administration may become more and more a mere instrument of "ring' rule, a tool to manufacture majorities and to organize plunder; and that finally, in the hollow shell of republican forms, this Government will become the mere football of rapacious and despotic factions."[18]

Grant's answer to Schurz's thunderous condemnation came barely two days later in a special message to the Senate accompanying his reply to a request for documents related to the Louisiana Statehouse incident. His prompt response alone suggests an acute personal sensitivity to the senator's stinging barbs, but its length and point-by-point refutation of Schurz's arguments are even more telling of just how deeply the one Union general turned Republican politician had wounded the other.

To begin with, Grant recalled in considerable detail the sordid history of political violence in Reconstruction Louisiana, beginning with the street battle and massacre at the Mechanics' Institute in 1866. He insisted that his every use of federal military power in the South had been justified by that violence, solidly affirmed in federal courts, and derived from the powers inherent in the Civil War amendments: "That the courts of the United States have the right to interfere in various ways with State elections so as to maintain political equality and rights therein, irrespective of race or color, is comparatively a new, and to some seems to be a startling idea, but it results as clearly from the fifteenth amendment to the Constitution and the acts that have been passed to enforce that amendment as the abrogation of State laws upholding slavery results from the thirteenth amendment of the Constitution." He refused to endorse the Louisiana state election of 1872, bluntly characterizing it as "a gigantic fraud," but insisted that "the great crime in Louisiana . . . is that one is holding the

---

18. Carl Schurz, "Military Interference in Louisiana" (speech in the U.S. Senate), Jan. 11, 1875, in *Speeches, Correspondence, and Political Papers of Carl Schurz*, 3 vols., ed. Frederic Bancroft (New York: G. P. Putnam's Sons, 1913), 3:123–26.

office of governor who was cheated out of 20,000 votes, against another whose title to the office is undoubtedly based on fraud and in defiance of the wishes and intentions of the voters of the State."

The president lashed out at the critics of his Reconstruction policy for their hypocrisy on voting and violence in the South: "Fierce denunciations ring through the country about office holding and election matters in Louisiana, while every one of the Colfax miscreants goes unwhipped of justice, and no way can be found in this boasted land of civilization and Christianity to punish the perpetrators of this bloody massacre." Grant conceded that military intervention "is repugnant to our ideas of government" but insisted that the real threat to liberty came, not from federal troops, but from the White Leagues. "I am credibly informed," he told the Senate, "that these violent proceedings were a part of a premeditated plan to have the house organized in this way, recognize what has been called the McEnery senate, then to depose Governor Kellogg, and so revolutionize the State government." Grant absolved his friend and old comrade-in-arms from any hint of impropriety connected with the "banditti message": "General Sheridan was looking at the facts, and possibly, not thinking of proceedings which would be the only proper ones to pursue in time of peace, thought more of the utterly lawless condition of society surrounding him at the time of his dispatch and of what would prove a sure remedy. He never proposed to do an illegal act, nor expressed determination to proceed beyond what the law in the future might authorize for the atrocities which have been committed, and the commission of which cannot be successfully denied."

Finally, in an almost querulous tone, Grant the former soldier defended the army as an institution from Schurz's charge of trampling on civil liberties. He protested that "the Army is not composed of lawyers. . . . The troops were bound to act upon the judgment of the commanding officer upon each sudden contingency that arose. . . . If error has been committed by the Army in these matters, it has always been on the side of the preservation of good order, the maintenance of law, and the protection of life."[19]

Despite the intense interest in the issue and weeks consumed in heated debate, the Senate made no headway on Louisiana. Acrimonious debate over Schurz's resolution continued until February 1, 1875, when it was finally tabled. Republican senators then tried to use Pinchback's reelection by the Louisiana Senate to a U.S. Senate seat as a way to revive the issue of congressional support for the Kellogg government

19. Ulysses S. Grant, "Special Message to the Senate of the United States," Jan. 13, 1875, in Richardson, *Messages and Papers of the Presidents*, 7:305–14.

in a different way. Sen. O. H. P. Morton of Indiana opened the new debate on February 15, arguing vigorously on behalf of Pinchback's credentials. Democrats counterattacked over the next two days, stalling all action and forcing the Republicans to retreat on February 17, when they conceded defeat and tabled their resolution approving Pinchback's nomination.[20]

Perhaps not surprisingly, the House of Representatives provided the impetus to substitute political compromise in exchange for continued military intervention in Louisiana. To a greater extent than in the Senate, House Republicans could feel time running out to strike a bargain with Democrats before the opposition took the reins of power in the new Congress. Stalwart Republicans like Benjamin Butler acknowledged the changing political wind and hastened to propose a package of measures to shore up Reconstruction, including a new civil rights bill, a new enforcement act, and an unusual two-year army appropriations bill designed to prevent incoming Democrats from tampering with the military's constabulary role before the presidential election of 1876. Out of this same milieu of frantic consolidation emerged a final effort to bolster the sagging Kellogg government in Louisiana.

In December 1874, responding to Grant's plea in his annual message for a definitive congressional policy, the House leadership had authorized a committee of seven to investigate Louisiana, with a subcommittee of three authorized to take testimony in New Orleans. The subcommittee's report, to the consternation of House Republican leaders, stated that the 1874 Louisiana election had been free, fair, and returned a Conservative majority in the lower house. Dissatisfied, the Republican leadership authorized the entire select committee, chaired by George F. Hoar but effectively led by William Wheeler of New York, to return to New Orleans and review Louisiana's tangled affairs since the 1872 election.

While Wheeler and his colleagues spent three weeks hearing witnesses, collecting documents, and producing a massive report, with published testimony running to more than a thousand printed pages, their entire investigation was in some respects a sideshow to their real goal, which was to broker an armistice between Louisiana Republicans and Conservatives. For this mission Wheeler was in one respect uniquely qualified. While Governor Kellogg had been a U.S. senator, he and Wheeler had worked together in the negotiations for the Texas and Pacific Railroad bill, which

20. Lonn, *Reconstruction in Louisiana*, 330–32.

sought to give the South its own transcontinental railroad line. The Texas and Pacific bill included a provision for construction of a three-hundred-mile branch line through Louisiana, terminating at New Orleans. Wheeler and Kellogg had grown personally close during these negotiations, and there is impressive circumstantial evidence that their relationship sprang from more than just friendship or party allegiance. Governor Kellogg and other members of the Custom House Ring were prominent stockholders in the New Orleans, Baton Rouge, and Vicksburg Company, chartered in 1869 and authorized to construct the Louisiana branch line connected to the Texas and Pacific. By 1875 the railroad had yet to lay a single mile of track, and its stock was essentially worthless, but if the Texas and Pacific bill became law, its provision for outright federal land grants and federally guaranteed bonds promised to make the company's shareholders wealthy men. Negotiating the final passage of the Texas and Pacific bill, however, required the cooperation of legislative statesmen more devoted to the fruits of future compromise than to the dictates of past principles.[21]

Governor Kellogg proved himself to be just such a man. From the moment Wheeler arrived in New Orleans, Kellogg cultivated his old friend (Conservative business leaders from New Orleans did too, it should be noted) and made it clear he wanted a compromise that would keep him in office for the rest of his term, whatever it might cost the state party. Wheeler obliged with a leading line of questioning during Kellogg's testimony before the congressional subcommittee, prompting the following exchange:

> WHEELER: Do you think there is any solution of the legislative difficulty except with the legislature itself?
> KELLOGG: I think that if this committee would determine who constitute the lower house, their decision would be accepted.[22]

The outlines of what became known as the Wheeler Compromise emerged in the first week of February, while the Hoar Committee was still taking testimony in New

21. For the Hoar Committee's report, see House, *Condition of Affairs in the Southern States*, H. Rpt. 261. On Wheeler's relationship with Kellogg, see James T. Otten, "The Wheeler Adjustment in Louisiana: National Republicans Begin to Reappraise Their Reconstruction Policy," *LaH* 13 (Fall 1972): 361–62. On Kellogg's personal financial stake in the Texas and Pacific Railroad, see C. Vann Woodward, *Reunion and Reaction: The Compromise of 1877 and the End of Reconstruction* (New York: Little, Brown, 1951), 88–89. Woodward refers to the charter for the Louisiana branch line as "unabashed jobbery" and notes that Kellogg's fellow carpetbagger and fellow U.S. senator from Louisiana, J. R. West, was one of the original incorporators of the Texas and Pacific as well as the chairman of the Senate Railroad Committee.

22. Testimony, W. P. Kellogg, in House, *Condition of Affairs in the Southern States*, H. Rpt. 261, 255–56.

Orleans. It consisted of three agreements, each of which had to be ratified by caucuses from both state parties in order to take effect. The first part called for the electoral returns of the Louisiana House elections of 1874 to be submitted to the Hoar Committee for final adjudication. All sides implicitly understood the committee would return a Conservative majority. The second part called upon Conservative senators to rejoin the Kellogg legislature and ratify the arrangement in an extra session the governor would call specifically for that purpose. The third part of the agreement required the new legislature to pledge not to make another attempt to overthrow or impeach Governor Kellogg.[23]

Factions emerged in both parties opposed to any hint of compromise. On February 6 a mass meeting was held at the Clay statue on Canal Street resembling the one held by R. H. Marr just before the street battle of 1874. Ogden, McEnery, and Penn all spoke before a crowd estimated at more than seven thousand, probably consisting of many White Leaguers. They denounced the Wheeler Compromise in a resolution as an "ignominious surrender" of the principles of white supremacy and white government. They nearly prevented a compromise. The Conservative caucus approved the compromise by only the narrowest of possible margins, 34–33, on February 24.[24]

In the Republican caucus black politicians took an early and consistent opposition to the Wheeler Compromise. C. C. Antoine, the black lieutenant governor and president of the Senate, denounced the agreement when its supporters broached the subject. Pinchback, mindful that his own election to the U.S. Senate still remained up in the air, objected on the grounds that the effect of a local deal would be "sure to denationalize the Louisiana question." Other black politicians studied the disputed election returns and concluded that a Conservative majority in the House could only be manufactured at the expense of black voters and black legislators.[25]

Assembling the components of the Wheeler Compromise took a few weeks, and the delay probably served to undermine some of the opposition. The members of the Hoar Committee left New Orleans in the first week of February and reconvened in March to deliberate over the 1874 returns at the New York law office of one of its members, William W. Phelps. In the interim each side made a number of attempts to amend the original terms of the agreement, all of which Wheeler refused. Deliberations over the election returns remained secret, and Wheeler kept his own counsel until he returned to New Orleans to announce the results to the Republican caucus

---

23. Otten, "Wheeler Adjustment," 361–62; Lonn, *Reconstruction in Louisiana*, 359–79.

24. *New Orleans Bulletin*, , Feb. 6, 1875 (evening ed.), 1.

25. Pinchback quoted in Lonn, *Reconstruction in Louisiana*, 374.

preparing for the extra session. On April 13, 1875, Kellogg, Wheeler, and the Republican State Central Committee met in the rotunda of the Capitol with the Republican legislative caucus to announce the adjusted roll call for the House. Wheeler informed the members that the new House would contain sixty-three Conservatives and forty-seven Republicans. The following day, as planned, the House assembled, and the clerk read Wheeler's revised roll of members. The Louisiana Senate also convened, with all Conservative members present as well. Only the election of an old Democrat, E. D. Estillette, as Speaker a few days later over the White Leagues' favorite, Louis Wiltz, produced any surprise in the consummation of Wheeler's Compromise.[26]

Pinchback and Antoine proved correct in their charges that the Wheeler Compromise would be made at the expense of black Louisianians. In 1872, Louisiana elected thirty-eight black state representatives, the highest number to hold office during Reconstruction. By 1874, even with a Returning Board dominated by Republicans, that number had dropped to twenty-nine. Under the Wheeler Compromise, there were to be just twenty black members in the House, close to a 50 percent reduction since Pinchback handed over the governorship to Kellogg. In addition to the loss in numerical strength, there was also the crippling loss of political influence in legislative committees since a Republican surrender of the House to the Conservatives meant that every black committee chairman would be unseated. A brief analysis of the specific black House seats lost from 1872 to 1875 also reveals that most of the losses came from parishes with significant White League activity in 1874, ample demonstration of how paramilitary terror in the countryside was being directly transformed into political power in the capital.[27]

THE ARMY'S RETREAT FROM RECONSTRUCTION

Buried amid the spectacle of charges that a militarized Grant administration had subverted American democracy with bayonet rule was the fact that Sheridan had pointedly offered the president the option to choose a more aggressive military policy against escalating white supremacist violence in the South. In his "banditti" message to Washington, he had actually gone beyond endorsing General Emory and Colonel Trobriand's use of federal troops to sort out the chaos of the Louisiana House. Sheridan had proposed that the federal government might sanction trials by what he termed "a military commission." Congress had taken the first steps toward federal pro-

26. Otten, "Wheeler Adjustment," 361–62.

27. See the appendices listing black members in each legislative session during Reconstruction in Vincent, *Black Legislators*, 228–35.

tection of civil and political rights in the Enforcement Acts, but Grant had chosen to suspend the writ of habeas corpus and deploy the army to quell the Ku Klux Klan's uprising only in South Carolina's upcountry in 1871 and 1872.[28]

Other actions by Sheridan after the statehouse incident reveal that he had been willing to abandon the army's peacekeeping role and embark on a much more aggressive strategy to stamp out White League terrorism. On January 12 the general sent a confidential message in cipher to the secretary of war asking him to send Secret Service funds by wire. The following day the War Department sent Sheridan a draft, also by confidential wire, for a thousand dollars. No one in the Grant administration ever spoke publicly about this, but both the action and the context of Sheridan's request suggests that he and Washington officials considered, at least for a few weeks, the possibility of creating a network of paid informants in the White Leagues who might help the general demolish the organization from within. Such actions might also have prepared the path for a series of successful courts-martial along the lines Sheridan had suggested to the president.[29]

In the end the prospect of a vigorous counterinsurgency strategy did not materialize. Grant appeared stunned by the popular wave of reaction against the military's actions in New Orleans and became defensive and vacillating by turns. Public attacks like those by Schurz made him even more determined that Congress should share some responsibility for policy on Louisiana and, by extension, Reconstruction as a whole.

Sheridan's proposal for more aggressive action also appears to have been out of step with shifting sentiment among the army's generals. A few weeks after the statehouse incident, Sheridan ordered Emory relieved as the local military commander, confidentially citing the need for more vigorous leadership to the War Department. While Emory made no public protest over his dismissal, he did write a long and bitter letter to Commanding General William T. Sherman in which he sought to vindicate his conduct by noting that Sheridan had been present and concurred in every one of his command decisions during the crisis. Emory retired from active duty the following year.[30]

A review of the careers of all the generals who commanded in Louisiana from 1865

---

28. Lou Falkner Williams, *The Great South Carolina Ku Klux Klan Trials, 1871–1872* (Athens: University of Georgia Press, 1996).

29. Telegram, P. H. Sheridan to W. W. Belknap, Jan. 12, 1875, RG 94; Telegram, E. D. Townsend to P. H. Sheridan, Jan. 13, 1875, ibid.

30. Maj. Gen. William H. Emory to Maj. Gen. Edward D. Townsend, Mar. 27, 1875, ibid. Sheridan had actually decided to replace Emory before the incident of January 4, 1875. See Telegram, P. H. Sheridan to W. W. Belknap, Jan. 2, 1875, ibid.

to 1877 helps explain how mounting professional hazards associated with such Reconstruction assignments turned army generals from supporters to opponents of such peacekeeping missions (see appendix 3). Over the course of the decade following 1865, this general-officer attrition produced an effect parallel to what political historians have described as a "retreat from Reconstruction." The persistent administrative turbulence meant that generals stayed in command on average less than a year, making it difficult for them to master the intricacies of local politics. This also created a kind of vicious cycle of replacement, crisis, relief, and interim assignment that repeated itself throughout Reconstruction.

Twenty-two generals commanded at one time or another in Reconstruction Louisiana. Of these, nine, or almost half, suffered politically motivated replacement, a surprisingly high rate of attrition (nine others left on bureaucratic transfers, two left by other routine transfers, and two died). Indeed, this demonstrates that occupation and constabulary duty in Louisiana became a sort of graveyard for the careers of a surprising number of army generals. The extent to which this attrition moved the officer corps against supporting Reconstruction is difficult to precisely gauge, but its overall effect is unmistakable. Reconstruction duty, simply put, was as professionally hazardous to a general's career as combat command during the Civil War. It is little wonder, therefore, that in the decade after the implementation of the Military Reconstruction Act of 1867 that the officer corps's support for Reconstruction policies waned. By the late 1870s few if any generals felt inclined to continue to support a frustrating, inconclusive, and politically controversial mission. Those likely to succeed Emory after his forced dismissal would not fail to read the writing on the wall.

7

The Street Battle of 1877

A Perfect Coup d'Etat

Despite its tangible diminishment of black political power, violent elements within the White Leagues refused to embrace the Wheeler Compromise. On the contrary, they extended their assent only grudgingly and then plotted endlessly for some new way to destroy Kellogg's administration. Part of their unhappiness over the idea of political compromise in Louisiana in 1875 came from the spectacle of white supremacy's violent triumph in neighboring Mississippi that year. The overthrow of that state's Republican government owed a special debt to the example of Louisiana over the previous two years; in some cases Louisiana White Leaguers crossed state lines to participate in the attacks.

Mississippi's "shotgun campaign" began with an assault against black municipal officials in Vicksburg. Aided by White Leaguers from northern Louisiana, white supremacists defeated the city's black sheriff and his posse in a minor skirmish in December 1874 and then launched a terrorist campaign in the surrounding countryside that may have claimed as many as three hundred lives. Over the following year Democratic rifle clubs proliferated across the state, followed by a number of deadly paramilitary actions. In September armed Democrats attacked a Republican campaign barbecue at Clinton, followed by a "negro hunt" in the surrounding counties in which dozens of blacks were killed or driven from their homes. Concerned that mobilizing local black militia companies would result in a full-scale race war, Mississippi governor Adelbert Ames appealed to President Grant for federal troops to supervise state elections in November. Grant's first instinct was to respond forcefully, but his cabinet dissuaded him from acting. Noting that a number of key northern states also hung in the electoral balance that year, they argued that sending troops might save Mississippi but would cost Republicans Ohio, a state they had carried in every national contest since 1856. Attorney General Edwards Pierrepont captured the growing fatigue in the national mood in a telegram denying Ames's request. "The whole public are tired out with autumnal outbreaks in the South," he said, "and the great majority are now ready to condemn any interference on the part of the government." Without the army's intervention, Democrats swept the Mississippi legislature races that November by a lop-sided margin; impeached the black lieutenant governor, Alexander K. Davis; and then forced Governor Ames to resign or face the same fate. By 1876 only Louisiana, South Carolina, and Florida remained in the hands of southern Republicans.[1]

THE RISE OF GENERAL NICHOLLS AND THE ORIGINS
OF THE BOURBONS' NEW STRATEGY

The "redemption" of Mississippi by white supremacists encouraged the White League wing of Louisiana Conservatives to emulate their example. On January 4, 1876, R. H. Marr and E. John Ellis, the defense attorneys for the Colfax paramilitaries, hosted a convention of White League Conservatives from across the state at St. Patrick's Hall in New Orleans, ostensibly to elect delegates to the Democratic national convention later that year. Their real object, according to Ellis, was not to actually overturn the Wheeler Compromise (which he claimed only adjusted the results of the 1874 election) so much as to find a way to reopen the question of the 1872 governor's election. White Leaguers hoped to unseat Kellogg in the upcoming session of the state legislature and install John McEnery as governor.

The approach to Kellogg's impeachment proved tentative. Most of the legislative session was taken up in wrangling over committee appointments in the Conservative-dominated House, a standoff on whether to allow the election of Conservative-sponsored J. B. Eustis to the U.S. Senate, and fruitless debate over a new election bill that would have jettisoned the Returning Board. On February 26 a select House committee indicted Governor Kellogg for "high crimes and misdemeanors" for mishandling the state's finances and recommended his impeachment to the full House. The House approved the impeachment resolutions on February 28 by a straight party-line vote of 61–45 and presented the resolutions to the Senate. The Republican-dominated Senate, to the dismay of House Conservatives, sat as a court the following day and summarily dismissed all charges against the governor by a vote of 25–9. Louisiana Conservatives had been frustrated once again.[2]

The accumulated frustrations of Louisiana white supremacists boiled over at the Democratic Party state convention, held in Baton Rouge over four hot days in July 1876. The location of the convention underlined the high level of disgust among rural parish leaders with the failed coup attempts by New Orleans White Leaguers, setting

---

1. Telegram, Atty. Gen. Edwards Pierrepont to Mississippi governor Adelbert Ames, Sept. 14, 1875, quoted in Kaczorowski, *Politics of Judicial Interpretation*,193. On Mississippi's "shotgun campaign," see Harris, *Day of the Carpetbagger*, 670–87.

2. Lonn, *Reconstruction in Louisiana*, 380–96.

the stage for a search for new leadership. Penn, Ogden, McEnery, and Wiltz all had support going into the convention, but they shared the disadvantages of splitting the support of the White Leagues along with the stigma of having failed to overthrow Kellogg's government. Even before balloting began, Francis Nicholls's name appeared in discussions by Conservative planters and local leaders searching for a new strategy against the Republicans. Through the first three ballots Wiltz, the leader of the 1875 parliamentary coup attempt in the Louisiana House, led the voting, but he failed to gain the required majority. Following the second ballot, though, minor candidates began to drop out. On the fourth ballot Nicholls gained enough delegates for the nomination. After his campaign manager moved to make the vote unanimous, Wiltz accepted the party's nomination for lieutenant governor.[3]

Up until the campaign of 1876, General Nicholls had played almost no role in Louisiana state politics, a factor that enhanced his appeal. The son of a parish judge, Francis Redding Tillou Nicholls was born in 1834 in Donaldsonville, Assumption Parish. He came from a family of distinguished citizen-soldiers: his father had fought against the British with Andrew Jackson at the battle of New Orleans in 1815, and both of his older brothers had commanded volunteer companies during the Mexican War. Francis graduated from West Point in 1855 but resigned his army commission after only a year to return to Louisiana, where he established a successful law practice. His career in the Confederate army was well known, heroic, and always on display. After raising a company of volunteers in Assumption Parish at the beginning of the war, Nicholls fought under Gen. "Stonewall" Jackson in 1862 and 1863. He was seriously wounded in battle twice, losing his left arm at Winchester in 1862 and then his left foot at the battle of Chancellorsville in 1863 on the same day that Jackson was mortally wounded. His wounds, however, did not interrupt his elevation in rank. In January 1863 Lee promoted Nicholls to brigadier general and command of a Louisiana brigade in the Army of Northern Virginia. In the summer of 1864 he transferred back to his native state, where he served as the chief of the Conscript Bureau of the Trans-Mississippi Department under Gen. E. Kirby Smith. After the war Nicholls resumed his law practice and became the president of the Assumption Parish Democratic Central Committee, where he acquired a reputation as a low-key leader who sometimes awarded minor posts to blacks and, at least in public, eschewed the overt terrorism of the White Leagues. While he was neither a polished public speaker nor a charismatic personality, the sight of the wounded Confederate war hero with an empty sleeve and a limping gait frequently moved Confederate veterans to unfeigned tears.

3. Taylor, *Louisiana Reconstructed*, 482–83.

After one campaign speech a grizzled and similarly maimed Confederate veteran approached him and exclaimed, "Giniral, all what's left of me is going to vote for all what's left of you!"[4]

Unlike Democrats' carefully crafted image of moderation and unity, the Republican convention produced a free-for-all that generated the bitterest discord yet in the brief but tumultuous history of the party. Even before the convention formally opened in New Orleans at the end of June, Marshal Stephen B. Packard and P. B. S. Pinchback openly feuded over control of the chairmanship. Pinchback had returned to New Orleans without his U.S. Senate seat, for which he blamed Packard and the Custom House Ring. Ex-governor Warmoth had also returned to the Republican fold and formed a new alliance with Pinchback. Together the two seasoned political veterans deployed every parliamentary scheme imaginable to prevent the Custom House Ring from dominating the convention and nominating a successor to Kellogg, who, quite understandably, had declared he was not interested in a second term as governor. All of their attempts failed, but eight days of dilatory maneuvers provided enough shouting matches, fistfights, and drawn weapons to keep an unsympathetic New Orleans press busy writing sensational stories of the proceedings. On July 3 Packard finally won the nomination for governor, and C. C. Antoine agreed to run for lieutenant governor again.[5]

It is difficult to categorize the Louisiana electoral campaign of 1876. It encompassed a number of violent incidents, but it was certainly not as violent as the White Leagues' unfettered campaign of violence preceding the 1874 election, let alone the presidential election of 1868. The results provoked charges of fraud that persisted for years afterward in both the casting and the counting of ballots, but this was hardly shocking news to Louisianians grown accustomed to the antics of the state Returning Board and the spectacle of congressional inquiries into their elections. Above all the 1876 election proved to be a climactic contest in which Republicans seemed desperately aware of the consequences of losing, and Conservatives seemed equally desperate to have Louisiana join the ranks of "redeemed" states.

Unlike McEnery, Nicholls made no rhetorical appeal to white supremacy, nor did he openly advocate violence against Republicans. Although he was nominated by a Democratic convention, he chose to run at the head of the Conservative ticket, hop-

4. Francis T. Nicholls, "An Autobiography of Francis T. Nicholls, 1835–1881," ed. Barnes F. Lathrop, *LHQ* 18 (Apr. 1934): 246–54; Ezra J. Warner, *Generals in Gray: Lives of the Confederate Commanders* (Baton Rouge: Louisiana State University Press, 1959), 224–25; unidentified Confederate veteran quoted in Henry E. Chambers, *A History of Louisiana*, 3 vols. (New York: American Historical Association, 1925), 1:691.

5. Taylor, *Louisiana Reconstructed*, 480–82.

ing to pick up the votes of Liberal Republicans, Whigs, Reformers, and even disaffected blacks. His campaign manager, the ubiquitous E. A. Burke, strove to cultivate an aura of moderation and incorruptibility around the general. There was, of course, a certain irony to this image, given that Burke later absconded to Honduras with over one million dollars stolen from the state treasury in 1889, but that event lay far in Louisiana's future.

White League–style paramilitary terror did continue (now referred to as "bulldozing"), but in fewer parishes than during the campaign of 1874. Part of the reason there was not more violence lay in the fact that the army sent more detachments (sixty-one in all) to guard federal election sites in Louisiana than it had ever done before. Nevertheless, Republican officials later produced ample evidence before congressional committees that white terrorism had robbed them of votes in at least six parishes: Morehouse, Ouachita, Richland, West Feliciana, East Feliciana, and East Baton Rouge. Interestingly, White League companies had commandeered none of these parishes in 1874, suggesting that white terrorism had not actually declined but had managed a strategic shift by moving into fresh territory. It seems that the political reconquest of white supremacy in Louisiana had settled into an incremental and therefore less visible pace.[6]

Packard, however, found himself forced by circumstances to wage a largely defensive campaign aimed at shoring up his electoral base. From the start he knew that hope for a Republican victory rested squarely upon a solid and heavy black vote, which the atmosphere of the party convention and Kellogg's assent to the Wheeler Compromise had already jeopardized. Unlike previous contests in which he had been the party's most loyal and consistent defender, Pinchback refused to campaign personally for Packard, devoting his energy to assisting individual black Republicans. Although Packard attempted to bridge the gap with black voters by endorsing an unprecedented number of black candidates for state office, the bitterness of his open feud with Pinchback lingered through the fall. Nicholls complicated his opponent's problem with black voters by waging a discrete campaign for black votes himself. Historians have debated how many blacks actually crossed party lines in 1876 (the balance of evidence suggests few did), but the unquestionable effect was to force Packard to abandon any potential effort to appeal for a broader white vote in favor of shoring up black support.[7]

6. Dawson, *Army Generals and Reconstruction*, 229–35; Testimony, David J. M. A. Jewett [secretary of the Louisiana Republican Party], in U.S. House, *Presidential Election Investigation*, 45th Cong., 3rd sess., 1878, H. Misc. Doc. 31, 1441–65.

7. Taylor, *Louisiana Reconstructed*, 483–86; Lonn, *Reconstruction in Louisiana*, 418–26; Garnie W. McGinty, *Louisiana Redeemed: The Overthrow of Carpetbag Rule, 1876–1880* (New Orleans: Pelican, 1941), 43–48.

To no one's surprise, Packard and Nicholls each claimed victory in the race for Louisiana governor. The Republican-dominated Returning Board, chaired by former governor J. Madison Wells, met in December and declared Packard the winner after excluding vote tallies tainted by terrorism, intimidation, and Conservative fraud. Conservative leaders accused Wells of fraud for soliciting a $200,000 bribe from the state's wealthiest planter, Duncan F. Kenner. They then produced their own set of election tallies, naming Nicholls the new governor. The critical novelty of the November elections, however, was not another disputed election in Louisiana but the dispute in the national election, where it appeared that the Democrat, Samuel J. Tilden, had won the popular vote but lost the Electoral College vote, 185–184, to Rutherford B. Hayes. Hayes's hope for victory, however, rested upon Republican victories in the disputed southern states of Louisiana, South Carolina, and Florida. Political turmoil once again thrust Louisiana into the national limelight.

THE STREET BATTLE OF 1877: COUP D'ETAT AND SIEGE

Louisiana Republicans prepared for a showdown with Conservative forces in New Orleans in January 1877, when the new governor would be inaugurated and the legislature convened. On January 1 Governor Kellogg ordered the Metropolitan Police to occupy the statehouse at the St. Louis Hotel around the clock. The following day the Republicans' new legislature convened with enough members present for quorums in both houses but slim margins in both chambers. The Packard House (as it became known) had sixty-six members present (sixty-one representing a quorum), and the Senate had nineteen members present (nineteen representing a quorum) for the new session. Kellogg immediately transmitted the Returning Board's findings for their approval, a legal requirement before Packard could be inaugurated. In appreciation for his services to the party and the state, the state senate elected Kellogg U.S. senator from Louisiana the following Tuesday. Incredibly, the legislature also hastily approved a $200,000 annual budget for the militia, which had been practically nonexistent since the street battle of 1874. Given that the amount approved was far larger than any other annual appropriation under any of Louisiana's Reconstruction governors as well as the chaotic condition of state finances in early 1876, the measure can only be interpreted as a desperate gamble designed to persuade Conservatives that Republicans would not surrender the state government without a fight. If so, that gamble failed miserably and only served to put the state on notice that Republicans anticipated serious trouble from General Nicholls and the White Leagues.[8]

8. Testimony, W. P. Kellogg, in House, *Presidential Election Investigation*, 634–43; *New Orleans Daily Picayune*, Jan. 5, 1877 (morning ed.), 2.

Republicans did not have to wait long. On January 8, as Packard's inauguration proceeded behind the closed doors of the French Quarter capitol, Conservatives inaugurated Nicholls at St. Patrick's Hall across town amid fanfare and public celebration; a crowd of ten thousand thronged Lafayette Square and spilled over into side streets. Conservative legislators had convened on January 1 and pledged to remain in continuous session until the federal government recognized their legitimacy. From the moment of his installation, Nicholls demonstrated a deft combination of political and military strategy that surprised and at times confused even his own supporters.

Nicholls had foreseen that his rivals would inaugurate a new government in January behind the shield of federal military protection. Any forcible attempt to oust Packard's regime, he feared, might provide the pretext that the Grant administration needed to intervene with troops and bolster support for the beleaguered Republicans. This was precisely what had undone McEnery's would-be government in 1874. Therefore Nicholls decided on what he termed "a general plan of action" to establish all three branches of his government "in a *de facto* position." After he ordered the White Leagues' overwhelming numbers to establish a fait accompli that Washington could not easily repudiate, he would then refuse to initiate "any aggressive or offensive move not actually required in my opinion for success." It was an ingenious design for a bloodless coup d'état that Louisiana Republicans might not be able to halt or reverse. It also offered the outgoing national administration no plausible rationale for ordering the army to intervene.[9]

General Nicholls's plan for a bloodless coup was more ambitious and intricate than anything previously attempted by white supremacists in New Orleans. He regarded an overt attack on Republican state forces in the streets or an assault on the heavily defended statehouse during broad daylight to be entirely too "risky." Instead he tried to create a complete and fully operational de facto government by seizing only those components not under his control before Packard or the federal garrison could react. Nicholls planned to order entire regiments of White League forces to cordon off Packard's principal supporters in the statehouse early on the morning of January 9, occupy the Louisiana Supreme Court offices in the Cabildo, and then overrun as many of the city police stations as possible. With all three branches of state government as well as the city government in his hands, he would appoint his own supreme court and city police force. After that he would need to sustain their presence until de jure recognition of his government from Washington compelled Packard to capitulate. Whether recognition would come from Grant or would have to wait on the res-

9. Nicholls, "Autobiography," 254–55.

olution of the Hayes-Tilden presidential contest could not be foretold in advance. This uncertainty demanded that Nicholls be prepared to deal simultaneously with each of three present or potential chief executives as well as the army commander in New Orleans. Executing such a complex plan would require the mustering of an even larger militia force than that used during the street battle of 1874. It would also require a diplomacy combining subtlety and intrigue in Washington.[10]

Late on the evening of January 8 and early on the morning of January 9, Nicholls set the coup in motion by signing a slew of commissions for his new government. He appointed five new supreme court justices (T. C. Manning, Alcibiades De Blanc, R. H. Marr, W. B. Eagan, and W. B. Spencer), an adjutant general and militia commander (D. B. Penn and Gen. F. N. Ogden), and an entirely new Board of Commissioners of the Metropolitan Police, who in turn immediately designated a new police chief. By 10:00 A.M. an estimated three thousand White Leaguers had assembled in formations on Lafayette Square and nearby St. Mary's marketplace. After forming up they marched off to seize their objectives and overthrow Republican rule in Louisiana once and for all.

The plan unfolded without a hitch. By mid-afternoon General Ogden's commanders reported the surrender of the supreme court and precinct police stations without a single casualty on either side. The Packard statehouse (with about four hundred legislators, Metropolitans, militia, and state officials inside) was now completely surrounded and isolated. Some state facilities fell that Nicholls had not even targeted for seizure. The Louisiana State Arsenal on St. Peter Street actually capitulated to forces sent to seize the supreme court offices in the Cabildo, supplying a new cache of weapons for additional White League companies. The coup was so thoroughly organized and so secret that former governor Kellogg later testified that he was unaware of what was happening until he was startled by the sound of men marching in the street outside his residence while he was having breakfast.[11]

News of Nicholls's coup left the Grant administration and the army in an unpalatable predicament. Ever since the public-relations disaster of the Louisiana Statehouse incident of 1875, the president had been retreating from his earlier policy of support for federal military intervention on behalf of beleaguered Republican governments in the South. In Mississippi's state elections of 1875, he had first considered

10. Ibid., 255–56.

11. See F. N. Ogden's commission as major general of Louisiana State Militia, Jan. 8, 1877 [signed by D. B. Penn and F. T. R. Nicholls], Frederick Nash Ogden Papers, 1856–1910, Special Collections Division, Howard-Tilton Memorial Library, Tulane University, New Orleans; Testimony, W. P. Kellogg, in House, *Presidential Election Investigation*, 644–45.

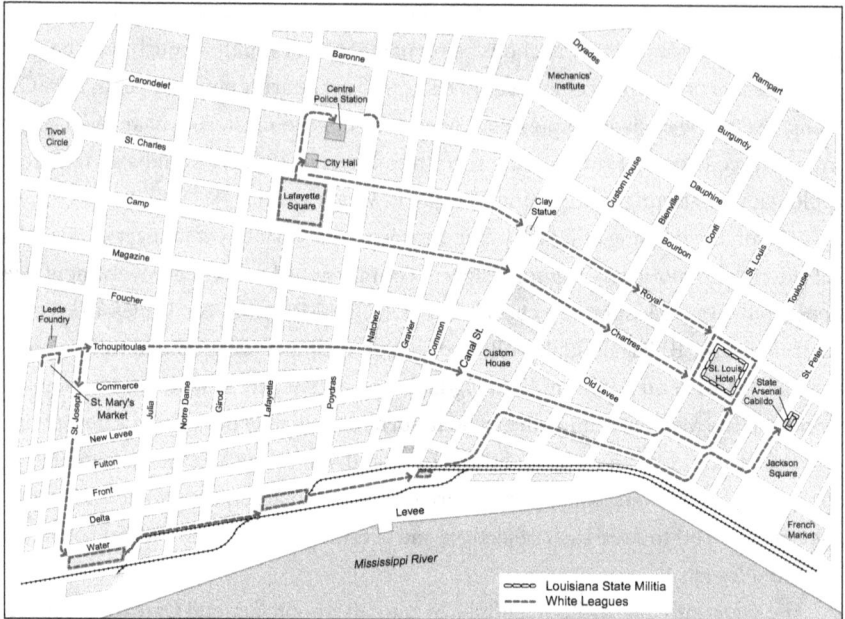

The Street Battle of 1877

and then rejected a request to send federal troops. In the fall of 1876, he had authorized the extensive stationing of soldiers to oversee federal elections in southern states. He did not, however, react forcefully when Red Shirt companies in South Carolina initiated a wave of pre-election terror, beginning with the Hamburg Massacre just across the state line from Augusta, Georgia. In a paramilitary action resembling Louisiana's battle of Colfax, white supremacists under the command of Gen. Matthew C. Butler overwhelmed a black South Carolina militia company and then executed their prisoners in cold blood. Grant reacted with a public statement filled with personal outrage in which he described the massacre as "cruel, blood-thirsty, wanton, unprovoked, and uncalled for," but he refused to invoke the Enforcement Acts as he had done to break the Ku Klux Klan in 1871–72, declare martial law, suspend habeas corpus, or order federal marshals and troops to hunt down Red Shirt terrorists. Like Louisiana, an undeclared civil war lurched forward in South Carolina during 1876, calling into question the legitimacy of its state and federal elections.[12]

12. U. S. Grant to Gov. D. H. Chamberlain, July 26, 1876, reprinted in Michael Perman, ed., *Major Problems in the Civil War and Reconstruction* (Lexington, Mass.: D. C. Heath, 1991), 537–38; Williamson, *After Slavery*, 267–70; Zuczek, *State of Rebellion*. It should be noted that the U.S. Supreme Court handed down its decision in *United States v. Cruikshank* (which grew out of the prosecution of paramilitaries at the 1873

Another factor, more pressing in the president's calculations than his growing personal distaste for federal military intervention, complicated his response to Nicholls's coup. This was the question of whether a new civil war on a national scale might erupt if Hayes became the next president over Democratic protests. Ugly rumors had reached Grant that Democratic rifle clubs and militias had mobilized across the North as well as the South to defend Tilden's popular election. In December the administration had begun taking some quiet and preliminary steps to prepare the army for the possibility of violence. Grant's use of troops during the federal elections of 1876, however inadequate it may seem in retrospect, had already triggered discussions among infuriated House Democrats about initiating impeachment hearings against him. Another incautious use of troops in New Orleans might have serious consequences reaching far beyond Louisiana.

Historians have strongly differed over how real the prospect for another civil war was in 1876–77. Some have dismissed it as little more than a Democratic bluff. However serious it may appear in retrospect, the *perception* of the possibility of renewed civil war was palpable in Washington and across the country at the time. In one protest against the Republican drive to inaugurate Hayes, the former Radical Republican turned ardent Democrat George W. Julian warned an angry crowd in Indianapolis that "[m]illions of men will be found ready to offer their lives as hostages to the sacredness of the ballot as the palladium of our liberties." Whatever the outcome of the national election, Grant did not want to go down in American history as the man who won one civil war but started another.[13]

Under these circumstances it was hardly surprising that Emory's replacement, Maj. Gen. Christopher C. Augur, reacted cautiously to the unfolding coup d'état in New Orleans. Augur, headquartered at the U.S. Custom House and commanding more than one thousand federal troops in the city on the morning of January 9, made no move to halt Nicholls's militia, though his staff officers observed and minutely reported the White Leagues' sweep across the French Quarter. Governor Packard telegrammed Grant to inform him of the coup and requested federal troops. Augur, in a long report to Secretary of War J. D. Cameron, merely recounted the events that had taken place that day, emphasizing that no violence had taken place and that he saw no need for his troops to act at the time.

---

battle of Colfax) in March 1876. This not only struck down provisions of the Enforcement Act of 1871 but also cast a chilling effect over further federal military intervention.

13. William A. Russ Jr., "Was There Danger of a Second Civil War during Reconstruction?" *Mississippi Valley Historical Review* 25 (June 1938): 39–58; George W. Julian quoted in Woodward, *Reunion and Reaction*, 110–12.

It seemed to take Grant several days to get a clear picture of what had just transpired in New Orleans, possibly waiting to see if Nicholls might make some misstep justifying military intervention. He finally responded to Augur with specific guidance five days later, on January 14. In his carefully worded telegram, the president reminded the general that it had been his policy to "take no part" in determining the rightful government of the state of Louisiana. That he explicitly left to the congressmen of both houses and parties who had come to New Orleans in December to oversee the Returning Board's count. But he did criticize Nicholls for seizing part of the government by "illegal means" and maintained that "if there be a necessity for recognition of either, it must be Packard." He did not elaborate on what he thought that necessity might be.[14]

Grant's guidance to General Augur left the rival governments with different strategic dilemmas to resolve. At the time some leading national Republicans urged Packard to break the standoff by creating an incident that would justify federal military intervention. Zachariah Chandler supposedly informed the governor that he should "die in the street" if that would create the incident permitting Grant to order the army's intervention. Packard is said to have replied to this suggestion with a heavy dose of sarcasm: "Your very polite invitation . . . 'to die in the street' is received. Owing to other pressing engagements I am constrained to decline, but would suggest the propriety of your coming to officiate in person."[15] The exchange may well be apocryphal, given that Chandler at the time was working closely with Hayes, who preferred to defuse rather than incite a crisis in New Orleans. The timing of the story's appearance in the Conservative press seemed calculated to heap ridicule on Packard's pretensions to command a *de jure* state government whose *de facto* existence had all but disappeared. Nonetheless, the exchange of telegrams, whether real or concocted, accurately reflects what might be called Packard's strategic dilemma.

Time was not on the would-be Republican governor's side. Packard was now utterly dependent upon federal recognition to legitimize his government. President Grant would leave office in less than two months, on March 5. After that Packard's prospects would evaporate because Hayes had vaguely opposed and Tilden wholly opposed further military intervention in the South. If there were to be any action by the army to restore his government, he would probably have to initiate something and quickly, whatever the hazards. For reasons that he never really explained (and even

14. McGinty, *Louisiana Redeemed*, 98; Telegram, U. S. Grant to C. C. Augur, Jan. 14, 1877, in House, *Presidential Election Investigation*, 962.

15. *New Orleans Daily Picayune*, Jan. 16, 1877.

Nicholls admitted that he could never quite comprehend), Packard shrank from seizing the initiative against Nicholls's coup. Instead he seemed content to bombard the president and northern Republicans with appeals to recognize his government and come to his aid.[16]

General Nicholls's strategic dilemma was not the mirror image of Governor Packard's. Unlike Packard, he was not barricaded inside a capitol besieged by an enemy army, but he did have to contend with serious hazards. His immediate problems were perhaps more considerable than might be imagined, given his de facto command over the capital city and much of the state. In the first few days after the coup, he could count on the enthusiasm of much of the white population to sustain him. As days turned into weeks, though, the weaknesses of an ersatz government supported by a volunteer militia would emerge. The costs of maintaining his own factious legislature in continuous session for months and a large militia force on duty around the clock would mount, particularly if it became necessary to continue until the inauguration of the new president in March. Nicholls also had to contend with the more *enragé* elements of the White Leagues. Always eager for a fight, they agitated for direct action to demolish the last remnants of Packard's government. They began complaining in New Orleans newspapers about Nicholls's apparent inertia. Grant's telegram to General Augur (which Grant authorized Augur to show to both Nicholls and Packard) suggested that some northern Republicans might welcome the prospect of just such a miscalculation by Nicholls or his followers.[17]

Nicholls responded by actively preparing for a long siege of the Republican state government on multiple levels. Alarmed at Grant's explicit preference for Packard, he dispatched Major Burke to Washington as his personal envoy on the day after the president sent his message to Augur. In New Orleans he encouraged General Ogden to expand his White League militia by enrolling new companies and regiments. A larger militia force would make it possible to rotate units on duty, dampening discontent in the ranks and allowing commerce in the city to resume even while the campaign against Packard continued. Most importantly Nicholls procured the financial support he needed to outlast and undermine the Republican government. Newspaper reports at the time declared that the white citizens of the state had agreed to a "voluntary taxation" scheme to support the Conservative government. This announcement made good public-relations copy by putting a popular face on an armed coup d'état, but it

16. Vincent P. de Santis, "Rutherford B. Hayes and the Removal of the Troops and the End of Reconstruction," in Kousser and McPherson, *Region, Race, and Reconstruction*, 417–50.

17. Nicholls, "Autobiography," 254–55; Telegram, U. S. Grant to C. C. Augur, Jan. 14, 1877, in House, *Presidential Election Investigation*, 962.

did not produce the hard cash Nicholls needed to pay his legislators to stay in session, encourage Packard's supporters to defect, and keep the militia on active duty. Other sources had to be found.

Several second- and third-hand sources confirm that both the New Orleans Cotton Exchange and the Louisiana Lottery Company provided hard cash to keep the Nicholls government operating over the next four months. Considering the Lottery's sordid reputation for corruption from the moment it received an exclusive state charter from Warmoth's legislature in 1869, it is hardly surprising that the surviving primary sources maintain a wall of silence regarding its support of General Nicholls in 1877—even after he killed the Lottery by vetoing the bill extending its charter in the 1890s.

J. G. Pitkin, who succeeded Packard as U.S. marshal in New Orleans, told a congressional committee several years later of a conversation with George Dupré, editor of the *New Orleans Democrat* in early 1877, that revealed the Louisiana Lottery's financial support for Nicholls. Dupré explained that he had been present at a lavish dinner at Moreau's Restaurant given by John A. Morris, a senior partner of Charles T. Howard, who founded the Lottery. Morris regaled Dupré with tales of how he had bribed key members of the Republican House and Senate to defect to the Conservative legislature, including such powerful black parish bosses as Henry Demas of Saint John the Baptist and T. T. Allain of West Baton Rouge. He claimed to have spent large sums of money to support the *New Orleans Daily Picayune* and the *New Orleans Bulletin* during the siege and wanted to do the same for Dupré's *Democrat.*[18]

Dupré mentioned no specific figure to Pitkin, but a number of sources suggest that between $30,000 and $60,000 changed hands early in 1877, with promises of more hard cash as needed. Given the stress of the ongoing crisis, the details of a quid pro quo were to be worked out later, but the Lottery's leadership expected a softening of Nicholls's opposition to their request to recharter. Despite explicit attacks on corrupt corporations chartered by Republicans, Conservatives tabled a bill to suppress the Lottery, and Nicholls never objected—even when one representative claimed that "Howard possessed the receipts of some of those members who got money from him." Combined with the unceasing psychological pressure of the White League siege, the Lottery's infusion of cash strengthened Nicholls's position immeasurably.[19]

While the Conservative regime worked to stabilize itself in New Orleans, Nich-

18. Testimony, J. G. Pitkin, in House, *Presidential Election Investigation*, 458. See also T. Harry Williams, *P. G. T. Beauregard: Napoleon in Gray* (Baton Rouge: Louisiana State University Press, 1955), 293–94; and Woodward, *Reunion and Reaction*, 220–21.

19. McGinty, *Louisiana Redeemed*, 104–5; *New Orleans Daily Picayune*, Mar. 6, 1877, 2.

olls's man in Washington performed masterfully. Working closely with Louisiana's Democratic congressmen, especially E. John Ellis, the New Orleans attorney who had risen to prominence as defense attorney for the Colfax paramilitaries, and Randall Lee Gibson, a Yale-educated lawyer who had commanded a Louisiana brigade in the Army of Tennessee, Burke encouraged the House Democratic caucus to threaten a filibuster of the count of the Electoral Commission. Such a parliamentary maneuver threatened to delay the presidential inauguration past March 5, possibly leaving the United States in the unprecedented situation of lacking a legal chief executive. Burke hoped at a minimum to secure Grant's continuing neutrality by emphasizing the discipline and peaceful intentions of Nicholls's forces. From Hayes (who increasingly appeared to be most likely to become the next president as the Electoral College count proceeded through February) and the weakened but still powerful contingent of congressional Republicans, Burke demanded additional guarantees.

Hayes's dilemma was that he needed all the electoral votes of the three disputed southern states to become president, but Burke and the southern Democrats in the House demanded the recognition of Conservatives in those same state governments. The prospective bargain created a dilemma for Republicans since they would have to convince the country and themselves that the southern states in dispute had all elected a Republican president but Democratic state governments. This was a particular problem for some of Hayes's closest supporters, such as John Sherman, the senator from Ohio and brother of the army's commanding general, William T. Sherman. Senator Sherman had already personally overseen the Louisiana Returning Board's count in New Orleans in December 1876 and had testified to the role played by intimidation and terror in the Conservative campaign.

Among Hayes's advisors during this critical time was Carl Schurz, Grant's nemesis during the congressional fight over the Louisiana Statehouse incident of 1875. In an insightful letter to Hayes on February 20, Schurz analyzed the Louisiana stalemate and suggested a course of action to defuse the crisis. Without question he understood that whatever the actual vote might have been, a coup d'état was now in progress in New Orleans. "The demand for the withdrawal of the Federal troops," he noted, "seems to indicate a purpose to blow the Packard government away by a popular rising, as they did with the Kellogg government in 1874." Schurz's main fear was that Conservatives in Louisiana might "precipitate a conflict" that would "complicate matters" before Hayes's inauguration. He insisted that abandonment of Grant's policy of military intervention was the only correct course to follow and advocated in its place a new policy of presidential conciliation. In a letter to Hayes he advised the following:

It occurs to me that you might, perhaps, through some confidential friend, admonish the Democratic leaders in Louisiana to keep the peace, with a view to arrange matters after your accession to power, possibly somewhat after the manner of the Wheeler compromise of 1875, although in this case not through Congressional action, as Congress will not be in session after the 4th of March, but through the moral influence of the Administration. It is a very delicate business, however, especially as it may become of great importance with regard to your Southern policy. I think I see a way out, but it will be open only when you have a good hold on the confidence of the Southern people.[20]

Hayes seemed impressed by the advice he received from Schurz. In his reply of February 25, he offered Schurz "a place in the Cabinet" as secretary of the interior. Hayes was probably also intrigued by the possibility of a more comprehensive version of the Wheeler Compromise because his own vice presidential candidate was none other than William Wheeler, whose previous effort at southern conciliation had been so esteemed by the Republican national convention that the delegates offered him the second spot on the ticket in 1876.[21]

The next day Burke and congressional Republicans struck their historic bargain at the Wormley House Conference in Washington. In exchange for lifting the Democratic filibuster against the Electoral College count, Hayes's intermediaries promised that the new president would end military intervention on behalf of Republican claimants in Louisiana and South Carolina. Senator Sherman, in addition, asked Burke to solemnly pledge that Nicholls would guarantee political equality, equal education, and civil rights. As C. Vann Woodward has demonstrated, the Compromise of 1877 also encompassed potential agreements on other issues, including southern internal improvements, Democratic support for a Republican Speaker of the House, and a Democratic nominee for the key patronage post of postmaster general. Not all of the individual items were carried out, but the core of the agreement at the Wormley Hotel, an exchange of a Republican presidency for a withdrawal of the army's last occupation forces, held fast.[22]

The outlines of this compromise became apparent two days later when House Democrats in Washington announced an end to their filibuster. In New Orleans the news fell on Governor Packard like a thunderclap. He telegrammed Grant to complain that Nicholls had been installed by White Leaguers who had been "suppressed by your order" in 1874 and that the failure to immediately recognize him could only

20. Carl Schurz to Rutherford B. Hayes, Feb. 20, 1877, in Schurz, *Papers*, 3:399–400.

21. R. B. Hayes to C. Schurz, Feb. 25, 1877, ibid., 403.

22. Woodward, *Reunion and Reaction*, 186–203.

end in "the annihilation of this Government." Grant replied by informing his secretary to tell Packard that his request was impossible: "In answer to your dispatch of this date, the president directs me to say that he feels it is his duty to state frankly that he does not believe public opinion will longer support the maintenance of the State government in Louisiana by the use of the military, and that he must concur in this manifest feeling. The troops will hereafter, as in the past, protect life and property from mob violence when the State authorities fail, but during the remaining days of his official life they will not be used to establish or to pull down either claimant for control of the State. It is not his purpose to recognize either claimant."[23]

The next day Grant showed this telegram to both Hayes and General Sherman at the White House. He authorized Sherman to transmit a copy to General Augur in New Orleans and sent copies to Major Burke and the Louisiana congressional Democrats. The day before his official inauguration on March 5 (he had already secretly taken the oath of office on March 3 at the White House), Hayes privately sent word to Packard advising him to abdicate.

In keeping with Schurz's recommendation, President Hayes did not embark on his southern strategy precipitously following his inauguration. Refusing all direct communication with Packard, he waited a full month before dispatching Vice President Wheeler and a commission to seek another compromise in New Orleans. Wheeler and his commissioners informed the remaining Republican members of the Packard Legislature that Hayes would soon order the army to withdraw the troops guarding the statehouse. They advised Louisiana Republicans to seek seats if they could obtain them in the Conservative legislature. Some Louisianians, including ex-Governor Warmoth, urged Hayes's envoys to reconsider. One commissioner replied: "It is no use to hope for troops. If you can make a fight here in Louisiana try it, but you will be wholly unsuccessful, and as they have the courts in their hands . . . they will hang every one of you to the lamp-post."[24] As if to emphasize how rapidly time was expiring, Hayes withdrew federal troops from the South Carolina Capitol in Columbia a few days later, on April 10. On April 21 Wheeler reported to Hayes back in Washington that most of the Republican legislators had agreed to depart the statehouse, either to join the Nicholls legislature or to return home.

The last days of the Republican regime in Louisiana amounted to a prolonged

23. Telegram, S. B. Packard to U. S. Grant, Mar. 1, 1877, reprinted in *New Orleans Daily Picayune*, Mar. 3, 1877, 1; Telegram, C. C. Sniffen [Grant's private secretary] to S. B. Packard, Mar., 1, 1877, in House, *Presidential Election Investigation*, 537.

24. Testimony, Marshal J. G. Pitkin, in House, *Presidential Election Investigation*, 459. Some Republicans continued to press for federal military intervention, though to no avail. See, for example, I. L. Hardin to B. F. Butler, Mar. 31, 1877, Benjamin Butler Papers, LC.

agony of the inevitable surrender. As a final gesture members of the House approved a special proclamation on April 19 that declared their "unalterable faith" in the legal election of Governor Packard and accused Hayes and the Wheeler Commission of failing to support legitimate self-government in Louisiana. They did not assemble again in the statehouse. Packard lingered for a few days longer. In his final written address to the people of Louisiana, he too declared his unalterable faith in the legitimacy of his expiring government. Reports circulated that Republicans in the statehouse had burned many of the records of government offices, including those of the state militia, for fear that they would be used by Nicholls's White Leaguers to carry out reprisals.

On the same day that Vice President Wheeler reported to him, President Hayes gave General Augur the order to withdraw the federal troops protecting the statehouse, sending copies of the message to both Nicholls and Packard. Cautious to the end, Nicholls waited an additional day before ordering the White League to occupy the building. Just after noon on April 25, 1877, General Nicholls personally took charge of the statehouse from a White League general, and as he entered the building, "an immense shout went up from the multitude which was massed in the streets." Reconstruction was over in New Orleans, in Louisiana, and in America.[25]

THE LOUISIANA COUP OF 1877 IN COMPARATIVE HISTORICAL PERSPECTIVE

Although it might appear exotic to specialists in American military history, the Louisiana coup of 1877 is certainly not unusual to military historians of other nations and eras. It bears many striking resemblances to the general features of the coup d'état throughout modern history, wherever Western-style armies have appeared. As with many coups, years of severe economic and political instability laid the groundwork for the final event. Even discounting the human and material damage inflicted during four years of declared war, the end of plantation slavery in the United States was a traumatic event. Emancipation of the slaves erased more than half of Louisiana's accumulated capital wealth in a single blow and dramatically disrupted cotton and sugar production, upon which the state's economy had been historically dependent. Enfranchisement of former slaves in 1868 and a severe economic depression leading to global agricultural price deflation in the 1870s fell like more hammer blows on the American South's already embattled economy. In this palpable crisis atmosphere, Louisiana planters wondered if they and the state's economy would survive, let alone recover.

25. *New Orleans Daily Picayune*, Apr. 24, 1877, 4; Uzee, "Republican Politics in Louisiana, 1877–1900," 1–2; *New Orleans Daily Picayune*, Apr. 26, 1877, 1.

Louisiana in 1877 resembled the new Latin American republics in their first generation after independence. From Mexico to Argentina, civil wars, foreign military interventions, slave emancipations, and economic crises followed revolution and independence from Spain. Military coups struck at the republics in every one of these states by the middle of the nineteenth century. Similar instability, internal unrest, and military coups accompanied the sudden dissolution of the ancient Austro-Hungarian, Russian, and Ottoman empires in Eastern Europe and the Middle East following World War I. Following World War II, a similar pattern prevailed in the dissolution of Western European colonial empires across Africa, the Middle East, and Asia. Curiously, most students of American civil-military relations have parochially ignored the considerable historical evidence that the effect of events external to the military as an institution is critical in assessing the military's inclination to overthrow its civil government.[26]

Underdeveloped ex-colonial states dependant on plantation economies have been particularly prone to domination by authoritarian military figures from landed and oligarchic elites who could raise and wield their own personalist-oriented irregular armies—the *caudillos*, as they became known in nineteenth-century Latin America. From his credentials as a member of the elite of southern Louisiana sugar planters to his family tradition of leadership of citizen-soldiers, Francis Nicholls enjoyed not just the advantages of a formal military education but also the powerful social prestige that marked him as a "natural leader" in his own time and place. His Confederate military service forged lifelong bonds with many White League officers and men who had fought with him during the Civil War. Nor was Nicholls unique in this regard. His counterpart in South Carolina in 1877, Wade Hampton (both a general and a governor), also came from a distinguished line of citizen-soldiers and was reputedly the richest planter in the entire South before the Civil War. Hampton's family holdings had been so vast that he outfitted and commanded an entire regiment during the war, suitably known as Hampton's Legion, before going on to leading the Red Shirts (who bore a striking resemblance to the White Leagues) to a similar victory over Republi-

---

26. Geoffrey Parker, *The Military Revolution: Military Innovation and the Rise of the West, 1500–1800* (New York: Cambridge University Press, 1988); Winters, *Civil War in Louisiana*, 428–29; Jay Kinsbruner, *Independence in Spanish America: Civil Wars, Revolutions, and Underdevelopment*, 2nd ed. (Albuquerque: University of New Mexico Press, 1994). On the coups d'état and military regimes of Eastern Europe, see Bernadotte E. Schmidt and Harold C. Vedeler, *The World in Crucible, 1914–1919* (New York: Harper and Row, 1984), esp. 402–54. Edward Luttwak relates an impressive list of successful coups, mostly in the emerging postcolonial nations of Africa, Asia, and the Middle East, from 1945 to 1967. *Coup d'Etat*, appendix C.

cans in the militarized campaign attending South Carolina's elections in 1876. The American South, it seemed, developed its own distinct version of the *caudillo* after the Civil War, proud in defeat, yet ready to deploy force in defense of their class and race.[27]

The Louisiana coup was typical of the general pattern of the military coup d'état in one other key aspect—it succeeded where previous attempts had not by focusing attention on the seizure of the central nodes in a network of communication, information, and transportation that composed the unique infrastructure converging in Louisiana's capital. The twentieth-century European writer Curzio Malaparte drew attention to this peculiar new vulnerability of the modern state in his 1931 book, *Technique du Coup d'état*. After analyzing an array of armed overthrows, from the Bolsheviks' 1917 seizure of power to Benito Mussolini's March on Rome, Malaparte concludes that the capture of only a few such critical nodes makes it feasible to subvert modern states. This internal overthrow, he argues, might be accomplished with a relatively small number of determined fighters possessing both the ideological conviction and the technocratic skill to plan such an operation. Malaparte would have appreciated Nicholls's deliberate refusal to attack the mere building of the Louisiana Statehouse in favor of the capture of more-vital and vulnerable institutions such as local newspapers or the rail stations and port facilities of New Orleans. Nicholls and his collaborators eventually demonstrated their understanding of New Orleans's peculiar vulnerabilities. In 1879 they held a new state constitutional convention that, in addition to dismantling many of the reforms of Louisiana's Reconstruction Constitution of 1868, decided to remove the state capital to the smaller and more provincial city of Baton Rouge, where the state government would, among other things, be less vulnerable to the forces of a countercoup.[28]

To be sure, the Louisiana coup of 1877 had features that at first glance seem to depart from the general pattern of coups d'états in the modern world. The multiple failed attempts of white supremacists in the 1870s might seem to suggest a particular "incompetence" on the part of Louisianians. By that time many Latin American militaries had demonstrated considerable ease in overthrowing civilian rule whenever it suited them. In this respect it would be well to recall that the first great military coup

---

27. The literature on the military's contentious role in domestic politics in Latin America is extensive. See especially Brian Loveman, *For la Patria: Politics and the Armed Forces in Latin America* (Wilmington, Del.: Scholarly Resources, 1999); and Frederick M. Nunn, *The Time of the Generals: Latin American Professional Militarism in World Perspective* (Lincoln: University of Nebraska Press, 1992). On the phenomenon of nineteenth-century *caudillismo*, see John Lynch, *Caudillos in Spanish America, 1800–1850* (New York: Oxford University Press, 1992).

28. Malaparte, *Technique du Coup D'Etat*; McGinty, *Louisiana Redeemed*, 159–61.

d'état of the modern era, Napoleon Bonaparte's coup of 18 Brumaire, which overthrew France's Directory in 1799, was itself preceded by two significant armed outbreaks by the French army, 13 Vendémaire in 1795 and 18 Fructidor in 1797. While neither of these revolutionary *journées*, strictly speaking, was a coup attempt, French historian Alfred Cobban has pointed out that the first "brought the army into politics," while the second habituated France to "military occupation." Both France in the 1790s and Louisiana in the 1870s suggest that the coup d'état is a learned practice of modern militaries, arrived at by a process of trial and error rather than something intrinsic to either their organizational structure or corporate ethos.[29]

29. Alfred Cobban, *A History of Modern France*, 3 vols. (London: Penguin, 1957), 1:250–51, 253–54, 257–59. France is an excellent case study in how awareness of a pattern of coups d'état in the past can adversely affect civil-military relations far into the future. See Alistair Horne, *The French Army and Politics, 1870–1970* (London: Macmillan, 1984). In what is otherwise an insightful study of the subject, Horne fails to consider the influence that coups by Napoleon I and Napoleon III had on the deep currents of tension between the French army and French civil authorities well into the twentieth century.

Conclusion

The Military Legacies of Reconstruction

Thus ended an era of "bayonet rule" in the American South. Or did it? The traditional story of Reconstruction draws neatly to a close with Rutherford B. Hayes's order to withdraw the army from its guardianship of the remaining Republican state governments in 1877, signifying the federal government's capitulation to aspirations for southern "home rule." But another way of understanding Reconstruction's lingering influence on the nation, the region, and the newly emancipated slaves is to look beyond 1877 and examine how the military institutions that shaped the undeclared war of the post–Civil War era were themselves affected by the ultimate defeat of southern Republican state governments.

THE INVENTED TRADITION OF THE "APOLITICAL ARMY" AFTER 1877

If the end of Reconstruction came with the end of federal military intervention into the southern states, then the continued refusal of the U.S. government to deploy the army to intervene in the internal politics of the ex-Confederate states was certainly a prominent pillar of the new political order. Given the unprecedented political turmoil of the quarter century since the Compromise of 1850 dissolved into a quasi-guerilla war in frontier Kansas, neither advancing Democratic redeemers nor retreating Republican reformers ought to have had much reason to suspect their bargain would prove permanent. Nevertheless, historians may now say, with the advantage that perfect hindsight grants them, that this feature of the Compromise of 1877 survived a comparatively impressive eighty years, until another famous general turned Republican president, Dwight D. Eisenhower, reluctantly ordered federal troops to enforce the Supreme Court–ordered racial integration of Little Rock Central High School in Arkansas in 1957. Not coincidentally, 1957 was also the year Congress passed its first civil rights bill since the end of Reconstruction. After the passage of eight decades, it took the combined pressure of all three branches of the federal government to produce another intervention by the army, which proved powerful enough to begin de-molishing the edifice of states' rights.[1]

It is doubtful that the framers of the Compromise of 1877 could have ever imag-ined their achievements might some day compare favorably to those of the congres-sional statesmen Stephen Douglas, Henry Clay, and Daniel Webster, who crafted the Compromise of 1850 in the hope of staving off disunion. Part of their reticence in championing what they had accomplished is attributable to a good deal of guilt over the secret negotiations, the brazen personal greed in matters of public interest, and the abandonment of lofty principle for temporary partisan advantage. But some of the explanation for a certain hesitation to trumpet the arrival of a new order can be traced to lingering uncertainty over how permanent the withdrawal of federal bayonets from the South would actually prove to be. Until 1890, northeastern Republicans steeped in the abolitionist tradition perennially introduced new enforcement acts in Congress designed to put legislative force back into the promise of the Fourteenth and Fifteenth Amendments. Every time they did so, they threatened the South with the specter of another military occupation.

Southern Democrats responded to this persistent threat of renewed federal in-tervention with what might be usefully described as the "military corollary" to the Compromise of 1877: an ongoing campaign in Congress to eviscerate the army's an-nual appropriations. They operated under the simple yet plausible assumption that if there was not much of a federal army, there could not be much federal intervention in southern affairs. While America's wealth and population surged during the last quarter of the nineteenth century, the army's annual budget (about forty million dol-lars per year) and overall troop strength (never more than twenty-seven thousand men) marked time. For the professional army as an institution, the decades following Reconstruction became an era of profound stagnation, ironically coinciding with a European era of intensive and extensive military growth ignited by the Prussian army's stunning victory over the French in 1870.[2]

This "military corollary" caused President Hayes and his Republican successors

1. Stephen E. Ambrose, *Eisenhower*, 2 vols. (New York: Simon and Schuster, 1984), 2:411–35.

2. For the army end-strength figures, see "Strength of the Active Army since 1789," in Weigley, *United States Army*, 566–69. On the general European military response to the Franco-Prussian War, see Michael Howard, *The Franco-Prussian War: The German Invasion of France, 1870–1871* (London: Routledge, 1961), 455–56. On the struggles over the army's postwar roles in the late nineteenth century, see Stephen Skowronek, *Building a New American State: The Expansion of National Administrative Capacities, 1877–1920* (New York: Cambridge University Press, 1982), 85–120.

no end of trouble over the following decades. During his own administration, southern Democrats repeatedly invoked the congressional power of the purse and their readiness to unite as a solid partisan phalanx to fasten their own interpretation on the withdrawal of federal troops from the South. At first Hayes tried gentle persuasion with his co-conspirators in the Compromise of 1877. Two weeks after he withdrew troops from New Orleans, the new president formally called Congress into an extra session with a solemn lecture on the need to pass an army appropriations bill to pay federal soldiers, whose salaries had been in arrears since the previous June.

Acquiescence of southern Democrats to the president's request came at a steep price. They attached an amendment forbidding the use of federal troops as a posse comitatus, the legal device Marshal Packard had employed to order soldiers to help him seize the Louisiana Statehouse from McEnery's Fusionists in 1872, to the new army appropriations bill for 1878. Hayes complained privately to his cabinet at this encroachment on his power as commander in chief, but he signed the bill, worried about the consequences of letting the entire army go unpaid for another year. After the troops stayed in garrison and Republicans suffered landslide defeats in the November 1878 congressional elections in Louisiana and South Carolina, however, Hayes reversed course and charged that the results "seem to compel the conclusion that the rights of the colored voters have been overridden and their participation in the elections not permitted to be either general or free." He demanded that Congress fully fund federal prosecutions under the terms of the 1871 Enforcement Act. House Democrats retaliated by refusing to make any army, executive, or judicial appropriations at all for 1879. Exasperated, Hayes immediately ordered Congress into another extra session and threatened to meet further southern obstructionism with presidential vetoes. During his final two years in office, Hayes refused to sign seven major federal funding bills, all of which had been amended by southern Democrats to hobble federal enforcement of civil and voting rights in the states of the former Confederacy.[3]

The first political fallout of this unanticipated tit-for-tat struggle was that Hayes's dream of creating a new southern Republican Party based upon wealthy white Whigs rather than poor black freedmen never materialized. Despite his assurances in 1877, Hayes's subsequent conduct gave white southerners continued reason to fear that he might one day decide to revert to Grant's example of military intervention. Despite

---

3. R. B. Hayes, "Second Annual Message" Dec. 2, 1878, in Richardson, *Messages and Papers of the Presidents*, 7:494. For the complete record of Hayes's struggle with Congress over appropriations and enforcement policy, see ibid., 447–598.

their earlier assurances, white southerners' conduct of "home rule" gave Hayes good reason to distrust their solemn pledges at the Wormley House Conference to respect black political and civil rights.

As if these mutual suspicions were not enough to blunt the emergence of a partisan realignment in the South, black southerners expressed a continuing enthusiasm for Grant and his supposedly discredited Reconstruction policies. In March 1880 P. B. S. Pinchback hosted a lavish reception for Grant in New Orleans as part of the movement to nominate the former president for an unprecedented third term. While feigning indifference to the most important social and political event of the year for black New Orleans, Louisiana's white leaders could hardly have failed to notice how the Republican Party continued to act as a magnet for their enemies. So long as a partisan chasm over enforcement policy remained a live issue charged with racial overtones, a "Solid South" devoted to the interests of one party and one race gathered momentum and became a cornerstone for national Democratic political campaigns far into the future.[4]

If Hayes's appropriations battles with Congress over military spending confounded the political strategy of his administration, they agonized the army's generals. The persistence of a partisan fault line over the army's enforcement mission became a constant reminder to its West Point–trained leadership that while they may have won victory and glory in the Civil War, thereby securing the permanent foundation for a professionalized officer corps, their institutional standing in Washington chronically suffered from being exclusively identified with the domestic political interests of one party.

Recent scholars of the army's role in Reconstruction have asserted that the "military administration of federal policy was creditable to the army as an institution" and that it "had not been the army's responsibility to guarantee the success of Reconstruction, only to carry out the policy."[5] Such sunny assessments seem remarkably oblivious to the contemporary ramifications of General Grant's decision to ally the army with congressional Republicans' determined drive to overturn Johnson's restored governments followed by President Grant's use of the army as an instrument to implement his own Reconstruction policies. The army's critical role in bitterly disputed policies of military government and intervention was not forgotten by south-

4. P. B. S. Pinchback to Blanche K. Bruce, Apr. 9, 1880, reprinted in Haskins, *Pinchback*, 245–46. On the persistence of the Republican threat to Democrats' hold on local power after Reconstruction, see Uzee, "Republican Politics in Louisiana, 1877–1900"; and William Ivy Hair, *Bourbonism and Agrarian Protest: Louisiana Politics, 1877–1900* (Baton Rouge: Louisiana State University Press, 1969).

5. Sefton, *Army and Reconstruction*, 253; Dawson, *Army Generals and Reconstruction*, 262.

ern Democrats after 1877, which meant that the institution would not escape bearing its portion of the recriminations after that policy failed.

Writing under the influence of the consensus school's conception of American political liberalism, Samuel P. Huntington, author of the classic work on civil-military relations *The Soldier and the State*, identifies the post–Civil War period as the cockpit of modern American military professionalism. Utterly ignoring the army's searing immersion in the politics of Reconstruction, Huntington insists that the military's tradition of apolitical service to the nation had been nurtured by "frontier isolation" and developed in reaction to the overwhelming dominance of "business pacifism" in the mainstream of American political thought after the Civil War.

In his enthusiasm to put the best possible face on one of the military's most difficult professional hours, Huntington even attempts to refashion William T. Sherman, the commanding general of the army from 1869 to 1883, into the apotheosis of the "apolitical tradition" of the officer corps—ludicrously ignoring the fact that no American of his time could boast a more-impressive personal network of political influence. The real General Sherman married into one of the most prominent political families in Ohio. Lucy Ewing Sherman was the daughter of a U.S. senator, Thomas Ewing. General Sherman's own brother, John Sherman, was a powerful U.S. senator himself for decades and an influential member of Hayes's cabinet. As if all those connections did not make him a political insider, General Sherman was the closest personal friend of the first U.S. president to serve two full terms since Andrew Jackson, Ulysses S. Grant.

General Sherman did indeed endeavor to create a tradition of apoliticism in the U.S. military after Reconstruction, but it was not one that he practiced himself. The stance of soldierly nonpartisanship made famous by his "if nominated I shall not run. If elected I shall not serve" declaration in 1880 was a wholly invented tradition, a defensive mechanism he bestowed upon subsequent generations of army officers by using Grant's postmilitary career and the Reconstruction experience as an illustrative tale of why professional officers should steer clear of the entangling alliances of domestic politics and enthusiasm for what now would be described as nation building.[6]

6. Samuel P. Huntington, *The Soldier and the State: The Theory and Politics of Civil-Military Relations* (Cambridge, Mass.: Harvard University Press, Belknap Press, 1957), 222–37. Huntington's conception of the dominance of liberal political ideology is drawn principally from the consensus politics found in Louis Hartz, *The Liberal Tradition in America* (New York: Harcourt, Brace, Jovanovich, 1955). Given the dramatic escalation in industrial warfare between organized capital and organized labor after the railroad strike of 1877, Huntington's formulation of "business pacifism" in late-nineteenth-century America seems dubious as well. Sherman's lifelong political connections are detailed in Lloyd Lewis, *Sherman: Fighting Prophet*

Reconstruction left painful institutional scars on the U.S. Army, the effects of which long outlived the memories of the post–Civil War years. Over time the high drama of Civil War battles and the low drama of Indian fighting provided more nostalgic memories than the petty frustrations of peacekeeping between ex-slaves and ex-Confederate soldiers. But the professional appeal of Sherman's argument for an apolitical army became apparent much sooner. To the very end of the twentieth century and beyond, it was always the same: the army would respond to demands for domestic deployments (in the case of drug enforcement along the Mexican border, for instance) or postwar nation building (in the case of the Balkans, Afghanistan, and Iraq, for instance), but it has always seemed to do so with a kind of wariness that has gone well beyond mundane institutional concerns about readiness and funding. Because of its experience in Reconstruction, the army entered the twentieth century without either the taste for domestic military intervention or the habits of colonial peacekeeping that had come to characterize the mainstream of modern European military practice.[7]

ORIGINS OF A NEW SOUTH STATE AND ITS NATIONAL GUARD

In another of Reconstruction's historical ironies, "bayonet rule" did not vanish from the American South after 1877 despite the Redeemers' incessant tirades against the dangers of domestic military intervention to democratic government. After 1877 the bayonets were in the hands of the enemies of Reconstruction rather than its friends. Learning more from the tactics and techniques of federal military occupation and intervention than it cared to admit, the new political regime that seized power in Louisiana repeatedly called upon a white supremacist militia that emerged during Reconstruction to shore up its legitimacy.

Given its reliance on strategies of violence to reconquer parish courthouses and the state capitol, it is hardly surprising that the white supremacist leadership in Louisiana continually resorted to force and a political economy of repression to stabilize their power over a state where they perpetually had to confront the opposition

---

(New York: Harcourt, Brace, 1932); and John Sherman and William T. Sherman, *The Sherman Letters*, ed. Rachel Sherman Thorndike (New York: Charles Scribner's Sons, 1894). For an impassioned restatement of the Huntington thesis with a slightly different rendition of origins of a "tradition" of apoliticism on the part of the military in American civil-military relations, see Russell F. Weigley, "The American Military and the Principle of Civilian Control from McClellan to Powell," *The Journal of Military History* 57 (Spec. Issue, Oct. 1993): 27–58.

7. Jerry Cooper, *The Army and Civil Disorder: Federal Military Intervention in Labor Disputes, 1877–1900* (Westport, Conn.: Greenwood, 1980).

of more than 50 percent of the legal electorate. Mindful of the persistent struggle over the enforcement question in Washington, however, they now proceeded with a studied caution that had eluded their predecessors in the 1860s. In general the regional counterrevolution against Reconstruction's revolutionary achievements stretched out over more than twenty years and necessitated cautious campaigns conducted on multiple fronts. Over time, emphasis shifted from political consolidation to economic consolidation to finally, with their grip on government secure, the social consolidation enshrined in *Plessey v. Fergusson*, the Supreme Court case that originated in Louisiana after Governor Nicholls signed a bill segregating public accommodations during his second term as governor in 1890.[8]

The prevailing interpretation of American political history as a series of partisan realignments in critical elections describes the coming of the "one party, one race" southern regimes as part of a normal political process in which state Republican parties gradually but inexplicably "sank into minority status."[9] While the eventual consolidation of the white supremacist reconquest of Louisiana could be foreseen in the death of the Republican state government during the long street battle of 1877, General Nicholls's victory did not result in an overnight establishment of a one-party system. For two decades the Louisiana Republican Party survived as a potential but unrealized threat to Democratic rule. Minor bastions of black political power bypassed during the White Leagues' campaigns of the 1870s continued to hold out under difficult odds and unrelenting pressure.[10]

The first order of business for Louisiana's white supremacist leadership was to ensure that Republicans could not regain power over the state government. In the campaign leading up to the 1878 elections, white paramilitaries attacked black Republican strongholds in the Mississippi Delta parishes of Carroll, Madison, Tensas, Concordia, and Pointe Coupée. The result was the Democratic landslide in the November 1878 elections that caught President Hayes's attention. Capture of these predominantly black parishes proved to be a critical incremental dividend for white rule in Louisiana, for their control helped assure a super-majority for Democrats at the state constitutional convention in 1879, called to rewrite the Radicals' state constitution. The new constitution curtailed the powers of the state legislature in favor of the

8. An interesting discussion of the attractions of political repression as a successful policy for regimes that come to power by extralegal means is found in Luttwak, *Coup d'Etat*, 183.

9. Sundquist, *Dynamics of the Party System*, 103.

10. The last black-ruled parish in Louisiana fell in 1896 when Henry Demas, the black political boss of St. John the Baptist Parish, lost power. A white militia armed with a cannon came to his home and forced him to surrender the parish ballot boxes at gunpoint. See Foner, *Freedom's Lawmakers*, 61.

governor, who received a line-item veto over all appropriations bills and broader appointive powers affecting local parish government. After the ratification of the 1879
Constitution, whenever a vacancy occurred on a parish jury, the governor filled the
position—and the governor of Louisiana after Reconstruction was always a native-
born white Democrat. This shift toward greater executive authority empowered Democrats to deeply entrench "ring rule" at parish courthouses across the state and within
the city government of New Orleans. This drive toward the centralization of power
in the hands of the chief executive belied the Redeemers' rhetoric of political local-
ism and economic laissez faire. It also considerably reduced the prospect that any
third party, such as the Populists, might emerge through grassroots organizing to
challenge Democratic hegemony. Not coincidentally, as one-party rule solidified, Louisiana's politics devolved into a carnival of factionalism, corruption, race baiting, and
demagoguery that dwarfed the comparatively petty theft of the carpetbaggers.[11]

The shift to one-party rule in Louisiana proceeded in tandem with the transfor-
mation of the White Leagues into the Louisiana National Guard, which became a vital instrument in the economic consolidation of the Redeemers' new order. For a
decade after 1878, P. G. T. Beauregard, the famous Confederate general and postwar
railroad executive, served as state adjutant general. Although he was too old to serve
as a field commander, Beauregard became a prominent supporter of this state-based
military force. He also served as the first vice president of the National Guard Association, the national lobby for state organizations in Washington, which gave state ad-
vocates for the National Guard a powerful lobby the U.S. Army could not match.
Thanks to the growing fear of industrial strife after the great railroad strike of 1877,
combined with the enforced stagnation of the federal military at the hands of southern Democrats, total enrollment of the National Guard in the United States rose to
nearly four times the size of the U.S. Army between 1877 and the late 1890s, making
it, in effect, an alternate army operated at the discretion of the state governors with
a minimum of federal intereference.[12]

At first glance the Louisiana National Guard did not strike most observers as a particularly impressive military organization. It never retained more than two thousand
troops on its muster rolls before World War I, and these were mostly assigned to com-

11. McGinty, *Louisiana Redeemed*, 159–61. A detailed study of the competitive formation of political
rings within the Democratic Party in New Orleans after 1877 is found in Jackson, *New Orleans in the Gilded
Age*, 30–78.

12. Williams, *P. G. T. Beauregard*, 321; Mahon, *Militia and the National Guard*, 113–23; Jerry Cooper, *The
Rise of the National Guard: The Evolution of the American Militia, 1865–1920* (Lincoln: University of Nebraska
Press, 1997); Skowronek, *Building a New American State*, 103–7.

panies at armories in the larger cities of New Orleans, Baton Rouge, and Shreveport. Regular-army officers assigned for duty with such state military organizations routinely disparaged the fitness of these units, in Louisiana and elsewhere, and questioned their effectiveness in combat against the armies of major foreign powers.

That appearance was deceiving because the National Guard's original focus was domestic rather than foreign. Unlike the poorly organized militia of the antebellum era, the National Guard became an organized militia equipped with modern military weapons (underwritten by state and federal subsidies), better junior officers trained in land grant college ROTC programs (such as Louisiana State University), and new armories constructed by solicitous state governments encouraged by powerful economic interests. After 1877 Louisiana also had a cohort of veteran officers from the White Leagues possessing the requisite military skills and reliable motivation to defend the interests of the Redeemer government. Beginning in the 1880s, the state government paid National Guard troops to drill and attend annual summer camps. Thanks to Beauregard's personal business connections to the railroads, the Louisiana National Guard also gained free passage on the state's rail network. Railroad executives, bankers, merchants, and agricultural associations that relied on its services underwrote its logistical needs for both training and active deployments. After Reconstruction ended, the Redeemers had an inexpensive, politically reliable, and tactically flexible force that could be deployed almost anywhere in the state in less than twenty-four hours with the capability to crush any threat to their interests.[13]

The effect of the Redeemers' reliance on the Louisiana National Guard can be seen most dramatically in the role it played in the revival of the state's sugar industry after Reconstruction. Profitable production of sugar cane in Louisiana during the nineteenth century demanded such large capital investments and labor inputs that the industry became a leader in the drive to mechanize agricultural production in America. Sugar plantations along the lower Mississippi River and its tributaries required costly construction and maintenance of levees, mechanized mills to process the cane into sugar, and a surplus of cheap, docile labor that could be flexibly called upon to work long hours, particularly at harvest time, when the mills ran continuously converting raw cane into syrup and processed sugar.

13. On the reorganization of the White Leagues into the Louisiana National Guard, see Louisiana Adjutant General's Office, *Annual Report, 1877*, 1–4. On the improved organization and funding of National Guard organizations throughout the United States between the end of Reconstruction and the Spanish American War, see Mahon, *Militia and the National Guard*, 108–37. On the post-Reconstruction surge in the construction of National Guard armories and its connection to concerns about working-class strikes and urban violence, see Robert M. Fogelson, *America's Armories: Architecture, Society, and Public Order* (Cambridge, Mass.: Harvard University Press, 1989).

At the end of the Civil War, Louisiana's sugar industry lay in ruins, devastated by the catastrophic financial blow of the emancipation of its labor force and the bankruptcy of the entire community of antebellum factors in New Orleans. In 1861 Louisiana produced 264,000 tons of sugar. In 1865 it produced less than 10,000 tons, an industry-wide collapse far surpassing the more temporary slump in wartime cotton production. Before 1861 sugar cane had been profitably grown almost as far north as Shreveport. On the largest plantations bordering directly on the Red River, wealthy planters paid cash to hire out additional slave labor after the cotton harvest but before killing frosts could ruin the highly temperature-sensitive sugar cane. A perfect example of a large antebellum plantation complex combining both cotton and sugar production in northern Louisiana was Calhoun Landing, the site of the 1873 battle of Colfax in Grant Parish. After the war, however, sugar's commercial range shrank southward more than one hundred miles, and planters rarely grew cane profitably north of Baton Rouge. In the wake of emancipation, planters complained incessantly about a chronic "labor shortage" and tried various schemes to promote immigration among Chinese or Italians, who were reputed to be cheaper and more-disciplined laborers than their former slaves. International competition also placed intense pressure on postwar Louisiana planters since sugar could be produced more profitably in Cuba and Brazil, where slave labor as well as frost-free growing seasons still prevailed. Mechanization and consolidation of sugar mills drove down prices relentlessly. Between 1864 and 1880, the retail price of refined sugar in the United States fell from $0.18 per pound to only $0.06 per pound, driving many smaller planters out of business permanently.[14]

A host of difficulties, therefore, plagued all efforts to revive sugar production in Louisiana after the war. All the major political parties (Conservative Unionists, Democrats, and Republicans) promised to extend state aid to the industry, but neither the planters nor the Reconstruction state governments could muster the capital to repair river levees, a dilemma that piqued Whiggish interest in the promise of more federal aid for southern internal improvements under the Compromise of 1877. After Sheridan's military government repudiated the postwar Black Codes, planters found Republican officials either deaf or hostile to their pleas to help restore antebellum labor discipline. Not only had sugar producers been unable to use the power of the state to

14. For an extended discussion of the revival of the sugar industry after emancipation, see especially John C. Rodrigue, *Reconstruction in the Cane Fields: From Slavery to Free Labor in Louisiana's Sugar Parishes, 1862–1880* (Baton Rouge: Louisiana State University Press, 2001). See also Charles P. Roland, *Louisiana Sugar Planters during the American Civil War* (Leyden, Netherlands: E. J. Brill, 1957); and J. Carlyle Sitterson, *Sugar Country: The Cane Sugar Industry in the South, 1753–1950* (Lexington: University of Kentucky Press, 1953).

shape labor relations to their advantage during Reconstruction, but by the mid-1870s they also faced a new threat in the intensive campaign of labor organizing in the canefields by the burgeoning national labor union, the Knights of Labor. Duncan Farrar Kenner, who was probably the wealthiest sugar planter in Louisiana before the Civil War and the author of Louisiana's 1865 Black Codes, eventually admitted defeat and gave up on sugar at his home plantation entirely. When his attempts at wage negotiations with his former slaves failed, he decided to shift to rice cultivation, which he thought would require less labor throughout the growing season.[15]

With the end of Reconstruction, Kenner sensed the possibility of a change in sugar's fortunes. In October 1877 he played a leading role in the founding of the Louisiana Sugar Planters Association (LSPA), a cartel of the two hundred largest sugar planters in the state. The LSPA lobbied extensively for a tariff on imported sugar, federal aid to construct and maintain river levees, and scientific research by the U.S. Department of Agriculture to raise sugar cane yields. It also united to support a decade-long campaign to regain control over its labor force. The LSPA intended to regain this by pledging its members to abide by a uniform pay scale for all sugar workers, mandating an 80 percent withholding of wages until the end of the harvest season, and abolishing the "job system," the practice of contracting for labor based upon specific tasks rather than time worked. The largest planters, who normally ran company stores on their plantations, also tried to impose a system of wage payment in scrip rather than cash. Their twin purpose was to immobilize their labor force and to sharply reduce its cost.[16]

Between 1880 and 1887, not a single harvest season went by in Louisiana's sugar country without a rash of strikes contesting some aspect of the LSPA's statewide labor pact. In March 1880, strikes among sugar workers seeking higher wages broke out in Saint Charles and Saint John the Baptist parishes. Workers in three other Mississippi River parishes soon followed this example. Units of the Louisiana National

---

15. For an example of the intense interest of Louisiana politicians in the issue of state and federal aid for levee construction and repair, see "Fourth Annual Message of His Excellency William P. Kellogg, Governor of Louisiana, Delivered at the Regular Session of the General Assembly, New Orleans, Jan. 3, 1876," in *Louisiana Legislative Documents: 1875* (New Orleans, 1876), 11–16; and Craig A. Bauer, *A Leader among Peers: The Life and Times of Duncan Farrar Kenner* (Lafayette: Center for Louisiana Studies, University of Southwestern Louisiana, 1993), 244.

16. Jeffrey Gould, "The Strike of 1887: Louisiana Sugar War," *Southern Exposure* 12 (Nov.–Dec. 1984): 45–55; Rebecca J. Scott, "Defining the Boundaries of Freedom in the World of Cane: Cuba, Brazil, and Louisiana after Emancipation," *AHR* (Feb. 1994): 70–102; Frederick Cooper, Thomas C. Holt, and Rebecca J. Scott, *Beyond Slavery: Explorations of Race, Labor, and Citizenship in Postemancipation Societies* (Chapel Hill: University of North Carolina Press, 2000).

Guard helped break the stoppages by evicting striking sugar workers from plantations and by guarding leased convict labor brought in from the state penitentiary at Angola. In October 1886 hundreds of cane cutters in Plaquemines Parish stopped work and refused to continue without a new contract promising cash wages and other concessions.[17]

The climax to the escalating struggle between the planters and their former slaves finally came in November 1887, when an estimated ten thousand sugar workers (90 percent of whom were black), organized by the Knights of Labor, went on strike in Terrebonne, Lafourche, and Saint Mary parishes. Given an early winter frost that threatened to destroy the entire crop in the field and a serious primary challenge for his renomination, Gov. Samuel McEnery (the brother of the 1872 candidate for governor, John McEnery) wasted no time in dispatching a force of ten infantry companies and an artillery company of the National Guard by train from New Orleans to Thibodaux, the parish seat of Lafourche and heart of the strike. Governor McEnery assigned Brig. Gen. William Pierce to command the field force. Pierce represented the rising generation of National Guard leaders in Louisiana and its connection to the overthrow of Reconstruction. While he had served as a private in the Civil War, he commanded one of the new companies that Governor Nicholls had raised to augment the New Orleans's White Leagues during the long siege against the Republicans in 1877.[18]

Upon arriving at Thibodaux, General Pierce appraised the situation and consulted with local leaders of the LSPA, who had thoughtfully underwritten the expenses of the expedition by providing food and quarters for the state troops. Some of the Lafourche planters initially counseled patience, but Pierce demanded "heroic and vigorous action" to break the strike immediately by evicting strikers and arresting Knights of Labor organizers. On November 5 a battalion of guardsmen supporting a sheriff's posse massacred as many as twenty people in the black village of Pattersonville, effectively breaking the strike in Saint Mary Parish. In Terrebonne Parish guardsmen protected eight hundred contract workers brought in from Mississippi to break the strike and then helped local authorities arrest fifty strikers wanted on various charges involving union activity. By November 20, Terrebonne planters reported to Pierce that the strike in their parish had collapsed and that most plantations were harvesting cane again. Shielded by the main National Guard detachment, planters

17. Hair, *Bourbonism and Agrarian Protest*, 172–74.

18. J. Curtis Waldo, "The Roll of Honor: Roster of the Citizen Soldiery Who Saved Louisiana," rev. and ed. R. J. Murphy (New Orleans: Works Progress Administration, 1938), 59, LLMVC; William Pierce, *Report to the Adjutant General* (Baton Rouge, 1888), 4.

from the Lafourche LSPA set to work raising their own paramilitary force of some three hundred whites in Thibodaux, ostensibly to defend the town after Pierce's force departed on November 21. After quarantining the town for three days, the Thibodaux paramilitaries launched a preemptive dawn attack on November 23 against the local Knights of Labor headquarters, massacring as many as fifty black strikers. In a pattern suspiciously similar to the mopping-up operations of the White League paramilitary assaults of the 1870s, a number of local Knights of Labor organizers disappeared over the following year, never to be seen again. One witness to the November 23 attack summed up the results by pungently observing, "I think this will settle the question who is to rule the nigger or the white man for the next fifty years."[19]

The Thibodaux Massacre crushed the Knights of Labor campaign in the canefields of Louisiana, the largest effort to organize agricultural workers in nineteenth-century America. The actions of the Louisiana National Guard and white paramilitaries alone did not revive the sugar industry in the state, but they did assure that the power of the state government, in the form of the National Guard, could be brought to bear in reconstructing labor relations to a closer (if not precise) approximation of those of the antebellum world than had been possible under Republicans in Reconstruction. Louisiana sugar production rose dramatically after the end of the "sugar war," registering a phenomenal increase of over 100 percent between 1887 and 1894. By the turn of the century, the industry had regained a return on equity it had not experienced since before the Civil War.[20]

THE DESTRUCTION OF THE BLACK RECONSTRUCTION MILITIA

The Thibodaux Massacre also dramatized how the loss of political power at the end of Reconstruction effectively disarmed black militias and left black institutions and black lives in the South more endangered than ever. In 1877 the triumphant Louisiana National Guard disenrolled all the black militia companies that had been raised during Reconstruction and ordered the return of all weapons and equipment to the state arsenal. Some southern states whose Reconstruction experiences had not been so violent or contested as that of Louisiana eventually permitted enrollment of a few black National Guard units. White officers, however, invariably commanded all such units mustered from southern states in 1898 for the Spanish-American War. The idea of black officers commanding regiments of armed black soldiers was simply beyond the pale to most white southerners, dredging up painful memories of both the Civil War

19. Mary Pugh to Edward Pugh, Nov. 25, 1887, Pugh Family Papers, LLMVC.
20. Gould, "Strike of 1887," 54.

and Reconstruction not likely to be fondly recalled by the Confederate veterans who gathered at the popular old soldier reunions.[21]

While the loss of legal status for black militias can be documented in straightforward fashion, it is not so easy to assess how the counterrevolution against Reconstruction affected black southerners' sense of their fundamental right to self-defense in an increasingly hostile world. To be certain, the vast mobilization of black soldiers during the Civil War and the smaller but no less politically significant mobilization of black militia companies during Reconstruction signified a fundamental shift in the freedmen's self-perception as citizens that could not be erased by decrees from the Redeemer state governments or even the protracted campaigns of vigilante, paramilitary, and militia violence that characterized late nineteenth-century Louisiana.[22]

Where black southerners achieved some measure of personal and collective autonomy, the impulse to self-defense against white attack survived and remained closely linked to the persistence of black political activity. Examples across the post-Reconstruction South are difficult to document, though still instructive. In the all-black community of small independent farm owners in South Carolina known as Promiseland, a tiny group of poor but fiercely independent black yeomanry acquired a formidable reputation for self-defense against the local Ku Klux Klan. Their descendants captured that stubborn determination in oral histories handed down from generation to generation and recalled with pride almost a century later. One remembered a story of how a nearby planter warned hostile whites not to provoke trouble: "Don't go down in that Promiseland. Josh Wilson and Colbert Jordan and them got some boys up there, and they got shotguns and Winchesters and old guns. Any white man come in to Promiseland to beat the niggers up, some body going to die. They'll fight 'til hell freezes over."[23]

Few blacks in the post-Reconstruction South possessed such autonomy providing either the means or the organization to construct effective extra-legal self-defense forces. Realizing their dangerous predicament and the worthlessness of the Redeemers' guarantees after the 1878 elections, thousands of poor black Louisianians followed the time-honored practice of the defeated by becoming refugees and going into exile in search of land they could own and communities they could defend. Against the ad-

21. Louisiana Adjutant General's Office, *Annual Report, 1877,* 4–5 (table).

22. On the continuing effort to use the federal government to defend voting rights after the end of Reconstruction, see Robert M. Goldman, *"A Free Ballot and a Fair Count": The Department of Justice and the Enforcement of Voting Rights in the South, 1877–1893* (New York: Fordham University Press, 2001).

23. Elizabeth Rauh Bethel, *Promiseland: A Century of Life in a Negro Community* (Philadelphia: Temple University Press, 1981), 17–40.

vice of many of their own leaders, they became "Exodusters" and left the Deep South to make new homesteads on the harsh plains of Kansas and Oklahoma, where they founded all-black towns with not only the hope of future opportunity but also the palpable possibility of self-defense.[24]

For the majority of blacks who remained in the Deep South, however, the steep decline in opportunities to hold political office or gain commissions in the militia after Reconstruction meant that black leadership increasingly migrated to other forms and eventually other strategies to regain in the second Reconstruction what was lost in the first Reconstruction. A distilled historical wisdom in dealing with the immutable facts of minority in numbers and the subservient economic condition of their constituency led the black religious leaders of the civil rights movement of the 1950s and 1960s to consciously eschew the past strategies of violence and embrace a strategy of nonviolence that was revolutionary in its own distinctive way. The legacies of Reconstruction's victories and defeats linger still.

24. Nell Irvin Painter, *Exodusters* (1977; reprint, New York: W. W. Norton, 1992).

Appendix 1
The Louisiana State Militia, 1871 and 1874

Table 1.1. Organization of the Louisiana State Militia, 1871

State Organization
Adjutant General
Maj. Gen. James Longstreet
New Orleans

1ST DIVISION
Maj. Gen. Hugh J. Campbell
New Orleans

——————————————— 1st Brigade ———————————————
(Vacant)
New Orleans

2ND REGIMENT (10 COS.)	4TH REGIMENT (6 COS.)
Col. James Lewis	Col. Napoleon Underwood
New Orleans	*East Baton Rouge* (2 cos.)
	Lafourche (2 cos.)
	Plaquemines (2 cos.)

——————————————— 2nd Brigade ———————————————
Brig. Gen. A. P. Mason
New Orleans

1ST REGIMENT (10 COS.)	5TH REGIMENT (5 COS.)	1ST FIELD ARTY. REGT. (3 COS.)
Col. William M. Owen	Maj. George H. Braughn	Col. Charles. W. Squires
New Orleans	*New Orleans*	*New Orleans*

CITY GUARDS COMPANY	1 CAVALRY COMPANY
Capt. Henry Street	Capt. H. E. Shropshire
New Orleans	*New Orleans*

——————————————— 3rd Brigade ———————————————
Brig. Gen. A. E. Barbour
New Orleans

3RD REGIMENT (9 COS.)
Col. James H. Ingraham
New Orleans

2ND DIVISION
Brig. Gen. J. Frank Pargoud
Monroe

——————————————— Brigade ———————————————
(Vacant)

2 INFANTRY COMPANIES	2 CAVALRY COMPANIES	6TH REGIMENT
Monroe	*Monroe*	(Vacant)
		1 co. under Capt. William Ward
		Colfax

Source: Louisiana Adjutant General's Office, *Annual Report, 1871*, 9–17.

Table 1.2. Organization of the Louisiana State Militia, 1874

State Organization
Adjutant General
Brig. Gen. Henry Street
New Orleans

1ST DIVISION
Maj. Gen. James Longstreet
New Orleans

——————————— **Metropolitan Brigade** ———————————
Brig. Gen. A. S. Badger
New Orleans

METROPOLITAN REGIMENT	METROPOLITAN CAVALRY	METROPOLITAN ARTILLERY
Col. Thomas Flanagan	(1 co.)	(1 co.)
New Orleans	Capt. Philip Taylor	Capt. Jacob Gray
	New Orleans	*New Orleans*

——————————— **1st Brigade** ———————————
Brig. Gen. A. E. Barbour
New Orleans

2ND REGIMENT (10 COS.)	3RD REGIMENT (5 COS.)
Col. R. B. Baquie	Col. A. J. Dumont
New Orleans	Lt. Col. Emile Detiege
	New Orleans

——————————— **4th Brigade** ———————————
Brig. Gen. T. M. Chester
New Orleans
(Vacant)

——————————— **5th Brigade** ———————————
Brig. Gen. Frank Morey
Monroe

——————————— **3rd Brigade** ———————————
Brig. Gen. Louis J. Souer
New Orleans

6TH REGIMENT (5 COS.)	B TROOP, CAVALRY
Lt. Col. Robert Ray	Capt. James Forsyth[a]
Clinton	*Harrisburgh* (Catahoula)
with companies at:	
Clinton (East Feliciana)	
Covington (St. Tamany)	
Thibodaux (Lafourche)	
Houma (Terrebonne)	
Napoleonville (Assumption)	

Source: Louisiana Adjutant General's Office, *Annual Report, 1874*, 17–25. This source also lists the First Louisiana Field Artillery Regiment, but that unit has been omitted here since most of its officers and men fought for the White Leagues in 1874. There is no evidence that it ever mustered under Republican officials after the militia mutiny of 1872. General Street's reasons for reporting the artillery regiment are not clear since he expelled all other white militia units under the command of Confederate veterans known to support the Conservatives. Its inclusion may have been an administrative error that occurred either in the preparation of the original report or possibly in the typed version prepared by Works Project Administration historians in the 1930s.

[a]Captain Forsyth is listed as "James Forsythe" in House, *Condition of Affairs in the Southern States*, 43rd Cong., 2nd sess., 1875, H. Rpt. 261, 377. Forsythe was the Republican tax collector and head of the parish executive committee of the Republican Party in Catahoula Parish in 1874.

Appendix 2
The White Leagues, 1874

Table 2.1. Growth and Actions of the White Leagues in Louisiana, 1874

PARISH	DATE FORMED	WHITE LEAGUE ACTIONS TAKEN
Avoyelles	June 1874?	Parish officials ousted. Assassination threat.
Bienville	May–July 1874?	White League organized.
Bossier	May–July 1874?	Parish officials ousted. Assassination threat.
Caddo	May–July 1874?	Parish officials ousted. Assassination threat.
Catahoula	May–July 1874?	Parish officials ousted. Assassination threat.
Claiborne	June 1874?	Parish officials ousted. Party meeting disrupted.
De Soto	May 1874?	White League organized.
Grant	July 25, 1874	White League organized. Two killings.
Iberia	August 12, 1874	Parish officials ousted.
Lincoln	June 1874?	Parish officials ousted. Assassination attempt.
Natchitoches	July 27, 1874	Parish officials ousted.
Orleans	July 1, 1874	Coup d'état
Rapides	May–July 1874?	White League organized. One killing.
Red River	June 1874?	Parish officials ousted. Six assassinations.
Saint Landry	April 27, 1874	White League organized.
Saint Martin	May–July 1874?	Parish officials ousted. Black pastor exiled.
Saint Mary	July 13, 1874	Parish officials ousted.
Terrebonne	May–July 1874?	White League organized.
Vermillion	May–July 1874?	White League organized.
Webster	May–July 1874?	White League organized.

Sources: Table compiled from Taylor, *Louisiana Reconstructed*, 282–86; Dawson, *Army Generals and Reconstruction*, 157–59; Lonn, *Reconstruction in Louisiana*, 256–64; House, *Condition of Affairs in the Southern States*, 43rd Cong., 2nd sess., 1875, H. Rpt. 261, 276; and Vincent, *Black Legislators in Louisiana during Reconstruction*, 183.

The rosters of White League officers in Tables 2.2 and 2.3 were compiled from "List of Those Who Took Part in the Battle of 14th September, 1874," in Landry, *Battle of Liberty Place*. This list was then cross-checked against Waldo, "Roll of Honor" (White League Papers, Tulane University), for accuracy and possible variations in spellings of names. The refined roster was then checked against the Confederate-veteran roster in Hewett, *Roster of Confederate Soldiers*, which was compiled from the card files of Confederate veterans, Record Group 109, National Archives, Washington, D.C.

Analysis of the roster reveals the following:

111 White League officers are listed by Landry.

4 in the Landry list have no first name listed (annotated "nfn" under "Name").

5 were sons of Louisiana veterans and did not fight in the Civil War (annotated "xf" under "Civil War Rank and Unit," with father's name and unit shown).

102 remaining names in sample are complete (92 percent).

From these data the following conclusions can be drawn:

1. The White League leadership was overwhelmingly drawn from Confederate veterans. Only 12 of 102 possible veterans had no Civil War record listed. Therefore, 90 of 102, or 88 percent, of White League officers in 1874 were Confederate veterans.

2. A high proportion of White League officers had been Confederate officers. Of the 90 Confederate veterans, 32 of 90, or 36 percent, were Confederate officers (3 colonels, 16 captains, 11 lieutenants, 1 surgeon, and 1 ordnance officer). Of the 90 Confederate veterans, 58 of them, or 64 percent, had been enlisted soldiers (12 sergeants, 16 corporals, 30 privates).

3. A *Herrenvolk* democracy–style social mobility was at work in the White Leagues. Many Confederate enlisted men rose to officer status during the Reconstruction battles.

4. All 90 of the White League officers identified were veterans of Louisiana Confederate units. Thus the White League was an intensely local movement. This was something of a surprising result given the known mobility of the population in New Orleans both before and after the Civil War.

Table 2.2. Civil War Records of New Orleans White Leagues Officers, 1874

NAME		1874 RANK AND UNIT		CIVIL WAR RANK AND UNIT
Addison, nfn	Lt.	La. Rifles	—	—
Allen, C. H.	Capt.	WL, 6th Dis.	Lt.	Ogden Cav. Regt.
Andress, F. M.	Capt.	WL, 11th Wd.	—	—
Angell, John G.	Col.	1st La. Inf.	Capt.	5th La. Inf.
Armstrong, W. J.	2nd Lt.	CCWL, Sec. E	Pvt.	Crescent Regt. Inf., Co. A
Arnauld, L. A.	1st Lt.	1st La. Inf., Co. B	1st Sgt.	Orleans Guards
Augustin, J.	Maj.	La. Rifle Club	Pvt.	Fenner's Btry.
Baker, Alfred T.	2nd Lt.	La. FA, Bat. A	Pvt.	22nd La., Co. G
Balfour, J. R.	1st Lt.	CCWL, Sec. A	—	—
Bardon, E. N.	1st Lt.	WL, Washington	Sgt.	Holmes's Btry.
Barton, William	1st Lt.	WL, Washington	Pvt.	Wash. Arty., Co. 3
Behan, W. J.	Col.	CCWL	Lt.	Wash. Arty., Co. 4
Bell William A.	Treas.	Ogden's staff	Pvt.	Orleans Light Horse
Bienvenu, N.	1st Lt.	WL, Co. H, 6th Wd.	Pvt.	Orleans Guards
Blanchard, D.	Capt.	1st La. Inf., Co. C	Pvt.	La. Guards Btry.
Boarman, C. B.	3rd Lt.	1st La. Inf., Co. B	Pvt.	Dreux's La. Cav., Co. B
Bond, R. C.	3rd Lt.	CCWL, Sec. A	Capt.	1st La. Heavy Arty.
Borland, Euclid, Jr.	1st Lt.	1st La. Inf., Co. A	—	—
Bouny, P. L.	1st Lt.	WL, Sec. A, 5th Wd.	—	—
Bozant, John	1st Lt.	WL, Co. B, 6th Dis.	Pvt.	Wash. Arty., Co. 1
Braud, E.	2nd Lt.	WL, Co. H, 6th Wd.	Pvt.	18th La. Inf.
Bruns, J. D.	Surgeon	Ogden's staff	Doctor	—
Buck, S. H.	Capt.	CCWL, Co. C	—	—
Buckner, James	Insp. Gen.	Ogden's staff	Capt.	10th La. Inf., Co. B
Buddendorf, nfn	Aide	Ogden's staff	—	—
Buisson, Theodule	2nd Lt.	CCWL, Sec. C, 5th Wd.	Pvt.	Dreux's La. Cav.
Burke, E. A.	Maj.	Penn's staff	Pvt.	1st La. Cav.
Chaffe, W. H.	Adj.	1st La. Inf.	—	—
Coleman, H. D.	Capt.	La. FA, Btry. A	Pvt.	Wash. Arty., Co. 2
Coleman, J. W., Jr.	3rd Lt.	CCWL, Sec. E	—	—
DeBlanc, A. E.	2nd Lt.	WL, Co. H, 6th Wd.	Pvt.	Orleans Guards
Dennee, R. S.	Capt.	WL, 2nd Wd.	—	—
Dupre, George W.	Capt.	WL, Co. H, 6th Wd.	—	—
Durand, E.	3rd Lt.	WL, Sec. A, 5th Wd.	Pvt.	1st La. Inf.
Ellis, E. John	Asst. Adj. Gen.	Penn's staff	Capt.	16th La. Inf., Cos. F and H
Eyle, Fred	2nd Lt.	CCWL, Sec. E	—	—
Fagan, William	1st Lt.	CCWL, Sec. E	2nd Lt.	2nd La. Inf., Co. C
Flood, Ed	Capt.	WL, Co. K	Lt.	6th La. Inf., Co. K
Flower, Samuel	Aide	Ogden's staff	Capt.	7th La. Inf., Co. G
Forman, B. R.	Capt.	1st La. Inf., Co. E	—	—

Table 2.2 (*continued*)

NAME	1874 RANK AND UNIT		CIVIL WAR RANK AND UNIT	
Forno, C. H.	1st Lt.	La. FA, Btry. A	xf-H. Forno	Lt. Col., 5th La. Inf.
Fremeaux, L. J.	Capt.	WL, Sec. C, 5th Wd.	Capt.	La. En., Co. A
Fulham, William	1st Lt.	WL, Co. I, 3th Wd.	Pvt.	Chalmette Regt.
Gaffney, Peter C.	2nd Lt.	CCWL, Sec. D	Sgt.	18th La. Inf., Co. H
Garcia, Joseph	2nd Lt.	WL, Sec. C, 5th Wd.	Pvt.	Eur. Brig., Spanish Regt.
Gehlbach, Charley	3rd Lt.	WL, Washington	Pvt.	Squad. Guides d'Orleans
Glynn, John, Jr.	Capt.	Chief FA, La. FA	Capt.	Orleans Guard Btry.
Greenleaf, Leeds	Aide	Ogden's staff	Sgt.	Orleans Light Horse
Greig, Frank	2nd Lt.	La. FA, Btry. C	2nd Lt.	30th La. Inf.
Guerin, Paul O.	Capt.	WL, 9 Wd.	Capt.	Orleans Guard Btry.
Guibet, E. Achille	1st Lt.	La. FA, Btry. C	Capt.	Orleans Guard Btry.
Hardie, Pierce	Aide	Ogden's staff	—	—
Hare, Walter	Aide	Ogden's staff	1st Sgt.	Wash. Arty., Co. 2
Harrod, BM	2nd Lt.	CCWL, Sec. A	2nd Lt.	1st La. Heavy Arty., Co. D
Hill, J. D.	Maj.	1st La. Inf.	Capt.	Orleans Fire Regt.
Holyland, Fred	Aide	Ogden's staff	Pvt.	Conf. Guards
Homes, Warren	2nd Lt.	CCWL, Co. F	—	—
Hyatt, A. W.	1st Lt.	CCWL, Co. F	Capt.	16th Btn., La. Inf.
Kelley, Dan	2nd Lt.	WL, Co. B, 6th Dis.	1st Lt.	5th La. Inf., Co. F
Kilpatrick, D. M.	Capt.	CCWL, Sec. G	Pvt.	Wash. Arty., Co. 1
Krumbhaar, W. B.	Capt.	Penn's staff	Ord. Off.	Wash. Arty. staff
Kurscheedt, E. I.	Aide	Ogden's staff	1st Lt.	Wash. Arty. staff
LeGardeur, G., Jr.	Maj.	CCWL, Sec. C, 5th Wd.	Capt.	Orleans Guard Btry.
Lord, George H.	Capt.	CCWL, Co. B	Sgt.	5th La. Inf., Co. D
Macheaca, Joseph P.	Capt.	1st La. Inf.	Pvt.	22nd La. Inf.
McBride, William	1st Lt.	CCWL, Co. D	Pvt.	Conf. Sts. Zouaves Btn., Co. A
McDonough, B. A.	1st Lt.	WL, Co. K, 10th Wd.	Pvt.	Wash. Arty., Co. 2
McGloin, Frank	Capt.	1st La. Inf., Co. B	Pvt.	2nd La. Cav., Co. C
McIntyre, Thomas	Capt.	CCWL, Sec. F	Sgt.	16th Btn., La. Inf.
Mire, B. C.	Capt.	CCWL, Co. H	Pvt.	Pelican Light Arty.
Mitchell, A.	Capt.	CCWL, Sec. D	Capt.	Leeds Guards Regt.
Moore, John V.	Aide	Ogden's staff	—	—
Moran, Thomas	2nd Lt.	WL, Co. I, 3rd Wd.	Pvt.	1st La. Inf., Co. C
Morgan, W. H.	Capt.	Ogden's staff	Pvt.	Wash. Arty., Co. 1
Muir, J. A.	Capt.	WL, 2nd Wd.	2nd Lt.	Crescent Regt., La. Inf.
Newman, John K.	1st Lt.	1st La. Inf., Co. A	Capt.	21st La. Inf., Co. A
Nixon, J. O., Jr.	1st Lt.	CCWL, Co. B	xf-Lt. Col. J. Nixon	1st La. Cav.
OBrien, Emile J.	1st Lt.	CCWL, Co. C	Sgt.	Wash. Arty., Co. 5
Ogden, Charles G.	2nd Lt.	CCWL, Co. F	xf-F. N. Ogden	Ogden's Cav. Regt.
Ogden, Fred N.	Maj. Gen.	Ogden's staff	Lt. Col.	Ogden's Cav. Regt.

Table 2.2. (*continued*)

NAME	1874 RANK AND UNIT		CIVIL WAR RANK AND UNIT	
Ogden, Octo N.	3rd Lt.	1st La. Inf., Co. D	xf-F. N. Ogden	Ogden's Cav. Regt.
Overton, John K.	2nd Lt.	1st La. Inf., Co. D	Pvt.	1st Special Btn., Co. A
Payne, John N.	Aide	Ogden's staff	Sgt.	Wash. Arty., Co. 1
Peck, Ossian F.	1st Lt.	La. FA, Btry. A	Pvt.	Wash. Arty., Co. 1
Penn, D. B.	Act. Gov.		Col.	7th La. Inf.
Peyroux, P. O.	Capt.	1st La. Inf., Co. D	Pvt.	7th La. Btn., Co. A
Philips, A. B.	Capt.	WL, 6th Wd., Washington	1st Lt.	Wash. Arty., Co. 3
Pleasants, R. B.	Capt.	CCWL, Sec. E	—	—
Prados, Louis	Capt.	1st La. Inf., Co. C	Pvt.	Wash. Arty., Co. 3
Renaud, nfn	Lt.	La. Rifles	—	—
Richardson, F. L.	1st Lt.	1st La. Inf., Co. D	Pvt.	Wash. Arty., Co. 5
Roman, Charles	Capt.	WL, Sec. A, 5th Wd.	Capt.	Orleans Guards Regt.
Sarrat, Belmont	2nd Lt.	WL, Sec. A, 5th Wd.	Sgt.	Orleans Guards Regt.
Selleck, J. R. S.	Capt.	WL, Co. I, 3rd Wd.	—	—
Selles, F.	2nd Lt.	1st La. Inf., Co. C	Pvt.	22nd La. Inf., Co. E
Shropshire, H. E.	Capt.	WL, Co. B, 6th Dis.	—	—
Shute, T. Lee	Col.	Ogden's staff	—	—
Smith, J. H.	Aide	Ogden's staff	Pvt.	Wash. Arty., Co. 4
Southamyd, F. R.	Aide	Ogden's staff	Pvt.	Crescent Regt., Co. B
Starks, Charles A.	2nd Lt.	1st La. Inf., Co. A	Pvt.	Crescent Regt., Co. A
Tennison, O. M.	Capt.	WL, 7th Wd.	—	—
Tobin, nfn	Aide	Ogden's staff	—	—
Vaudry, W. T.	Capt.	CCWL, Sec. A	Pvt.	Fenner's Btry.
Vautier, Charles	Capt.	WL, St. John	Pvt.	Watson's Btry.
Voorhies, William	3rd Lt.	WL, Co. H, 6th Wd.	Sgt.	2nd La. Cav., Co. G
Walker, Clem L.	2nd Lt.	1st La. Inf., Co. B	Pvt.	Jeff Davis Rangers
Walton, J. B.	Aide	Ogden's staff	Col.	Wash. Arty. staff
Watts, Harrison	Capt.	CCWL, Sec. A	Pvt.	Ogden's Cav. Regt., Co. G
Williams, G. A.	Aide	Ogden's staff	Pvt.	5th La. Inf.
Wiltz, P. S., Jr.	1st Lt.	WL, 9th Wd.	Sgt.	7th La. Inf., Co. A
Woelper, William	Lt.	La. Rifles	Cpl.	Fenner's Btry.

Abbreviations:

nfn = no first name

WL = White League

FA = Field Artillery, Field Artillerist

CCWL = Crescent City White League

xf = father's name

Table 2.3. Washington Artillery Veterans in the New Orleans White Leagues, 1874

NAME	1874 RANK AND UNIT		CIVIL WAR RANK AND UNIT	
Aby, Richard C.	Pvt.	CCWL, Co. G	Pvt.	Wash. Arty., Co. 1
Adams, J. S.	Pvt.	1st La. Inf., Co. D	Pvt.	Wash. Arty., Co. 4
Babcock, O. S.	Pvt.	La. FA, Btry. A	Cpl.	Wash. Arty., Co. 4
Baker, Alfred T.	2nd Lt.	La. FA, Btry. A	Pvt.	Wash. Arty.
Baker, H. H.	2nd Cpl.	CCWL, Sec. E	Pvt.	Wash. Arty., Co. 4
Barr, Joe	Pvt.	WL, Sec. A, 5th Wd.	Pvt.	Wash. Arty., Co. 2
Barton, William	1st Lt.	WL, Wash	Pvt.	Wash. Arty., Co. 3
Behan, W. J.	Col.	CCWL	Lt.	Wash. Arty., Co. 4
Bozant, John	1st Lt.	WL, Co. B, 6th Dis.	Pvt.	Wash. Arty., Co. 1
Cantzon, W. H.	Pvt.	La. FA, Btry. A	Pvt.	Wash. Arty., Co. 2
Carey, William	Pvt.	CCWL, Sec. D	Pvt.	Wash. Arty., Co. 4
Carter, Thomas	Pvt.	WL, Co. I, 3rd Wd.	Pvt.	Wash. Arty., Co. 1
Chalaron, Henry	Pvt.	CCWL, Sec. A	Pvt.	Wash. Arty., Co. 5
Coleman, H. D.	Capt.	La. FA, Btry. A	Pvt.	Wash. Arty., Co. 2
Farrell, James J.	Pvt.	CCWL, Sec. D	Pvt.	Wash. Arty., Co. 4
Farrell, John	Pvt.	CCWL, Sec. A	Pvt.	Wash. Arty., Co. 1
Guillote, Henry	Pvt.	La. FA, Btry. C	Pvt.	Wash. Arty., Co. 3
Hare, Walter J.	Aide	Ogden's staff	1st Sgt.	Wash. Arty., Co. 2
Holmes, J. K., Jr.	Pvt.	CCWL, Sec. A	Pvt.	Wash. Arty., Co. 3
Kilpatrick, D. M.	Capt.	CCWL, Sec. G	Pvt.	Wash. Arty., Co. 1
Krumbhaar, W. B.	Capt.	Penn's staff	1st Lt.	Wash. Arty. staff
Kursheedt, E. I.	Aide	Ogden's staff	1st Lt.	Wash. Arty. staff
Labarre, Lacestiere	Pvt.	La. FA, Btry. C	Pvt.	Wash. Arty., Cos. 1 & 3
Leverich, Henry	Sgt.	CCWL, Sec. A	Pvt.	Wash. Arty., Co. 5
Levy, E.	Pvt.	La. FA, Btry. C	Pvt.	Wash. Arty., Co. 1
Levy, S.	Pvt.	WL, Sec. A, 5th Wd.	Pvt.	Wash. Arty., Co. 3
McCartney, J. H.	Pvt.	CCWL, Sec. A	Pvt.	Wash. Arty., Co. 3
McCormack, J. A.	Pvt.	WL, Co. K, 10th Wd.	Pvt.	Wash. Arty., Co. 2
McDonough, B. A.	1st Lt.	WL, Co. K, 10th Wd.	Pvt.	Wash. Arty., Co. 2
Meux, John	Pvt.	CCWL, Sec. A	Pvt.	Wash. Arty., Cos. 4 & 2
Micou, Augustin	2nd Sgt.	1st La. Inf., Co. D	1st Lt.	Wash. Arty., Co. 1
Moran, W.	Pvt.	WL, Co. I, 3rd Wd.	Pvt.	Wash. Arty., Co. 1
Morgan, W. H.	Capt.	Ogden's staff	Pvt.	Wash. Arty., Co. 1
Murphy, John C.	Pvt.	CCWL, Sec. A	Pvt.	Wash. Arty., Co. 3
Murray, John R.	Pvt.	1st La. Inf., Co. C	Pvt.	Wash. Arty., Co. 5
O'Neil, John A.	Pvt.	CCWL, Sec. D	Pvt.	Wash. Arty., Co. 1
O'Brien, Emile J.	1st Lt.	CCWL, Co. C	Sgt.	Wash. Arty., Co. 5
Olivier, William	Pvt.	WL, Washington	Pvt.	Wash. Arty., Co. 1
Palfry, Charles	1st Sgt.	CCWL, Sec. E	Pvt.	Wash. Arty., Co. 4
Payne, John N.	Aide	Ogden's staff	Sgt.	Wash. Arty., Co. 1

Table 2.3 (*continued*)

NAME	1874 RANK AND UNIT		CIVIL WAR RANK AND UNIT	
Peale, Henry M.	Pvt.	WL, Wash	Cpl.	Wash. Arty., Co. 3
Peck, Ossian F.	1st Lt.	La. FA, Btry. A	Pvt.	Wash. Arty. staff
Philips, A. B.	Capt.	WL, 6th Wd., Washington	1st Lt.	Wash. Arty., Co. 3
Pinckard, William F.	Sgt.	CCWL, Co. C	Pvt.	Wash. Arty., Co. 3
Prados, Louis	Capt.	1st La. Inf., Co. C	Lt.	Wash. Arty., Co. 3
Richardson, F. L.	1st Lt.	1st La. Inf., Co. D	Pvt.	Wash. Arty., Co. 5
Russel, C. P.	Pvt.	CCWL, Sec. D	Pvt.	Wash. Arty., Co. 3
Smith, J. H.	Aide	Ogden's Report	Pvt.	Wash. Arty., Co. 4
Toledano, E. A.	Pvt.	CCWL, Sec. A	Pvt.	Wash. Arty., Co. 3
Walton, James B.	Aide	Ogden's staff	Col.	Wash. Arty. staff

Abbreviations:

WL = White League

CCWL = Crescent City White League

Appendix 3
General Officers Commanding in Reconstruction Louisiana

DEPARTMENT COMMANDER (*SUBORDINATE COMMANDER*)	DATES OF COMMAND	REASON FOR DEPARTURE
Maj. Gen. Benjamin Butler	5/1/1862–12/17/1862	Removed by Lincoln
Maj. Gen. Nathaniel P. Banks	12/17/1862–6/8/1864	Removed by Lincoln
Maj. Gen. Edward R. S. Canby	6/9/1864–5/17/1865	Replaced by reorganization
Maj. Gen. Stephen A. Hurlbut	*9/23/1864–4/22/1865*	*Resigned*
Maj. Gen. Nathaniel P. Banks	*4/22/1865–5/17/1865*	*Removed by Johnson*
Maj. Gen. Philip H. Sheridan	5/17/1865–9/5/1867	Removed by Johnson
Maj. Gen. Edward R. S. Canby	*7/17/1865–5/28/1866*	*Removed by Maj. Gen. Sheridan*
Maj. Gen. Absalom Baird	*5/28/1866–9/1/1866*	*Removed by Maj. Gen. Sheridan*
Maj. Gen. Charles Griffin	9/6/1867–9/13/1867	Interim appointment
Maj. Gen. Joseph A. Mower	9/16/1867–9/29/1867	Interim appointment
Maj. Gen. Winfield S. Hancock	11/29/1867–3/18/1868	Requested reassignment
Maj. Gen. Joseph J. Reynolds	3/18/1868–3/25/1868	Interim appointment
Maj. Gen. Robert C. Buchanan	3/25/1868–9/15/1868	Routine transfer
Maj. Gen. Lovell H. Rousseau	9/15/1868–1/7/1869	Died
Maj. Gen. Robert C. Buchanan	1/11/1869–3/31/1869	Interim appointment
Maj. Gen. Joseph A. Mower	3/31/1869–1/6/1870	Died
Maj. Gen. Charles H. Smith	1/7/1870–4/16/1870	Interim appointment
Maj. Gen. Joseph J. Reynolds	4/16/1870–11/28/1871	Replaced by reorganization
Maj. Gen. Charles H. Smith	*4/16/1870–11/28/1871*	*Replaced by reorganization*
Maj. Gen. William H. Emory	11/28/1871–3/27/1875	Removed by Maj. Gen. Sheridan
Maj. Gen. Christopher C. Augur	3/27/1875–6/21/1878	Routine transfer

Source: Biographical sketches for all the Louisiana commanding generals during Reconstruction can be found in Warner, *Generals in Blue.*

Bibliography

MANUSCRIPT COLLECTIONS

Amistad Research Center, Tulane University, New Orleans.
    American Missionary Association Papers.
Firestone Library, Princeton University, Princeton, N.J.
    William Worth Belknap Papers.
    Pierson Civil War Collection.
    Western Americana Collection.
Howard-Tilton Memorial Library, Tulane University, New Orleans.
    Battle of Liberty Place Papers, 1874.
    Louisiana Militia and National Guard Orders, January–April 1877.
    Nicholls Family Papers.
    Frederick Nash Ogden Papers.
    White League Papers.
Library of Congress, Washington, D.C.
    Nathaniel P. Banks Papers.
    Benjamin F. Butler Papers.
    Salmon P. Chase Papers.
    Hamilton Fish Papers.
    Ulysses S. Grant Papers.
    Rutherford B. Hayes Papers.
    Andrew Johnson Papers.
    Philip H. Sheridan Papers.
    John Sherman Papers.
    William T. Sherman Papers.
    Edwin M. Stanton Papers.
Louisiana and Lower Mississippi Valley Collections, Louisiana State University, Baton Rouge.
    William P. Kellogg Papers.
    McGhee Papers.
    Francis T. Nicholls Letterbook.

Pugh Family Papers.

William T. Sherman Papers.

Unification Movement Papers.

Henry C. Warmoth Papers.

Louisiana National Guard Museum, Jackson Barracks Military Library, New Orleans.

General Orders from Adjutants General, 1870–1912.

Special Orders from Adjutants General, 1870–1917.

National Archives, Washington, D.C.

Record Group 94, Records of the Adjutant General's Office, 1780–1917.

Record Group 393, Records of U.S. Army Continental Commands

Fifth Military District, 1867–70.

Department of the Gulf, 1874–77.

Southern Historical Collection, University of North Carolina, Chapel Hill.

Henry C. Warmoth Papers.

U.S. Military Academy Library, West Point, N.Y.

Abasalom Baird Papers.

Francis T. R. Nicholls Papers.

Phillipe Régis de Trobriand Papers.

PUBLIC DOCUMENTS

Federal

Department of Commerce. *Negro Population, 1790–1915.* Washington, D.C.: Government Printing Office, 1918. Reprinted with introduction by James McPherson. New York: Arno, 1968.

Fullerton, Joseph S. *Report of the Administration of Freedmen's Affairs in Louisiana.* Washington, D.C.: Government Printing Office, 1865.

Richardson, James D., ed. *A Compilation of the Messages and Papers of the Presidents, 1789–1897.* 10 vols. Washington, D.C., 1896–97.

U.S. House. *Condition of Affairs in Louisiana.* 42nd Cong., 3rd sess., 1873. H. Exec. Doc. 91.

———. *Condition of Affairs in Louisiana.* 43rd Cong., 2nd sess., 1875. H. Rpt. 101, pt. 2.

———. *Condition of Affairs in the Southern States.* 42nd Cong., 2nd sess., 1872. H. Exec. Doc. 268.

———. *Condition of Affairs in the Southern States.* 43rd Cong., 2nd sess., 1875. H. Rpt. 261.

———. *New Orleans Riots.* 39th Cong., 2nd sess., 1867. H. Exec. Doc. 68.

———. *Presidential Election Investigation.* 45th Cong., 3rd sess., 1878. H. Misc. Doc. 31.

———. *Report of the Secretary of War, 1868.* 40th Cong., 3rd sess., 1868. H. Exec. Doc. 1.

U.S. Senate. *Military Letters, Orders, and Telegrams.* 40th Cong., 1st sess., 1867. S. Exec. Doc. 14.

———. *Reports of Generals Grant and Schurz.* 39th Cong., 1st sess., 1865. S. Exec. Doc. 2.

War Department. *The War of the Rebellion: A Compilation of the Official Records of the Union and Confederate Armies.* 128 vols. Washington, D.C.: Government Printing Office, 1880–1901.

———. *Official Army Register of the Volunteer Force of the United States Army for the Years 1861, '62, '63, '64, '65*. 8 vols. Washington, D.C.: Government Printing Office, 1865.

Louisiana

Acts of the State of Louisiana. New Orleans, 1864–77.

Digest of the Statutes of the State of Louisiana, in Two Volumes. New Orleans, 1870.

Inaugural Address of Governor H. C. Warmoth and Remarks of Lieut. Governor Dunn. New Orleans, 1868.

Louisiana Adjutant General's Office. *Annual Reports*. New Orleans, 1870–74, and 1877.

Louisiana House Debates. New Orleans, 1864–77.

Louisiana House Journal. New Orleans, 1864–77.

Louisiana Legislative Documents, New Orleans, 1864–77.

Louisiana Senate Debates. New Orleans, 1864–77.

Louisiana Senate Journal. New Orleans, 1864–77.

Official Journal of the Proceeding of the Convention for Framing Constitution for the State of Louisiana. New Orleans, 1867–68.

BOOKS

Ambrose, Stephen E. *Eisenhower*. Vol. 2. New York: Simon and Schuster, 1984.

Banks, Nathaniel P. *The Reconstruction of States: Letter of Major General Banks to Senator Lane*. New York: Harper Brothers, 1865.

Bauer, Craig A. *A Leader among Peers: The Life and Times of Duncan Farrar Kenner*. Lafayette: Center for Louisiana Studies, University of Southwestern Louisiana, 1993.

Bell, Caryn Cossé. *Revolution, Romanticism, and the Afro-Creole Protest Tradition in Louisiana, 1718–1868*. Baton Rouge : Louisiana State University Press, 1997.

Bergeron, Arthur W., Jr. *Guide to Louisiana Confederate Military Units, 1861–1865*. Baton Rouge: Louisiana State University Press, 1989.

Berlin, Ira. *Slaves without Masters: The Free Negro in the Antebellum South*. New York, 1974.

Berlin, Ira, et al., eds. *Slave No More: Three Essays on Emancipation and the Civil War*. Cambridge: Cambridge University Press, 1992.

———. *Freedom: A Documentary History of Emancipation, 1861–1867. Selected from the Holdings of the National Archives of the United States. Series 2: The Black Military Experience*. Cambridge: Cambridge University Press, 1982.

Berry, Mary Francis. *Military Necessity and Civil Right Policy: Black Citizenship and the Constitution, 1861–1868*. Port Washington, N.Y.: Kennikat, 1977.

Bethel, Elizabeth Rauh. *Promiseland: A Century of Life in a Negro Community*. Philadelphia: Temple University Press, 1981.

Blackett, R. J. M. *Thomas Morris Chester: Black Civil War Correspondent.* Baton Rouge: Louisiana State University Press, 1989.

Blassingame, John W. *Black New Orleans, 1860–1880.* Chicago: University of Chicago Press, 1973.

Capers, Gerald M. *Occupied City: New Orleans under the Federals, 1862–1865.* Lexington: University of Kentucky Press, 1965.

Carleton, Mark T. *Politics and Punishment: The History of the Louisiana State Penal System.* Baton Rouge: Louisiana State University Press, 1971.

Carter, Dan T. *When the War Was Over: The Failure of Self-Reconstruction in the South, 1865–1867.* Baton Rouge: Louisiana State University Press, 1985.

Casso, Evans J. *Louisiana Legacy: A History of the State National Guard.* Gretna, La.: Pelican, 1976.

Chalmers, David M. *Hooded Americanism: The History of the Ku Klux Klan.* 3rd ed. Durham, N.C.: Duke University Press, 1987.

Chambers, Henry E. *A History of Louisiana.* 3 vols. New York: American Historical Association, 1925.

Clausewitz, Carl von. *On War.* Edited and translated by Michael Howard and Peter Paret. Rev. ed. Princeton, N.J.: Princeton University Press, 1984.

Coffman, Edward M. *The Old Army: A Portrait of the American Army in Peacetime, 1784–1898.* New York, 1986.

Cooper, Frederick, Thomas C. Holt, and Rebecca J. Scott. *Beyond Slavery: Explorations of Race, Labor, and Citizenship in Postemancipation Societies.* Chapel Hill: University of North Carolina Press, 2000.

Cooper, Jerry. *The Army and Civil Disorder: Federal Military Intervention in Labor Disputes, 1877–1900.* Westport, Conn.: Greenwood, 1980.

———. *The Rise of the National Guard: The Evolution of the American Militia, 1865–1920.* Lincoln: University of Nebraska Press, 1997.

Crouch, Barry A., Larry Peacock, and James M. Smallwood. *Murder and Mayhem: The War of Reconstruction in Texas.* College Station: Texas A&M University Press, 2003.

Current, Richard N. *Lincoln's Loyalists: Union Soldiers from the Confederacy.* Boston: Northeastern University Press, 1992.

———. *Those Terrible Carpetbaggers: A Reinterpretation.* New York: Oxford University Press, 1988.

———. *Three Carpetbag Governors.* Baton Rouge: Louisiana State University Press, 1967.

Dawson, Joseph. *Army Generals and Reconstruction: Louisiana, 1862–1877.* Baton Rouge: Louisiana State University Press, 1982.

Derthick, Martha. *The National Guard in Politics.* Cambridge, Mass.: Harvard University Press, 1965.

Desdunes, Rodolphe L. *Nos Hommes et Notre Histoire.* Montreal, 1911.

Du Bois, W. E. B. *Black Reconstruction in America.* New York: Harcourt, Brace, 1935.

Dunning, William A. *Essays on the Civil War and Reconstruction and Related Topics.* New York: Macmillan, 1898.

Fischer, Roger A. *The Segregation Struggle in Louisiana, 1862–1877.* Urbana: University of Illinois Press, 1974.

Fogelson, Robert M. *America's Armories: Architecture, Society, and Public Order.* Cambridge, Mass.: Harvard University Press, 1989.

Foner, Eric. *Freedom's Lawmakers: A Directory of Black Office Holders during Reconstruction.* Rev. ed. Baton Rouge: Louisiana State University Press, 1996.

———. *Nothing but Freedom: Emancipation and Its Legacy.* Baton Rouge: Louisiana State University Press, 1983.

———. *Reconstruction: America's Unfinished Revolution, 1863–1877.* New York: Harper and Row, 1988.

Franklin, John Hope. *After the Civil War.* Chicago: University of Chicago Press,1961.

Freeman, Douglas Southall. *Lee's Lieutenants: A Study in Command.* 3 vols. New York: Charles Scribner's Sons, 1942–44.

Gayarré, Charles E. A. *History of Louisiana.* 4 vols. 5th ed. New Orleans: Pelican, 1974.

Genovese, Eugene D. *From Rebellion to Revolution: Afro-American Slave Revolts in the Making of the New World.* New York: Vintage, 1981.

———. *Roll, Jordan, Roll: The World the Slaves Made.* New York: Vintage, 1972.

Goldman, Robert M. *"A Free Ballot and a Fair Count": The Department of Justice and the Enforcement of Voting Rights in the South, 1877–1893.* New York: Fordham University Press, 2001.

———. *Reconstruction and Voting: Losing the Vote in Reese and Cruikshank.* Lawrence: University Press of Kansas, 2001.

Gillette, William. *Retreat from Reconstruction, 1869–1879.* Baton Rouge: Louisiana State University Press, 1979.

Grant, Ulysses S. *The Papers of Ulysses S. Grant.* Edited by John Y. Simon. 18 volumes to date. Carbondale: Southern Illinois University Press, 1967–.

Hair, William Ivy. *Bourbonism and Agrarian Protest: Louisiana Politics, 1877–1900.* Baton Rouge: Louisiana State University Press, 1969.

Hanson, Victor Davis. *Ripples of Battle: How Wars of the Past Still Determine How We Fight, How We Live, and How We Think.* New York: Doubleday, 2003.

Harris, William C. *The Day of the Carpetbagger: Republican Reconstruction in Mississippi.* Baton Rouge: Louisiana State University Press, 1979.

Harrison, Mabel Fletcher, and Lavinia McGuire McNeely. *Grant Parish, Louisiana: A History.* Baton Rouge: Claitor's, 1969.

Hartz, Louis. *The Liberal Tradition in America.* New York: Harcourt, Brace, Jovanovich, 1955.

Haskins, James. *P. B. S. Pinchback.* New York: Macmillan, 1973.

Hayes, Rutherford B. *Hayes: The Diary of a President, 1875–1881, Covering the Disputed Election, the End of Reconstruction, and the Beginning of Civil Service.* Edited by T. Harry Williams. New York: D. McKay, 1964.

Heatwole, John L. *The Burning: Sheridan in the Shenandoah Valley.* Charlottesville, Va.: Rockbridge, 1998.

Hesseltine, William B. *Ulysses S. Grant: Politician*. New York: Dodd, Mead, 1935.

Hewett, Janet B., ed. *The Roster of Confederate Soldiers, 1861–1865*. 16 vols. Wilmington, N.C.: Broadfoot, 1995.

Hirsch, Arnold R., and Joseph Logsdon. *Creole New Orleans: Race and Americanization*. Baton Rouge: Louisiana State University Press, 1992.

Hobsbawm, Eric J. *Age of Extremes: The Short Twentieth Century, 1914–1991*. London: Michael Joseph, 1994.

———. *Revolutionaries: Contemporary Essays*. New York: Pantheon, 1973.

Hollandsworth, James G. *An Absolute Massacre: The New Orleans Race Riot of July 30, 1866*. Baton Rouge: Louisiana State University Press, 2001.

Holmes, Oliver Wendell, Jr. *Touched with Fire: Civil War Letters and Diary of Oliver Wendell Holmes, Jr., 1861–1864*. Edited by Mark DeWolfe Howe. Cambridge, Mass.: Harvard University Press, 1946.

Houzeau, Jean-Charles. *My Passage at the New Orleans "Tribune": A Memorial of the Civil War Era*. Edited by David C. Rankin. Translated by Gerard F. Denault. Baton Rouge: Louisiana State University Press, 1984.

Howard, Michael. *The Franco-Prussian War: The German Invasion of France, 1870–1871*. London: Routledge, 1961.

Huber, Leonard V. *New Orleans: A Pictorial History*. New York, 1971.

Huntington, Samuel P. *The Soldier and the State: The Theory and Politics of Civil Military Relations*. Cambridge, MA: Harvard University Press, Belknap Press, 1957.

Jackson, Joy J. *New Orleans in the Gilded Age: Politics and Urban Progress, 1880–1896*. Baton Rouge: Louisiana State University Press, 1969.

Johnson, Ludwell H. *Red River Campaign: Politics and Cotton in the Civil War*. Baltimore, MD: Johns Hopkins Press University, 1958.

Jones, Terry L. *Lee's Tigers: The Louisiana Infantry in the Army of Northern Virginia*. Baton Rouge: Louisiana State University Press, 1991.

Jones, Virgil Carrington. *Gray Ghosts and Rebel Raiders*. New York: Henry Holt, 1956.

Kaczorowski, Robert J. *The Politics of Judicial Interpretation: The Federal Courts, Department of Justice, and Civil Rights, 1866–1876*. New York: New York University Press, 1985.

Keegan, John. *The Face of Battle*. New York: Viking, 1977.

Kousser, J. Morgan, and James M. McPherson, eds. *Region, Race, and Reconstruction: Essays in Honor of C. Vann Woodward*. New York: Oxford University Press, 1982.

Labbé, Ronald M., and Jonathan Lurie. *The Slaughterhouse Cases: Regulation, Reconstruction, and the Fourteenth Amendment*. Lawrence: University Press of Kansas, 2003.

Landry, Stuart Omer. *The Battle of Liberty Place: The Overthrow of Carpet-Bag Rule in New Orleans—September 14, 1874*. New Orleans: Pelican, 1955.

Lewis, Lloyd. *Sherman: Fighting Prophet*. New York: Harcourt, Brace, 1932.

Lonn, Ella. *Reconstruction in Louisiana after 1868*. New York: G. P. Putnam's Sons, 1918.

Luttwak, Edward. *Coup d'Etat: A Practical Handbook*. New York: Alfred A. Knopf, 1968.

Mahon, John K. *History of the Militia and the National Guard.* New York: Macmillan, 1983.

Malaparte, Curzio. *Technique du Coup d'Etat.* Paris: Glasset, 1931.

Mayer, Arno. *The Dynamics of Counterrevolution in Europe, 1870–1956: An Analytic Framework.* New York: Harper and Row, 1971.

McConnell, Roland C. *Negro Troops of Antebellum Louisiana: A History of the Battalion of Free Men of Color.* Baton Rouge: Louisiana State University Press, 1968.

McCrary, Peyton. *Abraham Lincoln and Reconstruction: The Louisiana Experiment.* Princeton, N.J.: Princeton University Press, 1978.

McFeely, William. *Yankee Stepfather: General O. O. Howard and the Freedmen.* New Haven, Conn.: Yale University Press, 1968.

McGinty, Garnie W. *Louisiana Redeemed: The Overthrow of Carpetbag Rule, 1876–1880.* New Orleans: Pelican, 1941.

McPherson, James M. *Abraham Lincoln and the Second American Revolution.* New York: Oxford University Press, 1991.

———. *Battle Cry of Freedom: The Civil War Era .* New York: Oxford University Press, 1987.

———. *Ordeal by Fire: The Civil War and Reconstruction.* New York: Alfred A. Knopf, 1982.

Menn, Joseph Karl. *The Large Slaveholders of Louisiana—1860.* New Orleans: Pelican, 1964.

Millett, Allan, and Peter Maslowski. *For the Common Defense.* New York: Free Press, 1984.

Morris, Roy, Jr. *Sheridan: The Life and Wars of General Phil Sheridan.* New York: Crown, 1992.

Owen, William Miller. *In Camp and Battle with the Washington Artillery.* Boston: Ticknor, 1885.

Painter, Nell Irvin. *Exodusters: Black Migration to Kansas after Reconstruction.* 1977. Reprint, New York: W. W. Norton, 1992.

Parrish, T. Michael. *Richard Taylor: Soldier Prince of Dixie.* Chapel Hill: University of North Carolina Press, 1992.

Perman, Michael. *The Road to Redemption: Southern Politics, 1869–1879.* Chapel Hill: University of North Carolina Press, 1984.

———, ed. *Major Problems in the Civil War and Reconstruction.* Lexington, Mass.: D. C. Heath, 1991.

Petty, Elijah P. *Journey to Pleasant Hill: The Civil War Letters of Captain Elijah P. Petty.* Edited by Norman D. Brown. San Antonio: University of Texas Institute of Texas Cultures, 1982.

Pfanz, Harry W. *Gettysburg: Culp's Hill and Cemetery Hill.* Chapel Hill: University of North Carolina Press, 1993.

Rable, George C. *But There Was No Peace: The Role of Violence in the Politics in Reconstruction.* Athens: University of Georgia Press, 1984.

Ransom, Roger L., and Richard Sutch. *One Kind of Freedom: The Economic Consequences of Emancipation.* Cambridge: Cambridge University Press, 1977.

Rodrigue, John C. *Reconstruction in the Cane Fields: From Slavery to Free Labor in Louisiana's Sugar Parishes, 1862–1880.* Baton Rouge: Louisiana State University Press, 2001.

Roland, Charles P. *Louisiana Sugar Planters during the American Civil War.* Leyden, Netherlands: E. J. Brill, 1957.

Rousey, Dennis C. *Policing the Southern City: New Orleans, 1805–1889*. Baton Rouge: Louisiana State University Press, 1996.

Schurz, Carl. *Speeches, Correspondence, and Political Papers of Carl Schurz*. Edited by Frederic Bancroft. New York: G. P. Putnam's Sons, 1913.

Sefton, James E. *The United States Army and Reconstruction, 1865–1877*. Baton Rouge: Louisiana State University Press, 1967.

Seymour, William J. *The Civil War Memoirs of Captain William J. Seymour: Reminiscences of a Louisiana Tiger*. Edited by Terry L. Jones. Baton Rouge: Louisiana State University Press, 1991.

Sherman, John, and William T. Sherman. *The Sherman Letters: Correspondence between General and Senator Sherman from 1837 to 1891*. Edited by Rachel S. Thorndike. New York: Charles Scribner's Sons, 1894.

Shugg, Roger W. *Origins of Class Struggle in Louisiana: A Social History of White Farmers and Laborers during Slavery and After, 1840–1875*. Baton Rouge: Louisiana State University Press, 1939.

Shy, John. *A People Numerous and Armed: Reflections on the Military Struggle for American Independence*. Rev. ed. Ann Arbor: University of Michigan Press, 1990.

Singletary, Otis. *Negro Militia and Reconstruction*. Austin: University of Texas Press, 1957.

Sitterson, J. Carlyle. *Sugar Country: The Cane Sugar Industry in the South, 1753–1950*. Lexington: University of Kentucky Press, 1953.

Skowronek, Stephen. *Building a New American State: The Expansion of National Administrative Capacities, 1877–1920*. New York: Cambridge University Press, 1982.

Stampp, Kenneth M. *The Era of Reconstruction, 1865–1877*. New York: Vintage, 1965.

——— and Leon Litwack, eds. *Reconstruction: An Anthology of Revisionist Writing*. Baton Rouge: Louisiana State University Press, 1969.

Sundquist, James L. *Dynamics of the Party System: Alignment and Realignment of Political Parties in the United States*. Rev. ed. Washington, D.C.: Brookings Institution, 1983.

Taylor, Joe Gray. *Louisiana Reconstructed, 1863–1877*. Baton Rouge: Louisiana State University Press, 1974.

Taylor, Richard. *Destruction and Reconstruction: Personal Experiences of the Late War*. Edited by Charles P. Roland. Waltham, Mass.: Blaisdell, 1968.

Toomer, Jean. *Cane*. 3rd. ed. New York: Harper and Row, 1969.

Trelease, Allen W. *White Terror: The Ku Klux Klan Conspiracy and Southern Reconstruction*. New York: Harper and Row, 1971.

Tunnell, Ted. *Crucible of Reconstruction: War, Radicalism, and Race in Louisiana, 1862–1877*. Baton Rouge: Louisiana State University Press, 1984.

Urwin, Gregory J. W., ed. *Black Flag over Dixie: Racial Atrocities and Reprisals in the Civil War*. Carbondale: Southern Illinois University Press, 2004.

Vandal, Gilles. *The New Orleans Riot of 1866: Anatomy of a Tragedy*. Lafayette: Center for Louisiana Studies, University of Southwestern Louisiana, 1983.

———. *Rethinking Southern Violence: Homicides in Post–Civil War Louisiana, 1866–1884*. Columbus: Ohio State University Press, 2000.

Vincent, Charles. *Black Legislators in Louisiana during Reconstruction.* Baton Rouge: Louisiana State University Press, 1976.

Vinovskis, Maris A., ed. *Toward a Social History of the American Civil War.* New York: Cambridge University Press, 1990.

Warmoth, Henry Clay. *Letter of H. C. Warmoth, Claimant of a Seat in the House of Representatives as Delegate from the Territory of Louisiana, Addressed to Senator Williams, Chairman of the Sub-Committee on Reconstruction for Louisiana.* Washington, D.C., 1866.

———. *War, Politics, and Reconstruction: Stormy Days in Louisiana.* New York: Macmillan, 1930.

Warner, Ezra J. *Generals in Blue: Lives of the Union Commanders.* Baton Rouge: Louisiana State University Press, 1964.

———. *Generals in Gray: Lives of the Confederate Commanders.* Baton Rouge: Louisiana State University Press, 1959.

Weigley, Russell F. *The American Way of War: A History of the United States Military Strategy and Policy.* Bloomington: University of Indiana Press, 1977.

———. *History of the United States Army.* New York: Macmillan, 1967.

Welles, Gideon. *Diary of Gideon Welles: Secretary of the Navy under Lincoln and Johnson.* 2 vols. Boston: Houghton Mifflin, 1909.

Williams, Lou Falkner. *The Great South Carolina Ku Klux Klan Trials, 1871–1872.* Athens: The University of Georgia Press, 1996.

Williams, T. Harry. *Huey Long.* New York: Alfred A. Knopf, 1969.

———. *P. G. T. Beauregard: Napoleon in Gray.* Baton Rouge: Louisiana State University Press, 1955.

Williamson, Joel. *After Slavery: The Negro in South Carolina during Reconstruction.* Chapel Hill: University of North Carolina Press, 1965.

Wilson, Joseph T. *The Black Phalanx: A History of the Negro Soldiers of the United States in the Wars of 1775–1812, 1861–65.* Hartford, Conn.: American Publishing, 1888.

Winters, John D. *The Civil War in Louisiana.* Baton Rouge: Louisiana State University Press, 1963.

Woodward, C. Vann. *Reunion and Reaction: The Compromise of 1877 and the End of Reconstruction.* New York: Little, Brown, 1951.

Wright, Gavin. *Old South, New South: Revolutions in the Southern Economy since the Civil War.* New York: Basic Books, 1986.

Zuczek, Richard. *State of Rebellion: Reconstruction South Carolina.* Columbia: University of South Carolina Press, 1996.

ARTICLES

Berry, Mary F. "Negro Troops in Blue and Gray: The Louisiana Native Guards, 1861–1863." *Louisiana History* 8 (Spring 1967): 165–90.

Binning, F. Wayne. "Carpetbaggers' Triumph: The Louisiana State Elections of 1868." *Louisiana History* 14 (Winter 1973): 21–39.

Carleton, Mark T. "The Politics of the Convict Lease System in Louisiana, 1868–1901." *Louisiana History* 8 (Winter 1967): 5–25.

Carter, Dan T. "The Anatomy of Fear: The Christmas Day Insurrection Scare of 1865." *Journal of Southern History* 42 (August 1976): 351–57.

Castel, Albert. "The Fort Pillow Massacre: A Fresh Examination of the Evidence." *Civil War History* 4 (1958): 37–50.

Cimprich, John, and Robert C. Mainfort Jr. "Fort Pillow Revisited: New Evidence about an Old Controversy." *Civil War History* 28 (1982): 296–306.

Clendenen, Clarence C. "President Hayes' 'Withdrawal' of the Troops—An Enduring Myth." *South Carolina Historical Magazine* 70 (October 1960): 240–50.

Connor, William P. "Reconstruction Rebels: The *New Orleans Tribune* in Post-War Louisiana." *Louisiana History* 21 (Spring 1980): 159–81.

Dufour, Charles L. "The Age of Warmoth." *Louisiana History* 6 (Fall 1965): 335–64.

Everett, Donald E. "Emigrés and Militia Men: Free Persons of Color in New Orleans, 1803–1815." *Journal of Negro History* 38 (October 1953): 377–402.

Faust, Drew Gilpin. "Christian Soldiers: The Meaning of Revivalism in the Confederate Army." *Journal of Southern History* 53 (February 1987): 66–90.

Fischer, Roger A. "A Pioneer Protest: The New Orleans Street Car Controversy of 1867." *Journal of Negro History* 53 (July 1968): 228–45.

Fletcher, Marvin E. "The Negro Volunteer in Reconstruction, 1865–1866." *Military Affairs* 32 (December 1968): 124–31.

Foner, Laura. "The Free People of Color in Louisiana and St. Domingue: A Comparative Portrait of Two Three-Caste Slave Societies." *Journal of Social History* 3 (1970): 408–22.

Forman, William Harper, Jr. "William P. Harper in War and Reconstruction." *Louisiana History* 13 (1972): 47–70.

Gonzalez, John Edmond. "William Pitt Kellogg: Reconstruction Governor of Louisiana, 1873–1877." *Louisiana Historical Quarterly* 29 (1946): 394–495.

Gould, Jeffrey. "The Strike of 1887: Louisiana Sugar War." *Southern Exposure* 12 (November–December 1984): 45–55.

Grosz, Agnes Smith. "The Political Career of Pinckney Benton Stewart Pinchback." *Louisiana Historical Quarterly* 27 (April 1944): 527–612.

Harlan, Louis R. "Desegregation in New Orleans Public Schools during Reconstruction." *American Historical Review* 67 (April 1962): 663–75.

Harris, Francis Byers. "Henry Clay Warmoth, Reconstruction Governor of Louisiana." *Louisiana Historical Quarterly* 30 (April 1947): 523–653.

Hennessey, Melinda Meek. "Race and Violence in Reconstruction New Orleans: The 1868 Riot." *Louisiana History* 10 (Winter 1979): 77–92.

Hyman, Harold M. "Johnson, Stanton, and Grant: A Reconsideration of the Army's Role in the Events Leading to Impeachment." *American Historical Review* 66 (October 1960): 85–100.

Johnson, Manie White. "The Colfax Riot of April 1873." *Louisiana Historical Quarterly* 13 (July 1930): 391–427.

Jones, Howard J. "Biographical Sketches of Members of the 1868 Louisiana State Senate." *Louisiana History* 19 (1978): 65–110.

Lestage, Oscar, Jr. "The White League in Louisiana and Its Participation in Reconstruction Riots." *Louisiana Historical Quarterly* 18 (July 1935): 637–49.

Lowrey, Walter M. "The Political Career of James Madison Wells." *Louisiana Historical Quarterly* 31 (October 1948): 995–1123.

Nicholls, Francis T. "An Autobiography of Francis T. Nicholls, 1835–1881." Edited by Barnes F. Lathrop. *Louisiana Historical Quarterly* 17 (April 1934): 246–67.

Otten, James T. "The Wheeler Adjustment in Louisiana: National Republicans Begin to Reappraise Their Reconstruction Policy." *Louisiana History* 13 (Fall 1972): 349–67.

Perkins, A. E. "James Henri Burch and Oscar James Dunn in Louisiana." *Journal of Negro History* 22 (July 1937): 321–34.

Pitre, Althea D. "The Collapse of the Warmoth Regime, 1870–1872." *Louisiana History* 6 (Spring 1965): 161–87.

Prichard, Walter. "The Origins and Activities of the "White League' in New Orleans (Reminiscences of a Participant in the Movement)." *Louisiana Historical Quarterly* 23 (April 1940): 525–43.

Rable, George. "Republican Albatross: The Louisiana Question, National Politics, and the Failure of Reconstruction." *Louisiana History* 9 (Summer 1982): 109–30.

Rankin, David C. "The Origins of Black Leadership in New Orleans during Reconstruction." *Journal of Southern History* 40 (August 1974): 417–40.

———. "The Impact of the Civil War on the Free Colored Community of New Orleans." *Perspectives in American History* 11 (1977/1978): 379–416.

Reed, Wallace P. "Last Forlorn Hope of the Confederacy." *Southern Historical Society Papers* 30 (1902): 117–21.

Richardson, Frank L. "My Recollections of the Battle of the Fourteenth of September, 1874, in New Orleans, LA." *Louisiana Historical Quarterly* 3 (October 1920): 498–501.

Richter, William L. "Longstreet: From Rebel to Scalawag." *Louisiana History* 11 (Summer 1970): 215–30.

Russ, William A., Jr. "Was There Danger of a Second Civil War during Reconstruction?" *Mississippi Valley Historical Review* 25 (June 1938): 39–58.

Scott, Rebecca J. "Defining the Boundaries of Freedom in the World of Cane: Cuba, Brazil, and Louisiana after Emancipation." *American Historical Review* (February 1994): 70–102.

Swinney, Everette. "Enforcing the Fifteenth Amendment, 1870–1877." *Journal of Southern History* 28 (May 1962): 202–18.

Weigley, Russell F. "The American Military and the Principle of Civilian Control from McClellan to Powell." *Journal of Military History* 57 (Special Issue, October 1993): 27–58.

Weisberger, Bernard. "The Dark and Bloody Ground of Reconstruction Historiography." *Journal of Southern History* 25 (November 1959): 427–47.

Wetta, Frank J. ""Bulldozing the Scalawags': Some Examples of the Persecution of Southern White Republicans in Louisiana during Reconstruction." *Louisiana History* 21 (Winter 1980): 43–58.

Williams, T. Harry. "The Louisiana Unification Movement of 1873." *Journal of Southern History* 11 (August 1945): 349–69.

Woodward, Earl F. "The Brooks and Baxter War in Arkansas, 1872–1874." *Arkansas Historical Quarterly* 30 (Winter 1971): 315–36.

NEWSPAPERS AND PERIODICALS

Alexandria Louisiana Democrat.
Alexandria (La.) Caucasian.
Harper's Weekly, 1865–77.
Natchitoches Peoples' Vindicator.
New Orleans Commercial Bulletin.
New Orleans Daily Picayune.
New Orleans National Republican.
New Orleans Republican.
New Orleans Times.
New Orleans Tribune.
New York Herald.
New York Times.
The Weekly Louisianian.

THESES AND DISSERTATIONS

Binning, Francis Wayne. "Henry Clay Warmoth and Louisiana Reconstruction." Ph.D. diss., University of North Carolina, 1969.

Odom, Edwin Dale. "Louisiana Railroads, 1830–1880: A Study of State and Local Aid." Ph.D. diss., Tulane University, 1961.

Singletary, Otis Arnold. "The Reassertion of White Supremacy in Louisiana." Master's thesis, Louisiana State University, 1949.

Uzee, Philip D. "Republican Politics in Louisiana, 1877–1900." Ph.D. diss., Louisiana State University, 1950.

Windham, Allie Bayne. "Methods and Mechanisms Used to Restore White Supremacy in Louisiana, 1872–1876." Master's thesis, Louisiana State University, 1948.

Index

www.ingramcontent.com/pod-product-compliance
Lightning Source LLC
Chambersburg PA
CBHW070404270326
41926CB00014B/2689